THE KURDISH QUESTION AND
THE 2003 IRAQI WAR

Kurdish Studies Series
No. 5

THE KURDISH QUESTION AND THE 2003 IRAQI WAR

Edited by
Mohammed M. A. Ahmed
and
Michael M. Gunter

MAZDA PUBLISHERS, Inc. ◆ Costa Mesa, California ◆ 2005

Funding for the publication of this volume was provided by
grants from the Iranica Institute, Irvine California
and
Ahmed Foundation for Kurdish Studies, Sharon, Massachusetts.

Mazda Publishers, Inc.
Academic Publishers Since 1980
P.O. Box 2603
Costa Mesa, California 92628 U.S.A.
www.mazdapub.com

Library of Congress Cataloging-in-Publication Data

The Kurdish Question and the 2003 Iraq War/ edited by Mohammed M.A.
Ahmed and Michael M. Gunter.
p.cm.
Includes bibliographical references and index.

ISBN:1-56859-176-4
(alk. paper)
1. Iraq War, 2003—Kurds—Middle East—Politics and government.
I. Ahmed, Mohammed M.A. II. Gunter, Michael M.
DS79.76.K87 2004
956'.00491597—dc22
2004048975

Dedicated to our wives

Shirley Ahmed
and
Judy Gunter

CONTENTS

Preface

Mazda Publishers is delighted to present *The Kurdish Question and the 2003 Iraqi War* edited by Mohammed Ahmed and Michael Gunter as the fifth in our Kurdish Studies Series. We feel that recent developments in the Middle East reinforce our decision to start the Kurdish Series some five years ago. In the future it will be difficult to analyze the history and politics of the Middle East without consideration of the role that the Kurds have played and are playing in regional and, now, as the U.S. war against Iraq shows, global politics. I want to thank Mohammed Ahmed and Michael Gunter for bringing this timely and important book to fruition. The contributions address developments that affected the Kurds and Kurdish nationalism during the dozen years from the first Persian Gulf War in 1991 to the U.S. war against Iraq in March 2003. The editors were able to attract respected international scholars with expertise on the Kurds of Turkey, Iraq, Iran and Lebanon.

The publisher thinks this book will be of value not just to scholars of the Kurds, Kurdish nationalism, politics, history and culture, but to all scholars of the Middle East, policy makers, students and people interested in the Middle East. The past 12 years have shown the significance of the Kurds and Kurdish nationalism as being one of the most important issues of the Middle East and Caspian Sea region. The U.S. war against Iraq and its potential consequences have already demonstrated that the Kurds, their nationalism, politics and decisions will be a force to be reckoned with not only regionally, but globally. The essays in this volume contextualize and explain this leap of the Kurds from being a minority and regional issue to that of an important factor in global politics.

Robert Olson
Kurdish Series Editor

Foreword

This book is the product of a conference triggered by the 2003 coalition war on Iraq. The initial negotiations between the United States and Turkey to open a second front through Turkey raised deep concerns among the Kurds. Turkey threatened the Kurds with a war if they tried to exploit the situation to advance their national aspirations, including consolidation of political gains made in the "safe haven" zone, since 1991. Turkey drew several red lines for the Kurds not to cross, claiming that any political gain by the Iraqi Kurds would incite its own 15-20 million Kurds to demand similar political gains.

Turkey had already mobilized thousands of its troops along the Iraqi border in preparation to enter Southern Kurdistan (Iraqi Kurdistan) to dismantle the Regional Kurdistan Government, which was established under the protection of the United States and Britain in 1992. The declared U.S. war objectives were to rid Iraq of weapons of mass destruction and to use Iraq as a launching pad to spread democracy in the Middle East.

Rumors abounded before the war that Iran and Syria, who strongly opposed the Israeli policy against the Palestinians, were in line to be attacked after Iraq. Turkey, Syria, and Iran, with large Kurdish populations, became concerned that the conflict might accord the Iraqi Kurds an opportunity to gain influence and /or establish their own state, which could set a precedent for similar Kurdish demands in their own countries. A series of meetings was held by the neighboring countries in Damascus, Tehran, and Ankara with a view to harmonizing their position on the Kurdish question. Turkey's moves against the Iraqi Kurds were in line with the stance of the other neighboring states on the Kurdish issue. Despite Turkey's refusal to offer the United States a second corridor, it continues to threaten the Iraqi Kurds with war if they dare to declare independence or call for an ethnically and geographically based federal system of government in Iraq.

Accordingly, the narratives of the conference were articulated in a manner to analyze the impact of the war and the ongoing political discourse among the neighboring states on the future of the Kurds in the Middle East. A bright light was shed on the Kurdish movement and the survivability of the Kurds as a distinct ethnic group of people in the Middle East during the 21st century. The vigorous reemergence of Kurdish nationalism since the 1980s was given special attention. A set of well documented substantive papers was delivered at the conference by noted political scientists and historians covering different aspects of the Kurdish question in Turkey, Iraq, Syria, and Iran. Light was also shed on factors contributing to the plight of the Lebanese Kurdish community.

The quality and the importance of the topics covered at the conference motivated the Ahmed Foundation for Kurdish Studies to publish them in book form. This book presents up-to-date information about the Kurdish question. The diverse viewpoints presented by its different authors offer balanced analyses of the Kurdish people and will be of considerable interest to research fellows, scholars, and politicians who might be interested in Middle Eastern affairs. The editors do not necessarily agree with each individual author's statements and interpretations. Both editors are also very grateful to Shirley Ahmed for her editorial help in preparing the manuscript for publication.

Mohammed M. A. Ahmed
February 22, 2004

Introduction

The 2003 Iraqi War has proven to be a major landmark in the development of Kurdish nationalism, especially in Iraq, but also in Turkey, Iran, and Syria. Although the war has resulted in the potential for enormous opportunities for the Kurds, it also holds possibilities for great dangers. In Iraq, for example, the Kurds hope that the post-Saddam-Hussein era will result in a democratic, federal Iraq which would largely solve the longstanding Kurdish demand for political, economic, social, and cultural rights. Under certain circumstances, even independent statehood is possible, although few dare even to broach the topic. On the other hand, the post-Saddam-Hussein era in Iraq is laden with danger. If the United States withdraws prematurely from Iraq, a new oppressive Arab majority in that state might reimpose its will on the minority Kurds. Although the United States plans to transfer sovereignty back to Iraq on 30 June 2004, the jury will probably continue to remain out on these questions for some time into the future.

The 2003 Iraqi War has also heavily impacted the other regional states in which the Kurds live. Turkey, for example, fears the demonstration effect that any type of Iraqi Kurdish state would have on its own large and restive Kurdish minority. Only recently has the Kurdistan Workers Party (PKK)—renamed Kurdistan Freedom and Democracy Congress (KADEK) in February 2002 and then Kurdistan Peoples Congress (KHK) in November 2003—called off its 20-year-long guerrilla war against Turkey and haltingly turned to a peaceful strategy.

In addition, Turkey must come to grips with the results of its failure to support the U.S. war effort in Iraq. This failure led to a crisis in the 50-year-old U.S.-Turkish strategic alliance. With tremendous success, the Iraqi Kurds stepped into the breach abandoned by Turkey as the U.S. ally on the War's northern front. What will be the continuing implications of this situation for Turkey and its Kurdish population? Furthermore, how will this war also affect the future status of the Kurds in Iran and Syria?

On 6-7 September 2003, the Ahmed Foundation for Kurdish Studies sponsored an international conference in the Boston area to examine the implications of the 2003 Iraqi War for the Kurdish question. Dr. Mohammed Ahmed—an Iraqi Kurd and former United Nations official—is the founder and president of the Foundation. Through his enlightened vision and generous financial support, the Ahmed Foundation has now sponsored three international conferences and successfully published their proceedings. For this third conference on the 2003 Iraqi War, the Foundation again invited eminent scholars with different viewpoints from the United States and Europe to address various aspects of the situation in a balanced manner.

The resulting articles provide a useful background analysis for a situation that will continue to evolve for many more years. Although the editors do not necessarily agree with all the different opinions expressed in these articles, they strongly do believe that these ideas should be aired in order that the Kurdish question can be objectively analyzed.

David McDowall presents a thoughtful essay in which he ponders possible future trends for the Kurds based on their experiences in the 20th century. Despite the positive achievements in northern Iraq (often referred to by the Kurds as southern Kurdistan), McDowall notes such continuing problems as the corrupting influence of oil and patronage relationships, rather than complete democracy. Carole O'Leary takes issue with the viewpoint that the Kurds are a source of instability in the Middle East. Instead, she argues that it is their unjust situation of statelessness and lack of being allowed democracy that creates instability. She also maintains that continuing tribalism among the Kurds is not necessarily a primitive and anarchic source of instability, as many would argue.

Mohammed Ahmed examines the political consequences of past ethnic cleansing in Iraqi Kurdistan. He finds that attempts to forcibly assimilate the Kurds and Arabize their region have polarized inter-ethnic relationships and poisoned the minds of Arabs, fostering among them the erroneous belief that the Kurds have no history or culture, are prone to violence, and, therefore, must be assimilated. Michael M. Gunter analyzes the Kurdish future in post-Saddam Hussein Iraq. He finds reasons to be both optimistic and pessimistic. The Iraqi political culture will help determine the possibilities for establishing a federal and democratic regime; but, to put it bluntly, the Iraqis have little experience here. Instead, Iraq is a state that has been governed by strong men and dictators, and that also has deep ethnic, religious, and tribal cleavages. The Iraqi Kurdish future, therefore, is clouded with considerable uncertainties. Robert Olson examines the consolidation of Iraqi Kurdish nationalism and the Turkish reaction to it since the 2003 War.

Hamit Bozarslan demonstrates how the 2003 War helped demolish so-called Turkish "red lines" preventing the Iraqi Kurds from occupying Kirkuk and Mosul, as well as protecting the Turkish position in Cyprus. Gulistan Gurbey discusses recent Turkish reforms to meet the requirements of European Union (EU) membership and what their consequences will be for the situation of the Kurds in Turkey. Hakan Yavuz analyzes how the changing situation in Turkey, as well as the 2003 Iraqi War, is increasingly empowering the Kurdish minority.

Nader Entessar argues that the U.S. overthrow of Saddam Hussein and its advocacy of federalism for post-Saddam Hussein Iraq may have both negative and positive consequences for the Kurds in Iran. For example, Iranian officials fear that the United States may use Kurdistan as a staging ground to destabilize the Islamic Republic of Iran. On the other hand, if federalism proves a viable model to solve the Kurdish problem in post-Saddam Hussein Iraq, it may offer a useful model for Iran to consider within its own unique, but fast-changing political milieu. In her article, Farideh Koohi-Kamali demonstrates that the Kurds in Iran have not sought independence. Rather, they have seen themselves as part of the larger oppositional movement in Iran demanding political freedom and democracy, recognition and respect for ethnic rights, and women's rights.

Lokman Meho and Farah Kawtharani provide a general background on the divided Kurdish community in Lebanon, which had escaped persecution in Turkey and Syria. They analyze the Lebanese Kurds' history, geography, ethno-linguistic diversity, difficult citizenship and socioeconomic status, and associational organizations. David Fisher discusses evolving international legal norms regarding internally displaced persons and how these norms apply to the Kurds.

Although the editors have attempted to standardize spellings as much as possible, complete success on this score proved impossible. For example, documents cited by the various authors in this book used different spellings for the same term. In addition, the authors from different countries whose articles appear in this book used terms in their text that have different accepted spellings. Nevertheless, in most cases, the editors have attempted to standardize words by using the most common spellings employed in American English and to do so without cumbersome diacritical marks. Although the purist may object, these spellings do have the virtue of being easily recognizable by most readers.

Finally, although the editors closely read and frequently corrected the text in each of the following articles, they also felt it best to leave each author's style of writing alone as much as possible. The textual result at times may seem somewhat awkward, but accurately conveys the flavor of so many different authors who come from various academic traditions. In all cases, however, the authors' meaning should be amply clear. The inevitable lapses and errors, of course, are those of the editors.

Michael M. Gunter
April 15, 2004

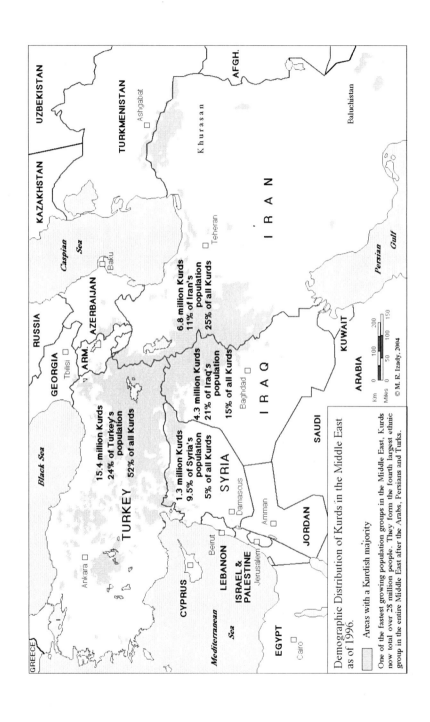

Demographic Distribution of Kurds in the Middle East as of 1996.

One of the fastest growing population groups in the Middle East, Kurds now total over 28 million people. They form the fourth largest ethnic group in the entire Middle East after the Arabs, Persians and Turks.

Areas with a Kurdish majority

15.4 million Kurds
24% of Turkey's population
52% of all Kurds

6.8 million Kurds
11% of Iran's population
25% of all Kurds

4.3 million Kurds
21% of Iraq's population
15% of all Kurds

1.3 million Kurds
9.5% of Syria's population
5% of all Kurds

© M. R. Izady, 2004

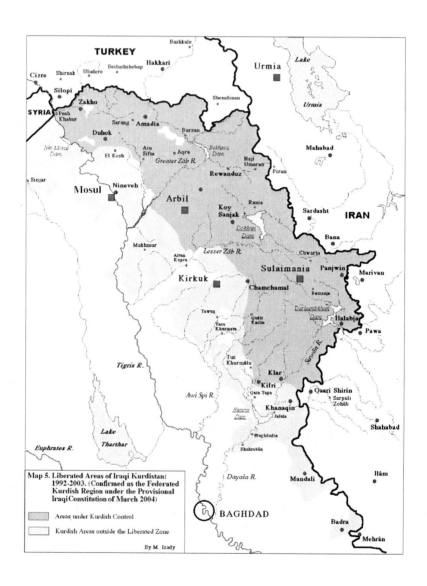

Map 5. Liberated Areas of Iraqi Kurdistan:
1992-2003. (Confirmed as the Federated
Kurdish Region under the Provisional
Iraqi Constitution of March 2004)

Areas under Kurdish Control

Kurdish Areas outside the Liberated Zone

By M. Izady

CHAPTER 1

Political Prospects of the Kurds in the Middle East

David McDowall

L ooking at the Kurdish communities of Iran, Iraq, Syria and Turkey, one can say that there are two very obvious and fundamentally shared characteristics: (a) a substantial proportion of these communities share a sense of common identity, and (b) in each of these four cases the fate of the Kurdish communities is affected (and possibly determined) by the majority community of the states in which they find themselves.

There is a third obvious and fundamental observation one may make: there is absolutely no guarantee that at the end of this new century, ethnic Kurds will still consider their ethnicity to be the major defining characteristic of their identity. This may seem a shocking statement. It is helpful to bear in mind that until the beginning of the twentieth century ideas of ethnic identity were current only among a tiny handful of people in the Ottoman and Qajar worlds. Middle Eastern society was divided much more meaningfully along religious and socio–economic lines; religiously, among the various millets of the Ottoman Empire; and socio-economically, among city dwellers of various kinds, and rural, desert and mountain dwellers of various kinds. Kurds, like Arabs and Turks, were thought of as an unlettered rural people, in the Kurdish case mainly nomadic and mainly mountain dwelling. We cannot guarantee that the "goal-posts" of identity will not change again.

Ideas of ethnic nationalism derived from Europe where they were a major force in the emergence of "nation states" before these ideas became discredited in the contradictions and barbarism of ethnic exclusivity. Western democracies now like to think of themselves in inclusive terms of plurality and civic nationalism. In Europe the nation state has undoubtedly started to give ground to other ideas, some individualistic, some regional and some supra-state ones. The troubled Balkans remain a field of ethnic blood-letting whereas in the rest of Europe this has now been largely confined to ritualized conflict on the football pitch. Who, then, is to say how the Middle East will treat questions of ethnicity by the end of this century?

Will Middle Eastern states follow the pattern of Europe? It is very difficult to say. The twentieth century has been characterized by a variety of secular ideologies, notably by a variety of Marxist or nationalist ideals. In almost every case, and certainly those cases that spring most readily to mind in the Middle East, ordinary people have eventually found the ideas to be bankrupt. The most important single reason is the authoritarianism with which these ideologies are propagated and maintained. The Kurds have been adversely affected by Kemalism, by forms of Arab Nationalism, most notably by the Baath, and in the case of Iran by the authoritarian behavior first of the Pahlavis, then of the Islamic Republic.

The Kurdish communities have also been affected internally, for example, by the Kurdistan Workers Party (PKK). (One should not belittle the achievement of the PKK: it created a mass movement in Turkey where previously it had not existed, and its legacy is that the question of the Kurds is now an unavoidable principal item on Turkey's agenda.) There is a negative side to the achievements of the PKK. Like the Turkish Republic itself, the PKK has proved doctrinaire, intolerant and ruthless with those Kurds who disagree with it. Such illiberal ideology and practice carry the seeds of their own self-destruction. For while it proclaims class and ethnic liberation, its real promise is of corruption and tyranny in the name of the Kurdish people, just as the people of the Soviet Union suffered corruption and tyranny in the name of the working class.

It is not difficult to trace the origins of such an intolerant state of mind. In part it comes from the inherent weakness of an oppressed minority. But it also comes from the intolerant monoculture proclaimed by the state. The Kurds of Turkey now have to work out how to map out their future. Where the PKK advanced an intolerant ethnic nationalism, Kurds must decide whether to continue to support its ideology, rooted in political violence, or whether there is not more to be said for striving for a quite different set of values: the basic rights and pluralistic characteristics of a fully-fledged parliamentary democracy for all Turkey.

There can be little doubt that a principal reason for these ideologies of intolerance is that they promised strength to societies that felt weak or oppressed. The question now is whether, having run the gamut of a variety of religious, class and ethnic nationalist "solutions," Middle Eastern societies will search for strength with more liberal values, or will they continue to be beguiled by the political snake oils that promise to be a panacea for internal weakness.

If Middle Eastern societies undertake this search, one can confidently expect this also to be reflected in Kurdish society. If Kurds find their neighborhood to be more tolerant and more accepting of the plurality of cultures that make the Middle East, then ethnic nationalism among the Kurds will also progressively soften as Kurdish communities feel they can be themselves and manage themselves without having to be overly assertive. It may be improbable that concepts like "Kurd," "Turk" and "Arab" return to their nineteenth century socio-economic meaning, but it is certainly possible during this century that they are seen to be more cultural than political statements. One can imagine Turks and Arabs, in particular, looking back with some embarrassment and possibly shame at the excesses of ethnic expression in the twentieth century. What we can be absolutely sure of is that socio-economic change is bound to occur in the Middle East during the twenty-first century. And as a consequence it is inevitable that the way people of the region think about themselves and their neighbors is bound to change, very probably in unpredictable ways.

One is constantly reminded of the way expectations can be confounded by the example of Beirut. In the 1950s and 1960s Beirut was confidently expected to be the crucible in which the different confessions and identities of the Lebanon would meld into a greater Lebanese identity. As we all know, it did not happen. Instead, different communities in Beirut retreated into a highly mythologized version of their confessional identity, resulting in civil war. So, it remains almost impossible to foretell what changes in identity are likely to develop.

A Crucial Turning Point in History

But let us look at where the Kurds are now and where they once were. In the wake of the overthrow of Saddam Hussein, the Kurds appear to stand at a crucial turning point in their history. For Iraqi Kurds, this juncture must without question be the most significant opportunity since the year 1919 to shape their future, and it may be that it proves to be of equal but indirect significance for Kurds living in adjacent states.

The year 1919 now seems lost in the distance. No one is alive today who can comment as an eyewitness of that fateful year. It will be recalled that Britain occupied Mesopotamia and the southern hills of Kurdistan in the autumn of 1918. It made some reckless and worthless statements about self-determination, just as the United States has made some reckless and worthless statements about bringing democracy to the region today. It made individual arrangements with a substantial number of chiefs, disturbing the existing balance within and between tribes, but augmenting the personal authority of those in whom it vested power,[1] creating a patron-client relationship with each of them.

---

[1] In late 1918 and early 1919 Britain would have happily gone along with a single Kurdish entity, either autonomous or independent of Arab Iraq. Indeed the terms of the Treaty of Sevres which allowed for southern Kurdistan to attach itself to a Kurdish state to the north, should that come into being, were drafted by none other than the British. Having looked in vain, as far afield as Istanbul, for a single leader acceptable to the mosaic of tribes within its area of military occupation, Britain de-

After an initially bumpy ride with various local tribal uprisings (because British administration proved more invasive than
the Ottoman one had been), things settled down between the im-
perial power, Britain, its puppet ruler King Faisal and the tribal
chiefs. The chiefs fell in with Britain's scheme for Iraq while
more politically aware urban Kurds began to recognise the cata-
strophic implications for Kurdish self-rule.[2] Britain emerged
from this page of history with little honor. The story of 1919
through to, say, 1922, raises interesting questions for us now.

Being largely tribal at the beginning of the twentieth century,
Kurds had great difficulty, like other tribal communities of the
region, in shaking off one mode of political thought in favor of
another. One may ascribe to that fact the fundamental reason
why Kurdistan (whether one thinks of what became Iraq or Turkey) failed to emerge as a political entity during the creation of
the modern state system of the Middle East. This raises a fundamental question for today. Is the political structure of Kurdish
society in Iraq ready to forge the kind of polity that will benefit

---

cided to make individual agreements with a substantial number of
chiefs, augmenting their own direct powers. As late as December 1922,
when the British were in a difficult situation and the Kemalist troops
seemingly had the upper hand with the tribes around Rawanduz, it was
decided to "recognise the right of the Kurds living within the boundaries of Iraq to set up a Kurdish Government within those boundaries..."
But it was left to "the different Kurdish elements to arrive at an agreement between themselves as to the form which they wish that Government should take..." Not only was the offer published in Baghdad but
C.J. Edmonds conveyed the offer orally to Sheikh Mahmud Barzinji's
brother, Sheikh Abdul Karim, a man whose ambition "was to see the
establishment of a Kurdish state under the Barzinja Shakhs." C.J.
Edmonds, *Kurds, Turks and Arabs* (London: Oxford University Press,
1957) p. 311. It remains an enigma why the offer was never taken up.

[2] That sense of catastrophe was confirmed when Britain comprehen-
sively failed to ensure its modest undertakings to the League of Nations. Although these undertakings fell short of autonomy, Britain had
promised to ensure that ethnic Kurds would administer the Kurdish
region and that the official language would be Kurdish. As is well
known, Britain failed in this undertaking and signed with the Iraqi government a treaty of independence which did not even mention the
Kurds.

its members most? Some reactions to that question are implicit in what will follow below.

Will it be possible to create a stable pluralistic Iraq in which the Kurdish region, whatever shape it finally assumes, is seen as an exemplar for Kurds elsewhere? If so, what threat will this good example pose to the governments that hold other Kurds in subjection? Will the Kurdish leadership in Iraq be able to forge genuine trust with the leaders of other solidarity groups and communities in Iraq? Will the Kurdish leaders jeopardize the long-term position of Kurds in Iraq by throwing their weight around while they are currently relatively powerful? Will they possibly engender distrust of other Iraqis either by being perceived too much in the lap of the United States, or by being perceived as the principal beneficiary of the US war on Iraq? These are dangers essentially of Kurdish leaders overplaying their hand. Or will the Kurdish leadership be too trusting of the United States, only to discover that its promises are as worthless as those of Henry Kissinger 30 years ago, or as worthless as those of Britain 80 years ago?

Of course, much has changed since 1919, and the kinds of question posed above sit now in a very different context. Since the year 1919 the Kurds have struggled with profound internal weaknesses of which those associated with tribal identity are the most significant, and with formidable external ones, of which the direct and repressive control of non-Kurdish state forces is the most obvious. But there are other immensely important and significant developments which have critical impact on the Kurdish question today.

Economic change, most notably the radical change or decline in agrarian activity—both agriculture and stock rearing—has led to massive migration from the countryside to town and city. This has been exacerbated by the conflict between Kurdish nationalists and the state, with village evacuations being one consequence. These processes have created a large urban proletariat. In the countryside the changes in agricultural economy and technology and loss of land has produced a de-tribalized proletariat in some parts, notably in Turkey and Iran, while leaving tribally-based people in others. The outlook of Kurds will almost certainly be affected by their location, be it urban or rural. It must be borne in mind, too, that Kurds are increasingly dependent on the most productive economic centers of the state as locations where they can make their living. This must inevitably impact upon their political outlook. So we can expect those Kurds still in their ancestral habitat to see things somewhat differently from those inhabiting towns and cities beyond Kurdistan.

There is an educational corollary. Those who leave the village to obtain secondary education in the local town will be unlikely to go back. Those who go from the local town to the city beyond Kurdistan in pursuit of higher education are even less likely to return. This pattern of constant brain-drain from the periphery to regional capitals is true for all urbanizing societies. Migrant individuals cross invisible demographic borders from predominantly Kurdish to predominantly non-Kurdish environments. This migration is bound to affect these individuals' thinking. Finally there is a large expatriate Kurdish population beyond the states which incorporate Kurdistan. This population has been immensely important in helping to forge the political ideas and support for Kurdish political activity, ever since the publication of *Kurdistan* in 1898. The diaspora Kurdish community has enjoyed access to democratic levers that may not be available inside Kurdistan. But it runs the risk of a retrospective and romanticized view of Kurdistan that may not reflect a changing reality. It is extremely hard to predict how important this expatriate community will be in the future, especially if or when Turkey gains membership of the European Union.

There has been an ideological change, too. As noted, in 1919 most Kurds would probably have defined themselves in tribal and religious terms. The reason is simple. Almost all of them belonged to intimate communities where leaders (and all others with whom business of one kind or another had to be done) were personally known. During the middle years of the twentieth century, with changes in socio-economic organization, questions of class and ethnicity became central to the Kurdish dilemma. One of the most articulate exponents was the great literary and political figure, Ibrahim Ahmad. This author can remember interviewing Dr Ahmad a decade ago. For him class and ethnicity remained indissolubly one issue. These two powerful ideas had been central to his political life. He was unwilling to state the primacy of one over the other. He had seen a harmony in the resolution of both issues in a reformed Iraqi society that recognized and embraced both Kurds and Arabs. Issues of class and ethnicity have not disappeared. They remain relevant, and yet one senses they are viewed as less important now than, say, 25 years ago. Indeed, we now seem to be in a period of religious revivalism in the Middle East, an attempt to discover strength against the pervasive influence of the West. And against it the United States has pitched its own ideological campaign to promote an American value system.

We cannot be sure of the outcomes. We can, however, be sure that the immense social transformations that have radically affected Kurdish society over the past century have not finished. Nor will they ever finish. It is the most obvious fact we all too easily lose sight of when we focus on the present or on the immediate future.

All of what has been said above gives rise to a formidable number of questions. But before asking one or two of these questions, it might be useful to list the most obvious problems imposed upon the Kurdish community from outside. The most obvious problem is the daily infringement of basic human rights, but one wishes to be more specific with regard to the states in which Kurds find themselves. (1) Constitutional denial. Kurds are only fully recognized as a specific ethnic community in Iraq. (2) Denial of citizenship. This affects about 250,000 people in Syria. (3) Denial or severe restriction of culture and Kurdish medium education. This affects Kurds in all countries except Iraq. (4) Denial of religious freedom or active discrimination against adherents of certain sects. This affects Sunnis in Iran, Alevis (though mainly for political reasons) and Yezidi Kurds in Turkey, Yezidi Kurds in Syria and until very recently, Faili Kurds in Iraq. (5) Severe economic neglect or discrimination. This occurs in Turkey, Iran and Syria; until recently it also occurred for Iraqi Kurds with regard to the Kirkuk oilfield.

One can also think very crudely in terms of two fundamentally different contexts in which Kurds find themselves in the region: (1) Countries in which the fate of the Kurds seems to be wholly contingent on the fate of the wider society to which willy-nilly they belong. These are Iran and Syria (and also

Lebanon and the ex-Soviet Union). The brand of national ethos which among other things has inflicted repression on the Kurdish community is now widely discredited in the eyes of the people of Iran and Syria. The economy of Syria and Iran both urgently require fundamental reform. These reforms cannot take place without political liberalization, which may now be more likely to happen as a consequence of events in Iraq. The Syrian and Iranian presidents Bashar Assad and Mohammad Khatami probably wish to initiate reforms but are probably not strong enough to face down the old guard. Ironically, all the bullying pressure exerted by the United States legitimizes the hardliners' claims in both countries that they remain under external threat and therefore no liberalization can take place. As in other parts of the Middle East, the US seems to have very little comprehension of how to lure those states it sees as a problem into a more productive relationship or how most effectively to advance human rights. The Kurds are to a great extent in the same boat as everyone else in Syria and Iran.[3] They, like everyone else, await the dawn. One can be optimistic that like everyone else in Syria, they will be beneficiaries of that awakening.

(2) Countries where substantial opportunity exists for the Kurdish community to determine its relationship with the majority: Iraq and Turkey. In the case of Iraq there is now great promise (but also great dangers) in forging relationships in which all communities can gain: Kurd, Turkman, Arab, Sunni and Shiite. In the case of Turkey the Kurdish community can hopefully en-

---

[3] One is struck by the observation of Riad Seif, an Amnesty International prisoner of conscience in Syria: "We are all the same. As a minimum, we want to create a state of rights and laws, where every Syrian has equal rights and where every Syrian has the chance to compete fairly and equally. To attain that, we need the fundamentals, the basic elements of democracy: free elections, an independent parliament, independent courts of law, a free media and a civil society with non-governmental organisations." And of Haitham al-Maleh, President of the Syrian Human Rights Association: "I thank Hafiz al-Assad because he put me in jail. All ideologies in Syria were in jail. Now we have a new understanding." Both quoted in Alan George, *Syria: Neither Bread nor Freedom* (London: Zed Press 2003), pp. 31 & 62.

sure its rights are both recognized and enabled along the road to European Union membership.

Should and Will Kurdistan Achieve Statehood?

That the Kurds have the right to self-determination must be incontestable. In the light of the body of basic principles and laws concerning human and civil rights, starting with the Twelfth of President Woodrow Wilson's Fourteen Points for World Peace,[4] it would be difficult to argue against that right.

The Kurds are undoubtedly the largest ethnic community in the Middle East denied a state of their own and possibly the largest in this predicament world-wide. They enjoy a wide measure of sympathy particularly among the world's most powerful states. True though this observation may be, it is certainly not enough to guarantee the Kurds a seat in the United Nations. No Kurd can be unaware of the fundamental misfortune: to miss out on the creation of the modern state system at the end of the First World War. The thirty million or so Kurds have watched as one by one, other communities have been granted statehood. In some cases it can seem outrageously unjust. For example, in 1999, Nauru became a UN member state. It is a Pacific island less than 9 square miles in size. It has a population of 12,000 and it derives its income from exporting phosphates in the form of bird droppings. And yet 30 million Kurds still remain unrepresented.

A more difficult question, however, is the practical feasibility of Kurdish statehood, if it were to alter the present international borders. First, given the unanimity of the regional states not to allow such an eventuality, it is extraordinarily difficult to imagine a situation arising in which a Kurdish state was able to emerge. And if it did, for example in southern Kurdistan (Iraqi Kurdistan), one may be sure that it would have to withstand immense pressure from its significantly more powerful neighbours.

---

[4] "The Turkish portions of the present Ottoman Empire should be assured a secure sovereignty but the other nationalities which are under Turkish rule should be assured an undoubted security of life and an absolutely unmolested opportunity for autonomous development." Woodrow Wilson, Twelfth of Fourteen Points for World Peace, January 1918.

Each would wish to reduce it to a satrapy. On balance, therefore, we may consider the proposition that a fully independent Kurdish state will emerge as less rather than more likely.

Can the Kurds of Iraq develop a relationship of functional equality within the new Iraq? Here they are faced with a real dilemma. While Kurds may romantically think of Kurdistan as a separate country, there is the prospect of greater economic well-being as a component (whether a federated state or an autonomous region) within a prosperous Iraq which would not have been possible in a separate landlocked Kurdish state. That, of course, presupposes the stability and economic growth of Iraq. Probably, the Kurds of Turkey also have more to gain in a Turkey that becomes pluralistic (assuming that this happens) than as an independent ethnically Kurdish entity. In both cases large numbers of Kurds will need access to the non-Kurdish cities of Iraq and Turkey. These factors, will likely militate powerfully against a wholly independent Kurdish state, regardless of the progressive growth of the Kurdish national movement.

Can Kurdistan Cease To Be Politically Peripheral?

Alongside the ill-fortune that Kurdish society was unready politically and socially to seize the opportunity at the end of the First World War, lies another fundamental reality. In terms of economic power, Kurdistan has always been on the periphery of things, in the marginal terrain between the power centers of the Near East. Think of the principal Kurdish cities and towns: Amid/Diyarbakir, Van, Mahabad, Sinna/Sanandaj, Sulaymaniya, Kirkuk and Arbil. Even had there been no economic neglect of Kurdistan, they could never compare in economic might with the regional capitals: Istanbul, Izmir and Ankara in Turkey; Tabriz, Tehran and Isfahan in Iran; Mosul, Baghdad and Basra in Iraq; and Aleppo and Damascus in Syria. The economic potential of Kurdistan has always flowed into a more powerful economy on the plain. Even with its oilfield, the Kurds' most valued economic asset, Kirkuk has always been an unlikely competitor with the core cities of Mesopotamia. The brutal fact is that while Kurdistan remains of intrinsic political, social and cultural importance to its inhabitants (and that should in no way be belittled), it is always likely to be eclipsed by the power of the states that surround it. However one views Kurdistan's future, it is important to root it in the realities of its geopolitical relationship with the wider region. Regardless of its political configuration, whether remaining parts of other states or even as a state on its own, it can never hope to rival the economic power centers of the region. It is destined to remain economically (and therefore politically) weaker.

Yet undoubtedly Kurdistan could be very much more prosperous than it is at present. In the case of those Kurds living in Iraq, as stated above, the prospect of much greater prosperity rests largely with the possibility of a stable polity replacing Saddam Hussein's regime. Here, however, a warning note needs to be sounded. The dismal events following US president George W. Bush's declaration in May 2003 that major conflict had ended indicate that Iraq may be heading for chaos rather than order. Iraq's Kurds have a natural fear of a strong Baghdad, and their experience between 1975 and 1991 gives good grounds for that fear. But supposing Iraq implodes into chaos, with the Anglo-American occupation ending without a UN force both willing and able to draw Iraq back from the abyss of civil breakdown? What will happen then? One can suggest some possibilities: the Kurdish region will remain more orderly than elsewhere, but its economy is likely to stagnate. Few outsiders will wish to invest in it. It will be returned to the unsatisfactory kind of political limbo that existed from 1991. Then there are external dangers. What will Turkey do? If the US withdraws and Iraq implodes into chaos, it may prove difficult for neighboring states not to intervene to secure areas of Iraq of vital interest to themselves. It could create a situation in which Kurds find themselves rather improbably yearning for a strong and stable Iraq, even one which restricts the Kurds own freedom of action. We shall have to wait and see what happens.

Let us briefly turn to the Kurdish question in Turkey. Accession to the European Union might lead to the provision of regional development funds to the patently impoverished region of Kurdistan. But the basic disparity of wealth between the Kurdish region and western Anatolia has no realistic prospect of disappearing. This disparity of wealth was a reality in the nineteenth century. Looking at the prosperous countries of the European Union we can see that there, too, there are regions of longstanding and intractable economic weakness. A classic example, which finds echoes of similarity in Kurdistan, is the highland and islands region of Scotland. Perhaps one can say the same of eastern Kurdistan, where Iran could make much more effort to develop the area if it were minded to do so but that, even so, this region is never likely to match the regions around Tabriz or Tehran for economic prosperity. As for those Kurds in Syria, they, like the rest of the people of Syria, await the demise of a bankrupt economic system and the revival of Syria's once considerable prosperity. The question therefore arises whether Kurdish political movements will be content in the knowledge that Kurdistan cannot compete as a political equal with its neighbors, even were a Kurdish state to come into being. Or will new parties like the PKK come into being, set upon an ideal of Kurdish secession?

Will the Kurds Achieve Internal Democracy?

Some Iraqi Kurds may feel indignant at this question, in view of the Kurdistan Regional Government's (KRG's) achievement in northern Iraq over the past decade. During that period the Kurdish community has sustained a measure of representative government, allowed a semi-free press, and allowed a semi-independent judiciary. One might—patronizingly—say that the progress has been good. Beyond all doubt the KRG brought a more accountable form of government than the region has ever enjoyed before. But it cannot yet be described as democracy in the sense this word is understood in the West. There is still an important way to go if it aspires to this form of democracy. Here are some of the issues.

The armed forces of the Kurdish region are still loyal to one political party or the other. It is essential that those armed forces as a whole serve the state (Kurdish or Iraqi) regardless of the political hue of the elected party. It is also essential that political parties themselves have no militia and no people ready to use guns for a partisan purpose. The security forces must owe their loyalty to an abstract idea of the Kurdish state or nation, not to any political group. In this regard the collapse of the Lebanese army in 1976 remains a cautionary tale.

The media and the judiciary must be genuinely independent. Ordinary people must know that ideas may be freely propagated in the press without fear of reprisals. Foreign investors must know that their investments are protected from illegal seizure by the existence of a respectable and independent judiciary. Women must know that the judiciary will treat all citizens as equal, and that their rights as equals will be respected.

Wealth creation must be in the hands not of the state, but of the widest possible constituency of wealth creators to whom the government remains accountable for its survival. The creation of such a class of wealth creators in Kurdistan strikes one as still quite a way off.   Perhaps in this regard a note of warning is also not amiss. Ordinary Kurds in Iraq will probably be anxious they get their share of oil. But they and all the others in Iraq who believe oil will solve their problems should beware. Oil could prove a curse rather than a blessing. It has a real potential to destroy the chances for democracy.

Of all OPEC members there is only one that enjoys a fully functioning western-style parliamentary democracy: Venezuela. The reason? Venezuela acquired democracy before it acquired oil. How was Saddam able to ignore the massive flight of intellectuals and businessmen that so impoverished the potential of Iraq for 30 years? The answer is very simple. He could rely on a massive income from oil. Moreover, those Western countries which placed greatest emphasis on the importance of democracy, like the US and UK, were the very ones that ignored Iraq's need for democracy in their own thirst for oil.

So there is a real warning here. Oil wealth relieves a government of its need to be truly accountable to the other wealth creators within the country. And it also relieves parliamentary democracies which trade with oil-producing states of the desire for them to become democratic. No one outside—least of all those of the West—are likely to rescue Iraq's democracy once they are bribed with the prospect of Iraqi oil. Those in doubt on this point should look at US relations with Saudi Arabia and Kuwait.

At the heart of the internal problems faced not only by the Kurds but also by many communities in the Middle East lies the issue of patronage. Patron-client relations are in contradiction with democracy. They occur where the government is unable to extend security and when the national economy is unable to offer an open marketplace for employment. Ordinary people inevitably turn to local strongmen who are able to mediate these two fundamental requirements. That is what has happened in many parts of the Middle East. For example, an uncle or a cousin is able to persuade a patron to offer employment to a young man in search of work. In return that young man, among other things, will surrender his vote to the intentions of his patron. If a political group is able to mediate employment and security, it will command people's votes and the consequence will be a form of neo-tribalism, not a form of democracy. We all know that this has been a widespread phenomenon, for example in Turkish and Iraqi Kurdistan.

Herein lies a major dilemma. A stable, open and lawful environment based on universal suffrage is necessary in order to generate a level of investment that will create a robust economy and full employment. We normally call that state "democracy." Yet the erosion of patron power comes only when a prosperous, open and stable economy renders patrons unnecessary and consequently obsolete. Patrons depend on exercising control in an otherwise unstable environment and providing employment in an otherwise destitute existence. Iraqi Kurdistan may have achieved greater movement towards democracy than elsewhere in Kurdistan, but patronage power clearly remains the basis of the two sectors of the Kurdish autonomous region. Furthermore, patrons inevitably make their priority the increase of the extent and depth of their scope of patronage.[5]

The currently gloomy prognosis for stable governance of Iraq, let alone democracy, renders patronage networks all the

---

[5] For example it is reported that Jalal Talabani has been supplying arms and mobile phones to members of Arab tribes. It is difficult to see what this might be for except to extend his own political influence, possibly with the intention of forging cross-ethnic electoral alliances. David Baran, "Iraq: filling the vacuum," in *Le Monde Diplomatique* (English language edition), June 2003.

more likely to increase rather than decrease in strength. This prospect must be viewed with immense concern. Achieving a transition from patronage power to an openly accountable society is the most crucial challenge the Kurds face. It is also a very hard path to take.

In conclusion, one may quote two great Palestinian sages (no accident for, like the Kurds, the Palestinian people have been cynically denied their birthright). First, Professor Edward Said, a stalwart champion of truthfulness, reminds us that there is something much more important than unthinking patriotism: "I have always reserved the right to be critical, even when criticism conflicted with solidarity or with what others expected in the name of national loyalty."[6] The quality of Kurdish political development is equally dependent on the willingness of people to criticize the leadership.

From 1990 until 1993, Dr Haidar Abd al-Shafi was part of the Palestinian delegation in talks in Madrid and in Washington. The talks collapsed, something widely viewed by Palestinians as a catastrophe. That was not how he saw it. "I tell you plainly," he said on his return to Gaza, "that the negotiations are not worth fighting about. The critical issue is transforming our society. Only once we achieve this will we be strong."[7] In any country such a challenge raises the question of the kind of society one seeks. And, if one's concern extends beyond public recognition of Kurdish identity and rights, it is *the* question which must eclipse all others.

---

[6] Edward Said, *Reflections on Exile and Other Essays* (Cambridge MA: Harvard University Press, 2001), p. 565.
[7] *Middle East International*, No. 459, 24 September 1993.

CHAPTER 2

Are the Kurds a Source of Instability in the Middle East?

Carole A. O'Leary

Introduction

The Kurds, an Iranian ethno-linguistic group, like Persians, Lurs, Baluchi and Bakhtiari, inhabit the mostly mountainous area where Turkey, Iran, Iraq, and Syria converge on the map. Following World War I and the breakup of the Ottoman Empire, the Kurds were promised their own country under the terms of the 1920 Treaty of Sevres only to find the offer rescinded under the 1923 Treaty of Lausanne which formally divided Ottoman Kurdistan among Turkey, Syria and Iraq. Numbering more than 25 million people today, the vast majority of Kurds are divided among Turkey, Iraq, Iran and Syria. The area of greater Kurdistan is about 230,000 square miles, equal to Germany and Britain combined. The so-called "Kurdish Question" refers to the fact that such a large number of distinctive people do not have a country of their own. Indeed, the Kurds are, by far, the largest ethnic group in the world without their own nation-state. The term "Kurdish Question" is also used in a country specific sense, with reference to, for example, the Kurdish question in Iraq or Turkey. The term "Kurdistan" is widely used in Iraq to refer to the Kurdish area of northern Iraq and in Iran to refer to the Kurdish area of northwest Iran. Turkey and

Syria, however, avoid this term for political reasons, although under the Ottomans the term was widely used.

Pelletiere's Instability Thesis

In 1984, Westview Press published Stephen Pelletiere's study entitled *The Kurds: An Unstable Element in the Gulf.*[1] The thesis of this paper is simply this: the assertion that the Kurds are a source of instability in the Middle East is patently false because the underlying assumption about what constitutes "stability" in Middle Eastern states is false. Few policy makers or scholars would argue with the proposition that establishing stability in Middle Eastern states is a necessary precondition for the development of good governance and a vibrant civil society. However, there is no such consensus on what kind of stability we are talking about and what it takes to achieve it.

"Stability," as understood by Pelletiere and others, is predicated on the belief that U.S. support for autocratic regimes assumed to be pro-American promotes stability and is, therefore, in the U.S. strategic interest. In contrast, "stability" defined here refers to the presence of a political and social environment wherein concepts of democracy, pluralism, human rights and civil society can take root within states.[2] Absent a just and lasting resolution to the Kurdish question in Iraq, Iran, Turkey and Syria, it will prove impossible for these states to achieve stability in the sense defined here. Continued instability in Iraq, Iran, Turkey and Syria will inhibit the development of democracy and civil society, threatening long-term U.S. interests in the region. It will be argued here that the Kurdish experience of state-sponsored oppression and violence in Iraq, Iran, Turkey and Syria, including mass murder and ethnic cleansing, requires an organizing framework for governance that accommodates cul-

---

[1] Stephen C. Pelletiere, *The Kurds: An Unstable Element in the Gulf.* Westview Special Studies on the Middle East. (Boulder, Co: Westview Press, 1984).

[2] Carole O'Leary, "The Kurds of Iraq: Recent History, Future Prospects," *Middle East Review of International Affairs (MERIA) Journal*, 6 (December 2002), p. 5 and endnote 12.

tural diversity or pluralism and thereby promotes stability. Federalism is one such model.

Pelletiere's thesis is simply that the Kurds represent an unstable element in the Middle East because they "have a great potential for making trouble." This thesis rests on three assumptions: (1) that the Kurds are a "fighting people"; (2) that Kurdish society is "anarchic"; and (3) that the Kurds are "continuously disrupting the peace in an area that is adjacent to the Persian Gulf where the superpowers want to maintain stability."[3] Pelletiere notwithstanding, no serious scholar today would utilize phrases like "the Kurds are a fighting people" or "they have a great potential for making trouble." How does one even evaluate these statements in terms of the standards of modern socio-cultural analysis, of socio-cultural theory and methodology? Putting aside for the moment the problem with Pelletiere's approach to socio-cultural theory and methodology, could anyone seriously suggest the Kurds are the only entity in the Middle East that could be described as warlike or as having a potential for making trouble?

Pelletiere's misunderstanding of Kurdish tribalism in particular and Middle East tribalism in general is a key to understanding why he concluded that the Kurds are anarchic and, therefore, a force of instability in the region.[4] Pelletiere assumes that tribalism itself is both primitive and anarchic. Ergo, the Kurds are primitive and anarchic because they are tribally organized. Cultural or social identity can be defined by concepts such as kinship, tribe, religion or sect, ethnicity, or nationality. All of these concepts are cultural constructs. They are imagined, negotiated and contested in changing historical, political and economic contexts. They are not primordial or biologically determined, although people often conceive of their cultural identities as if they were inherited or passed on through DNA.

Like the term state, tribe refers to a form of socio-political organization. In the case of tribes, this form of organization is based on shared concepts of kinship (real or imagined), loyalty and territory. Tribe also refers to a form of social or cultural

---

[3] Pelletiere, *The Kurds*, p. 11.
[4] *Ibid.*, pp.17-19.

identity.   The term "culture" or "ideology" refers to sets of be-
liefs constituted by implicit, shared assumptions concerning such
basic aspects of the social order as notions of kinship relations,
citizenship, religion and national identity.   Locally held under-
standings about tribal identity vary throughout the Middle East,
but they are generally based on a concept of political identity
formed through common patrilineal descent.[5] Tribes are neither a
relic of the past nor a "primitive" vestige of social organization.
In fact, tribes can be a constructive element in sustaining modern
national identity (i.e. Saudi Arabia, Jordan, Oman, and the
United Arab Emirates).[6] As Dale Eickelman has argued, "both
now and in the past many states work through tribes, rather than
against them."[7] Tribalism pervades the Middle East from Mo-
rocco to Afghanistan. Whether tribes can be described as forces
of anarchy or instability depends on context. Throughout Middle
East history, tribe-state dynamics, as well as interactions within
and between tribes, have produced both stability and instability.
Therefore, the presence of tribalism in a given society is not in
and of itself an indicator of instability.

In concluding this brief analysis of Pelletiere's thesis, let us
focus for a moment on the Cold War period and Pelletiere's argument that the Kurds were trouble makers because they were
disrupting the peace in an area near the Persian Gulf where the
superpowers sought to maintain stability. One could argue that in
refusing to seriously engage the Shah of Iran on issues pertaining
to human rights, pluralism, democracy and civil society, the US
was at least partially responsible for the Islamic Revolution
which by any measure seriously destabilized the Persian Gulf
region. When one looks beyond the Persian Gulf region to the
entire Middle East it is patently clear that in supporting
"friendly" autocratic regimes in an attempt to block the influence
of the Soviet Union, the U.S. impeded the development of civil

---

[5] See Dale Eickelman's chapter "What is a Tribe?" in his *The Middle
East and Central Asia: An Anthropological Approach*, 3rd ed. (Upper
Saddle River, NJ: Prentice-Hall, Inc., 1998).

[6] *Ibid.*, p. 127.

[7] *Ibid.*, p. 124.

society and democratization which resulted in the rise of an anti-American, anti-Western form of political Islam.

Pluralism and "Official Nationalisms"

Returning to the definition of stability used in this article, let us turn to the concept of pluralism. The word pluralism has multiple meanings. It can refer to an observable social fact – i.e. the presence in a society of more than one cultural identity (e.g. ethnic, national, linguistic or religious), or to a political theory such as the theory of interest-group political pluralism developed by Robert Dahl in the 1950s and 1960s which provided a model for democratic governance and social cohesion in pluralistic societies.[8] Pluralism also refers to an ideology or belief system which assumes that diversity in all of its manifestations is beneficial to society.

Reflecting on challenges to pluralism in India, Muchkund Dubey wrote in the *Times of India* that in Third World countries, years of neglect of various cultural communities, at times their "brutal suppression, and the failure of the nation state project to deliver the goods has made pluralism a major source of tension, conflict and violence." He further noted that "in an increasing number of cases, cultural minorities are converting themselves into political minorities in order to seek recognition and protection of their distinctive identities, claim autonomy and self-governance, and demand segregation and sometimes even secession."[9]

Dubey also argued that in failing to deliver basic goods and services at the mass level, the response of the state-elites was to subvert democratic institutions where they existed by making these states even more highly centralized and coercive. The solution, according to Dubey, was for the controlling elites to

---

[8] Avigail Eisenberg, "Pluralism, Consociationalism, Group Differentiated Citizenship and the Problem of Social Cohesion," unpublished paper, 2000, p. 2.
[9] Muchkund Dubey, "Challenges of Pluralism: Reaching Out to Minority Communities," *Times of India*, February 25, 1999.

abandon the idea of majoritarian dominance—of "hitching the state to the cart of any majoritarian identity."[10]

Benedict Anderson's seminal 1983 study of nationalism raises a key issue for any consideration of stability in the context of plural societies in the Middle East. Of specific interest is his analysis of the rise of "official nationalisms" in Europe during the second half of the 19th century.[11] "Official nationalism" imagines a nation without diversity. It is the antithesis of a pluralistic form of governance. Often violently imposed, "[official nationalisms] developed after and in reaction to, the popular national movements proliferating in Europe since the 1820s."[12] Czarist Russification policy is perhaps the best known example of the institution of "official nationalism" in 19th Century Europe. "Official nationalism" subsequently became the model for many of the new states in the Middle East, Africa and Asia.[13]

The adoption of the ideology of "official nationalism" by Iraq, Iran, Turkey and Syria, as well as other new states that emerged out of the Ottoman Empire, exacerbated tensions among various ethnic and religious communities and between those communities and the new states. While it is not the goal here to rewrite history, it can be argued that a more "elastic" understanding of national identity, of "nationness" as Anderson terms it, could have limited or perhaps even prevented the occurrence of ethnic and religious tensions in the multi-cultural states of the Middle East. In an analysis of nationalist identity-making on the parts of states and ethnic groups, Arjun Appaduri suggests that "the central problem of today's global interactions is the tension between cultural homogenization and cultural heterogenization,"[14] by which he means the struggle on the part of

---

[10] *Ibid.*

[11] Benedict Anderson, *Imagined Communities: Reflections on the Origin and Spread of Nationalism* (London: Verso, 1983), p. 82. See his footnote, which refers to Hugh Seton-Watson's *Nations and States: An Enquiry into the Origins of Nations and the Politics of Nationalism* (London: Methuen, 1982), pp. 147-48, wherein the term is first used.

[12] Anderson, *Imagined Communities*, p. 83.

[13] *Ibid.*

[14] Arjun Appaduri, "Disjuncture and Difference in the Global Cultural Economy," *Public Culture* 2 (1990), p. 5.

states to produce cultural uniformity and the opposing efforts of sub-national ethnic groups to gain cultural and political rights, autonomy and even statehood. Appaduri argues that for many people around the world, the fear is not Americanization, but something much closer to home. Thus, for the Kurds in Iraq and Turkey, Arabization and Turkification are more worrisome than Americanization.[15]

Federalism As a Model

Arguably, federalism, as an organizing principle for at least some of the new states in the Middle East, could have provided a better model for accommodating cultural diversity than existing models in which national identity is understood in terms of one nation, one language, and one people. Iran, Turkey and Syria—who see eye to eye on very little with respect to foreign policy concerns—are in complete agreement when it comes to their mutual obsession with what they perceive as their common "Kurdish problem." Why? The ruling elites of Iran, Turkey and Syria, who have yet to provide full political and cultural rights for their own Kurdish communities, fear that the decade-long Kurdish experiment in democratization and self-rule which has flowered in the Kurdish autonomous enclave in northern Iraq will be institutionalized through a federal arrangement with a new central government in Baghdad. A new Iraq in which Kurds express their internationally recognized right to self-determination through a federal arrangement with Baghdad constitutes an existential threat to states like Iran, Turkey and Syria whose vision of national identity is rooted not in concepts of citizenship, pluralism or common values, but in exclusionism.

Reza Pahlavi and his son, Mohammad Reza Pahlavi, in Iran, Mustafa Kemal Ataturk in Turkey and the Baath party in Syria adopted the later variant of European nationalism wherein national identity was constructed on the basis of ethno-linguistic factors—the Persian language and culture in the first case and the Turkish or Arab language in the other two. Constructing a national identity on this basis in a homogeneous society is one

---

[15] *Ibid.*

thing—if there is such a society—imposing it on a pluralistic reality is yet another. Thus, as recently as the early 1990s, Turkish diplomats in Washington were still referring to Turkey's large Kurdish community as "mountain Turks."

A key question here is whether the current model for maintaining stability in the Middle East, predicated on U.S. support for friendly autocratic states, will cause the Bush Administration to back away from the challenge of constructing a federal, pluralistic and democratic Iraq – and, in the longer term, supporting the development of pluralism and democracy in Iran, Turkey and Syria. There is a precedent for this. In 1991, the first Bush Administration made a strategic decision not to support the Iraqi uprising due to concerns about the stability of key U.S. allies in the region—Turkey and the oil producing Arab states. U.S. troops in Iraq stood on the sidelines as Saddam's security apparatus brutally crushed the uprising that was spearheaded by Kurds in the north and Shiites in the south. Turkey focused on the ramifications of a future democratic and pluralistic Iraq for its own Kurdish policy, while the Persian Gulf states focused on the same ramifications with respect to their minority Shiite communities, as well as fears about Iranian intentions. Contrary to the model of stability embraced by the first Bush Administration in 1991, real stability emerges from meeting the basic human needs of a society, including political and cultural rights for all ethnic and religious communities.

Many states, including Iraq, Iran, Syria and Turkey have attempted to either marginalize ethnic groups or to create an imagined, homogeneous ethnic group or nation out of a reality that is pluralistic. Since the establishment of the British Mandate in Iraq in 1921, the Arab Sunni community—some 20 per cent of the population or less—has ruled with an iron hand over a multi-ethnic, multi-religious society in which Kurds outnumber Sunni Arabs and Shiites form the largest communal group. As President George W. Bush rightly recognizes, regime change in Iraq does not assure the end of dictatorship and aggression; it does not guarantee a post-Saddam Hussein Iraq at peace with its own citizens and its neighbors. Any roadmap for a peaceful transition in Iraq must take into account the multi-ethnic, multi-religious nature of Iraqi society. Iraqis and their American partners in liberation must commit themselves to establishing a system of governance rooted in the principle of pluralism.

While regime change can open the door for transition to a pluralistic democracy in Iraq, the transition process will only succeed in the long run if it is an indigenous process—rooted in the active participation of a broad spectrum of Iraqis in the political process. Although no one can yet speak for some 20 million newly liberated Iraqis, the nearly 4 million Kurds who live in Duhok, Arbil and Sulaymaniya have been free to express their views for a decade. They overwhelmingly support a democratic, pluralistic and federal Iraq and have been debating the fine points of a new Iraqi constitution in their regional parliament. Likewise, since 1992, the Iraqi opposition in exile—including the Iraqi National Congress—has been consistent in its support for a democratic and federal Iraq precisely because it recognizes that Kurds and Shiites must have a place at the table and that federalism is the best framework for governance in a pluralistic society.

In thinking about a federal solution for Iraq as a way to manage diversity, it is important to note that until very recently, Turkey supported a UN plan to create a Swiss-style federal government in Cyprus in which the Republic of Cyprus would be replaced by two component states—one Turkish and one Greek—each with its own constitution, in addition to a common state with a presidential council and a two-chamber legislature.[16] The Turkish government withdrew its support for the UN plan for Cyprus in advance of the 2003 Iraqi war because of the possible precedent it would establish for a federal solution to the Kurdish question in Iraq and the implications of that precedent for its own Kurdish policy. A key question for American and European policy makers—as well as for Iraqis, Iran and Turkey—is whether federalism is the only viable solution to Iraq's still unresolved Kurdish question that will ensure the territorial integrity of the state. A second question relates to how federalism in Iraq

---

[16] Tozun Bahcheli, *Greek-Turkish Relations Since 1955* (Boulder: Westview, 1990), pp. 19-128; and Necati Ertekun, *The Cyrpus Dispute and the Birth of the Turkish Republic of Northern Cyprus* (Nefkosa, Northern Cyprus: K. Rustem & Brother, 1984).

will be structured. A third is whether federalism, as an organizing framework for governance in pluralistic societies, can provide stability in Iraq after regime change —a necessary condition for the development of democracy, human rights and an active civil society.[17]

It is clearly not in the interests of the United States to have sacrificed American, British and Iraqi lives only to see another dictator emerge in Baghdad. It is in the U.S. strategic interest to assist the Iraqi people in establishing a pluralistic and democratic system of governance to avoid the prospect of civil war. The Bush Administration has ready access to millions of Iraqis inside Iraq who have already begun the process of democratization. These Kurdish allies are natural partners for the Administration as it articulates its plans for the transitional phase. Why? The creation of the Kurdish safe haven and northern no-fly zone in 1991 produced a unique situation in which democratization and civil society building have begun to take root through the efforts of the Kurdistan regional government and the millions of Kurds who live in the autonomous region.

As Paul Wolfowitz, Paul Bremer and others in the Administration have recently suggested, the Kurdish experiment in democracy can provide a model for the rest of Iraq in the transitional phase. Moreover, there are important lessons to be learned from it. The critical role of Turkey, Syria and Iran in fueling the Kurdish civil war during the mid-1990s should be revisited by Pelletiere, American policymakers and Iraqis alike. Moreover, there are lessons to be drawn from examining how pressure from below—the role of ordinary Kurdish citizens—influenced the process of negotiation and compromise between the Kurdish leaders that resulted in the stable power sharing arrangement that exists in Iraqi Kurdistan today.

When this author returned from a visit to the region in June 2001, she wrote that an unintended but welcome consequence of the establishment of the Kurdish safe haven in 1991 was an ongoing experiment in democracy.[18] Based on subsequent field-

---

[17] Carole O'Leary, "The Kurds of Iraq: Recent History, Future Prospects."
[18] Carole O'Leary, *Washington Post*, July 15, 2001.

work conducted in July 2002, this author suggested that a second unintended but welcome consequence of the establishment of the safe haven is an ongoing experiment in pluralism and cultural tolerance that has, paradoxically, encouraged the emergence of a communal identity shared by Kurds, Assyrian-Chaldeans and Turkmans.[19]

In other words, tolerance of cultural diversity or pluralism has in fact promoted stability and social cohesion in Iraqi Kurdistan. This emerging form of collective identity may be termed "Kurdistani-ness" for lack of a better word. In trying to contextualize the frequent use of the term "Kurdistani" by Kurdish, Assyrian-Chaldean and Turkman informants, this author was reminded of how Americans use the descriptors "New England" and "New Englanders" to define not only geographic, but also cultural and historic aspects of their localized American identity.

Interviews with some 100 Assyrian-Chaldean and Turkman intellectuals, political and religious leaders, and cultural activists suggest that the decade long experiment in self rule and democratization has been beneficial not only for the Kurdish majority but for these smaller communities as well. Informants suggest that this new sense of Kurdistani identity is taking root precisely because it accommodates pluralism or cultural diversity by not threatening deeply rooted ethno-linguistic identities. The Kurdish Democratic Party--established in 1946 and renamed the Kurdistan Democratic Party in 1953--supported a broad-based political platform for all Kurdistanis regardless of ethnic identity. The Patriotic Union of Kurdistan has advocated the same view since its creation in 1975. However, it is only in the post-1991 period that the people of Iraqi Kurdistan have experienced self-rule and the beginnings of democratization.

The emerging Kurdistani identity allows Kurds, Assyro-Chaldeans and Turkmans to maintain their respective ethno-linguistic identities, while at the same time establishing a wider sense of collective identity based on three key factors: (1) common geography; (2) the ongoing experiment in self rule, democratization and cultural tolerance; and (3) a shared experience as

---

[19] O'Leary, "The Kurds of Iraq: Recent History, Future Prospects."

non-Arab Iraqis who have all known repression and marginali-
zation within the modern state of Iraq.

Suham Wali, one of the many Turkmans interviewed, is an
educator and cultural activist, as well as director-general of
Turkman Studies in the Ministry of Education in Arbil. She argues that the establishment of the Kurdistan Regional Government in 1992 was a milestone. For the first time in Iraq's modern
history, the cultural and political rights of all communities were
truly guaranteed. According to Wali, while the Kurdish majority
may have first sought to address the rights of their own community, the new political structure under the Kurdistan Regional
Government has benefited all communities. She describes political life in the safe haven since 1991 as "a work in progress in
which all communities, not just the Kurdish majority, participate."

Interviews with Turkmans and Assyrian-Chaldeans, suggest
that a growing confidence in the Kurdistan Regional Government's protection of the political and cultural rights of all communities—not just the Kurdish majority—has enabled these two
smaller communities to embrace a shared Kurdistani cultural
identity, in addition to their respective ethno-linguistic identities.
The Kurdistan Regional Government and the Kurdish majority
recognize that stability, democratization and some degree of social cohesion can only be achieved through institutionalizing
equal rights for all communities. For these reasons, this author
would argue that the growing sense of communal solidarity
among Kurds, Assyrian-Chaldeans and Turkmans in the
autonomous region has implications for the debate on how to
organize governance in a highly pluralistic Iraq in the post-
Saddam era.

Given its failure to confront the Iraqi regime's history of
crimes against the Iraqi people, including a policy of ethnic
cleansing and mass murder in Iraqi Kurdistan, support for a pluralistic and democratic post-Saddam Hussein Iraq is a clear
moral imperative for the US. It is also a strategic imperative if
the goal is a stable and unified Iraqi state. The Kurdistan Regional Government and the millions of Kurds it represents have
proven that Kurds can be architects of stability and progress in
Iraqi Kurdistan and in Iraq as a whole. The question is whether

Turkey, Iran and Syria, as well as the new government of Iraq, will also become elements of stability in the region and engines of positive change in their respective states.

CHAPTER 3

The Political Fallout of Ethnic Cleansing in Iraqi Kurdistan

Mohammed M. A. Ahmed

Background

Ever since World War I, Southern Kurdistan-Iraq (Iraqi Kurdistan) has become a major target first for Arabization and then for ethnic cleansing in order to change its Kurdish character. Pull and push factors have been set in motion to expedite the dispersal and assimilation of the Kurdish population. Despite its rich oil fields, fertile agricultural land, and abundance of irrigation water, Southern Kurdistan has been deprived of major capital investments in order to keep the region underdeveloped with a view to obliging its population to seek employment elsewhere in the country. The resources of the region have been mined to enrich and develop other parts of Iraq. Until the early 1960s, Kurdistan produced enough farm products, especially grains, to meet the basic needs of the entire Iraqi population.

Failing to assimilate the Kurdish population through discriminatory practices and Arabization, the government eventually resorted to ethnic cleansing in Kurdistan. Thousands of Kurdish villages and towns were bulldozed, and their population was relocated elsewhere in the country. Arabs from other parts of the country were offered financial incentives to move to homes and farms of Kurds who were forcibly relocated. Thousands of Kurds became internally displaced as a result of government policies. The purpose of this article is to shed some light on the past and recent events and their political implications for the future of the Kurds in Southern Kurdistan.

Causes of Internal Displacement

To properly address the issue of internal displacement and its political implications, one must understand not only its root causes, but also its political and humanitarian consequences. There are two kinds of internal displacement; one is development induced and the other is politically motivated. In civil societies, internal displacement of individuals resulting from government encroachment on their properties occurs in the public interest and in the context of law. The affected persons are compensated fairly for their losses based on the market value of comparable properties. However, in lesser developed states, members of certain ethnic groups are often forcibly removed from their homes and farms and replaced by others with nominal or no compensation for their losses.

Those people who were forcibly relocated in Kurdistan lost not only their lifetime accumulated savings, but also their jobs, friends, and education of their children. In the absence of financial means to start anew, these people were often obliged to undertake any type of work, including begging, just to make ends meet. The disruption of children's education could cause irreparable damage to their future lifestyle.

Forcible displacement, which is used as a means to settle political scores, is socially and economically harmful not only to the displaced families but also to the society at large; it hinders social and economic progress and harms inter-ethnic harmony. The economic and social backwardness of the Kurdish provinces in Turkey, Syria, Iran and Iraq may partly be attributed to the denial of their population of equal opportunity to actively participate in their own social and economic development.

The incidents of ethnic cleansing in Bosnia-Herzegovina, Kosovo, Rwanda, Iraqi Kurdistan, Turkish Kurdistan, and Syrian Kurdistan provide excellent examples of politically motivated social engineering. The governments of these states have used ethnic cleansing and other means of social engineering to "purify" their societies from ethnic minorities such as the Kurds. The weaker segments of these societies have quietly suffered irreparable damage in the hands of their governments under the pretext of safeguarding national security or protecting the sovereignty and territorial integrity of the state. For political expediency and in the name of national interests, members of the United Nations and its Security Council have often turned a blind eye to atrocities committed by these governments against their ethnic minorities.

Forcible displacement has often been used in conjunction with other means to accelerate assimilation of ethnic minorities. For example, aside from relocating thousands of Kurds from central Anatolia, Northern Kurdistan-Turkey, to the west, the Kemalists denied them recognition of their ethnic identity, the use of their mother tongue, and the practice of their cultural heritage. The Kurds were called mountain Turks, people who had forgotten their Turkish mother tongue. This was done not only to suppress Kurdish nationalism, but to expedite the assimilation of the Kurdish population. Kemalists "denounced Kurdish nationalism, along with any other manifestation of Kurdishness, as feudal and reactionary, opposed to progress and civilization."[1] Those Kurds who sought independence were either brutally executed or forcibly relocated to the west of the country and their villages were razed to the ground.[2] Despite these atrocities against the Kurds, the European states embraced Turkey as one of the most progressive and civilized Islamic states in the Middle East.

Similarly, Arab nationalists in Iraq and Syria and Persian nationalists in Iran portrayed the Kurds as being backward, illiterate, uncivilized, uneducated, and highway bandits. They put

---

[1] Hamit Bozarslan, "Some Remarks on Kurdish Historiographical Discourse in Turkey, 1919-1980," *Essays on the Origin of Kurdish Nationalism*, ed. by Abbas Vali (Costa Mesa, CA: Mazda Publishers, Inc. 2003), p. 29.

[2] David McDowall, *A Modern History of the Kurds* (New York: I.B. Tauris, 1996), p. 196.

Kurdish activists on the defensive by claiming that their people have no history or culture of their own and that they are a major source of violence and instability in the region.[3]

In the absence of vigorous international protests, Turkey, Syria, Iraq, and Iran became emboldened in their efforts to assimilate their Kurdish population. Aside from physical and emotional abuse of the Kurds, they have also deprived them of equal rights to education and employment. The Kurds have been denied sufficient space to develop, nurture and practice their own cultural heritage and language.

Since World War I, the Kurds have been left to the device of these states, who have used all available means to reshape them in their own images. Recent reports of Amnesty International, Human Rights Watch, and the international media have described Turkey, Syria, Iraq, and Iran as among the worse abusers of human rights, supporters of terrorism, corrupt, and backward. Since the greater Kurdistan was fragmented and annexed to these newly created states with the blessing of the League of Nations, it is logical to assume that the international community, the United Nations in particular, will take some responsibility for the predicament of the Kurdish people.

The self-rule experiment in Iraqi Kurdistan since 1991 has demonstrated to the international community and the neighboring countries that the Kurds are quite capable of not only ruling themselves but of making substantive contributions to the security, stability, and the economic prosperity of the region. The accomplishments of the Iraqi Kurds do not bode well for the past claims of their neighbors that Kurds are a bunch of mountain bandits. The neighboring countries, however, have recently made it abundantly clear that they do not see it in their national interests to grant the Kurdish people, as a distinct ethnic group, any special political or civil rights.

---

[3] Ismet Cheriff Vanly, "The Oppression of the Kurdish People in Syria," *Kurdish Exodus: From Internal Displacement to Diaspora*, eds. Mohammed Ahmed and Michael Gunter (Sharon, MA: Ahmed Foundation for Kurdish Studies, 2002), p. 57.

Historical Perspective

Ever since the 1920s, the Kurdish region of Iraq has been the scene of sustained social engineering, with a view to changing its historic and demographic features. This practice started with the annexation of the Ottoman Mosul *Wilayat* (province) to Arab Iraq, which consisted of the Basra and Baghdad *Wilayat*s.[4] While the Kurds sought self-rule, British colonial administration promised them local autonomy which never materialized.

With the exception of religion, the Kurds have nothing in common with the Arabs in the center and south of the country. Britain lumped the Mosul *Wilayat* with Arab Iraq for the sole purpose of benefiting from its rich oil resources. The British Royal Air Force was instrumental in breaking up the Kurdish opposition to their plan. As the government in Baghdad gained strength, the promise of self-rule for the Kurds was abandoned in order to appease the Arabs inside and outside the country.[5]

British officials divided Kurdistan-Iraq into three governorates and a number of counties and townships with a view to fragmenting its political power base. Those Kurds who joined the British and Iraqi government ranks were awarded political positions concomitant with their tribal lineage, while those who opposed them were branded bandits. The Kurdish bloc was used to extract economic and political concessions from the Arab dominated Iraqi Parliament. The frequent uprisings by Sheikh Mahmud Barzinji and Mustafa Barzani were put down with brute military force. This in turn resulted in dislocation and imprisonment of thousands of Kurds.

Education in Arabic and the establishment of Arab settlements were used early on as major instruments to assimilate the Kurdish population into the Arab culture. In order to clarify the case in point, one must shed some light on the evolution of the Iraqi government's assimilation policy in the province of Kirkuk and its environs. Arabization of this province started after Britain gained control of the Turkish Petroleum Company (T.P.C.) in Southern Kurdistan in 1925. Instead of relying on local man-

---

[4] McDowall, Modern History of the Kurds, pp. 144-46.
[5] *Ibid.*, p. 151.

power, British officials brought in Arabs, Assyrians, and Chaldeans from other parts of the country to work at the oil company. Preferential treatment was also given to the Turkman minority in the province. The Kurds at the oil company were offered only menial jobs, which did not require managerial, technical, or clerical skills. Britons did not wish to see the Kurds gain a political foothold in this oil-rich province of Kirkuk.[6]

The following statistics should serve not only as a benchmark for measuring future changes in the composition of the population of the city of Kirkuk and its environs, but should also help settle the argument as to which ethnic group accounted for the majority of the population of the province. Table 1 shows that the overwhelming majority of the population of the province in 1925 were Kurds, with a three-to-one numerical advantage over the Turkmans and Arabs. Discrepancies between the population estimates of the League of Nations and those of the Iraqi government can be attributed either to methodological errors in data collection or to the manipulation of census results by local government officials.

Table 1[7]

League of Nations Estimates		**Government Estimates**	
Kurds	87, 500	63%	81,400	59.5%
Arabs	25, 250	18%	26,654	19.5%
Turkmans	26,100	19%	28,741	21.0%

The Haweija irrigation project, which was designed and implemented with the help of British engineers in 1937, was the first major step to Arabize this strategic region under King Ghazi's leadership. The project is about 20 miles southwest of the city of Kirkuk and north of the Hamrin mountain chain which demarcates the southern boundary of Kurdistan-Iraq. The apparent purpose of this project was to erode the geographic boundaries of Kurdistan and to change its demographic reality in favor of Arabs. Its vast oil reservoirs, fertile agricultural land,

---

[6] Layla Namik Al-Jaf, *Kirkuk: Lamahat Ta'areekhiya* (Arabic) (Iraq, 1992), p. 8

[7] *Ibid.*, p. 9.

and abundant irrigation water increased the importance of the province. For the Iraqi government, Kirkuk became the gateway to Sulaymaniya, Arbil and Mosul.

In order to strengthen its power base in Kurdistan, the government settled large numbers of Al-Obeid and Al-Jubour tribal members in the Haweija project. These people had in the past roamed the southern plains of Kirkuk in search of pasture for their camels and goats. The new settlers lived a semi-nomadic life despite the fact that they were allotted free housing units in the project area. They remained in Haweija during spring and looked for pasture elsewhere during the rest of the year. While some family members roamed with their livestock, others remained stationary in the project area.

This is in contrast to the sedentary lifestyle of the majority of the Kurdish population who lived in mud-brick adobe houses and worked as tenants or sharecroppers for large-scale Kurdish landholders. Had the objective of the project been economic, the farmland of the Haweija project would have been allotted to thousands of landless indigenous Kurdish farmers who had a rich farming experience. This was soon followed by settling the Arab tribes of the Al-Kurwy and the Al-Lahib in the plains of Qara-Tappa, south of Arbil, and the Al-Jubour and the Al-Tayi tribes in the Makhmour district of Arbil. These settlements, which were created in strategic locations, gradually penetrated deep into Kurdistan.

The official Iraqi census shows that by 1957, 11,000 members of the Al-Obeid, 12,595 members of the Al-Jubour, and 2,140 members of the Albuhamdan tribes were settled in a number of newly created settlements on the southern fringes of the city of Kirkuk.[8] These tribes later became government sponsored militias entitled "Fursan Khalid Ibn Al-Walid," who harassed and attacked Kurdish towns and villages during 1963 and afterward in order to force their population to leave the area.

The 1957 census shows that there were 5,018,962 Arabs, 1,042,774 Kurds, 136,806 Turkmans, 61,053 Assyrians and Chaldeans, and 217,171 other ethnic minorities in Iraq. This

---

[8] Nouri Talabani, *Mantikat Kirkuk Wa Muhawalat Taghyeer Wk̞iihal Kowmy* (Arabic) (London, 1999), pp. 48-54.

meant that Arabs constituted 79.2 percent of the total population of Iraq, Kurds 16.4 percent, Turkmans 2.2 percent and Assyrians and Chaldeans about 0.1 percent. Table 2 shows the ethnic composition of the population of the city and the province of Kirkuk in 1957.

Table 2[9]

	Kirkuk City		Kirkuk Province		Total	
Arab	27,127	23.8%	82,493	30.8%	109,620	28.7%
Kurd	40,047	35.1%	147,546	55.0%	187,593	49.1%
Turkman	45,306	39.8%	38,065	14.2%	83,371	21.8%
Assyrian	1,509	1.3%	96	____	1,605	0.4%
Total	113,989	100.0%	268,200	____	382,189	100.0%

The above two tables show that while the proportion of the Kurds in the total population of Kirkuk province declined from about 60 percent to 49 percent during 1925-1957, those of Arabs increased from 19 to 29 percent and of Turkmans from 21.0 to 21.8 percent. Since there was no ethnic cleansing during these years, the percentage of the Turkman population should have declined by the same proportion as that of the Kurds. Furthermore, since there is no evidence of Turkman population movement from Turkey to Southern Kurdistan during 1925-1957, the census results must have been manipulated in favor of the Turkmans. Also, there is no evidence to indicate that the birthrate among the Turkmans is higher than that among the Kurds. It is reported that since many Kurds could not read or write, the census conductors in the province, who were mostly Turkmans, registered many Kurds as Turkmans.[10]

Though the Arabization of Kurdistan had been a continuous process, it accelerated after the downfall of the monarchists in 1958 in a military coup led by Abdul Karim Qasim. The overthrow of President Qasim by the Baathists in 1963 was the beginning of a vicious campaign against the Kurds by Arab nation-

---

[9] Directorate of Population, Ministry Of Interior, *Iraq's General Statistical Census for 1957.*
[10] *Ibid.*

alists and Baathists. Compared with Baathists and Arab nationalists, the monarchists had a more gradual approach to the assimilation of Kurds and other ethnic minorities. Though the Baath regime was soon unseated by Arab nationalists in November
1963, they returned to power in 1968 with greater determination
to eliminate the Kurdish opposition in Iraqi Kurdistan.

The new ethnic cleansing program initiated by the Baathists
started with bulldozing some 13 Kurdish villages to the ground
and dispersing their population to other parts of the country under the pretext that they were too close to the oil fields of
Kirkuk. This was followed by the forcible removal of Kurds
from 34 other villages in the Dubiz district of Arbil and replacing them with Arabs, who were provided with free farmland,
houses, and financial incentives. The program aimed at encir-
cling the city of Kirkuk with Arab settlements. A settlement of
600 housing units in Al-Karama, with military outposts to protect its population, was erected on the eastern outskirts of Kirkuk
en route to Sulaymaniya. This was followed by hundreds of
other settlements such as Al-Muthnna and Al-Nablus, near the
city of Kirkuk. Many of these settlements were given Arabic
names and others were named after Palestinian towns such as
Nablus and Al-Karama.

In an effort to further erode the Kurdishness of Kirkuk province, some of its administrative units were soon annexed to Diyala and other adjacent governorates (provinces). Tuz Khurmatu
county was annexed to the predominantly Arab governorate of
Salahaddin, Kifri to Diyala, Kalar and Chamchamal to Sulaymaniya, and Altun Kupri (Perda) to Arbil. The name of the governorate of Kirkuk was changed to Al-Tamim (Nationalization)
on June 1, 1972, marking the nationalization of foreign oil companies in Iraq.[11] By 1976, this important governorate had been
reduced in size from eight counties to three: Kirkuk, Dubiz
(Dibs), and Haweija.

The Baath regime forced thousands of Kurds into retirement,
and others were transferred from Kirkuk to Arab towns and cities
in the south. Positions vacated by the Kurds were soon filled
with Arabs from the center and south of the country. Numerous

---

[11] Al-Jaf, *Kirkuk: Lamahat Ta'areekhiya*, p. 11.

military outposts mushroomed to protect these settlements from attacks by their original Kurdish property owners. Private citizens, including Kurdish shepherds, were barred from entering the depopulated areas which were classified as security zones.

Arab tribesmen who were settled in Kurdish villages were armed with a view to supporting government troops against Kurdish fighters who sought autonomy for their region. The old Kurdish names of schools, streets, shops, and places were changed to Arabic. Aside from demolishing Kurdish homes and villages, extensive military campaigns were launched to intimidate, harass, and pressure Kurds to move farther north or south. Thousands of Kurds, who were falsely accused of collaborating with Kurdish peshmerga fighters, were imprisoned, executed, and dispossessed of their property. The executed Kurds were buried in a cemetery known as the "unknown people's cemetery" on the eastern outskirts of Kirkuk .

New factories and government buildings were constructed on the southern and western outskirts of the city of Kirkuk for Arab settlers only. Arabs who volunteered to settle in the city of Kirkuk and its environs were offered jobs, free housing, and 10, 000 Iraqi Dinars. The houses and farmlands seized from Kurds were allotted to these newcomers. Kurds were pressured to either change their ethnic identity and join pro-government militias or leave the province. The Kurds were not allowed to either buy or build new houses in the province and could sell their property to Arabs only.

Since the Baathists were still weak when they came back to power in 1968, they showed a degree of moderation towards Kurdish demands for local autonomy. By March 1970, a 15-point autonomy agreement had almost been reached between the government and the Kurds, except for their differences over the future status of the Kirkuk province which was under relentless Arabization. The two sides were deadlocked on the status of Kirkuk, which the Baathists wanted to keep under direct control of the central government. The Kurds turned down the government's offers to share the administration and oil revenues of the province once in 1973 and again in 1974.[12] As a result, the Kurds returned to armed struggle with support from Iran, United States, and Israel in 1974. These countries' support for the Kurds was not to help them gain greater autonomy, but to weaken Iraq in favor of Israel and to gain Iranian access to the Shatt Al-Arab waterway. By 1975, the Baath regime was receiving a considerable amount of arms from the former Soviet Union and had extended its power base to every government institution in the country.

During the non-aligned nations' conference of 1975 in Algiers, the former U.S. Secretary of State, Henry Kissinger, had engineered an agreement which gave Iran access to the eastern portion of the Shatt Al-Arab waterway and the withdrawal of the allies' support for the Kurds. The agreement was followed by the closure of the Iranian border and the collapse of the Kurdish uprising. Some 275,000 Kurds took refuge in Iran in order to avoid persecution by the Iraqi regime. Under the so-called amnesty, some Kurdish refugees returned from Iran to Iraq, but were not allowed to go back to their homes and farms which had already been allotted to Arab settlers. Thousands of families were banished to the south and others were sent farther north. Most of these people suffered from utter poverty in refugee camps in Iran or in squalor in Iraq; their children lost lifetime schooling and employment opportunities.

By 1977, the population mix in the governorate of Kirkuk had dramatically shifted in favor of the Arabs. Table 3 shows while the percent of Kurds in the total population declined by 11.6 percent, Arabs increased by 15.71 percent, and Turkmans decreased by only 5.5 percent. Because of Turkey's influence and their own cordial relationship with the Baath regime, the Turkmans must have escaped the brunt of the ethnic cleansing which the Kurds were exposed to.

---

[12] Jonathan Randal, *After Such Knowledge, What Forgiveness? My Encounters with Kurdistan* (New York: Farrar, Straus and Giroux, 1997), pp. 155-158.

Table 3[13]
Composition of Kirkuk population

	1957 Census	1977 Census
Kurd	49.1%	37.53%
Arab	28.7%	44.41%
Turkman	21.8%	16.31%
Assyrian	0.4%	N/A

By 1988, political, economic and social repression of the Kurds had reached its climax, when the Iraqi government leveled over 4,000 Kurdish villages and gassed 200 other villages. The final phase of this campaign, which was called Anfal (the spoils of war) consumed about 182,000 Kurdish lives. Some 8,000 Barzani youth disappeared overnight without a trace. Over 5,000 civilians were killed as a result of chemical attacks on the town of Halabja only. The survivors of chemical attacks continue to suffer from deformation and cancer.

After Saddam Hussein's defeat in the first Persian Gulf war in 1991, the Iraqis were encouraged by former President George H.W. Bush to rise up and overthrow their government. When the Shiites in the south and the Kurds in the north rose up against Saddam Hussein, the American army stood aside and allowed Saddam's retreating troops to squash both uprisings. The chemical attacks of 1988 being vivid in their mind, the Kurds fled to the mountains in the middle of winter with very little clothing on their backs. Iraq's military helicopter gunships pursued the fleeing Kurds to the mountains. Aside from attacking with machineguns, the Iraqi air force cynically sprayed the fleeing Kurds with wheat flour to remind them of the 1988 chemical attacks. Over a million Kurds fled to the Turkish and Iranian borders. Those who reached the Turkish border were prevented from crossing it by border guards and soldiers. The refugees were beaten back with sticks and rifle butts. Thousands of Kurds, including sick, elderly, pregnant women and infants, were stranded on steep mountain slopes covered with winter snow for days. The short-

---

[13] Talabani, *Mantikat Kirkuk Wa Muhawalat Taghyeer Wakiiha Al-Kawmy*, p. 81.

age of food, drinking water, and shelter took their toll on these people. The number of daily casualties reached 1,000. The world media shamed the allies into action in order to prevent a greater human tragedy. As a result, the allies created a safe haven zone above the 36th parallel and protected it from Saddam Hussein's attacks.

The Scale of Injustice and Suffering

It is extremely difficult for most Kurds to understand why the World War I allies betrayed them by turning their back on the Sevres Treaty which contemplated creation of a Kurdish state, and then watched them from afar as they were being brutalized by their rulers. "What sins have we committed," the Kurds ask, "to deserve all this endless brutality?" While the Jewish people continue to pursue Nazi criminals for crimes they committed against their people some 55 years ago, the Kurds are being told to forget and forgive the crimes committed against them by their Arab countrymen during the past 35 years.

Despite Kurdish suffering at the hands of their Arab rulers, the international community continues to view the Kurds as non-persons. Otherwise, they would have taken their national cause as seriously as those of the Bosnians, Croatians, Kosovars, and East Timorians. Since the 1920s, the Kurds have been betrayed again and again by the international community for their own short-term and narrowly defined national interests.

During the 1991 Persian Gulf war, the Iraqi Kurds were betrayed twice by the allies; once by failing to aid the Kurds after they encouraged them to rise up against their rulers, and then by excluding a large segment of Southern Kurdistan-Iraq from the safe haven zone they (the allies) created. The exclusion zone stretches from Khanaqin on the Iranian border to Kirkuk in the center, and Sinjar on the Syrian border.[14] This served as a green light to the Iraqi government to continue its unholy ethnic cleansing in the Kurdish region under its control. From 1991,

---

[14] John Fawcett and Victor Tanner, *The Internally Displaced People of Iraq* (Washington, D. C.: Brookings Institution, 2002), p. 11.

when the safe haven zone was created, until April 9, 2003, when Baghdad fell to the coalition forces, expulsion of ethnic minorities, mostly Kurds, from Kirkuk province continued. The exclusion of these areas from the safe haven zone has become one of the most contentious issues to address since Baghdad fell in April 2003. While the internally displaced Kurds are anxious to return to their homes and farms from which they were forcibly expelled, Arab settlers are refusing to vacate them.

Table 4 shows that by 2001, there were some 805,805 Internally Displaced Persons (IDPs) in the safe haven zone.

Table 4[15]

Expelled in the 70s and 80s	372,347
Victims of 1988 Anfal campaign	222,939
Victims of ethnic cleansing	58,796
Victims of internal fighting among Kurds	77,104
Returnees from Iranian refugee camps	40,155
Iranian refugees	491
Refugees from Turkey	2,552
Victims of conflict with PKK	15,335
Others	16,086
Total	805,805

However, it is important to point out that the above table makes no reference to the internally displaced Kurds relocated to the center and south of the country or those who have been dissolved in larger population centers in Kurdistan. Also no mention is made of some 12,000 Kurdish refugees from Iran who were settled west of Baghdad. It should also be mentioned that the Kurdish refugees from Iran (491) and those from Turkey (2,552) have been lumped with the internally displaced persons in Iraqi Kurdistan. Excluding the Kurdish refugees from Iran and Turkey in the safe haven zone leaves us with 802,762 internally displaced persons. The survey was conducted only in designated

---

[15] United Nations Centre for Human Settlement, *IDP Site and Family Survey* (Nairobi: HABITAT, 2000), Table 2.2.

locations, where the internally displaced persons had been as-
sembled.

About 23.3 percent of the population covered by the survey
was displaced during 1975-1979, 2.2 percent during 1980-1984,
39.9 percent during 1985-1989, 18.7 percent during 1990-1994,
15 percent during 1995-1999, and 0.9 percent during 2000-
2003.[16] This shows that about 75 percent of the internal displacement in Kurdistan took place after 1985, including the victims of the 1988 Anfal campaign and chemical attacks on Kurdish population centers.

The internally displaced persons were practically stripped of
their lifetime accumulated wealth and denied any help to resettle
elsewhere in the country. Most of these people ended up in
squalor with no jobs and survived on handouts from relatives and
/or charity organizations. About 55.4 percent of these people
squatted in abandoned buildings and dilapidated structures, 2.1
percent in apartment buildings vacated by former government
workers, 2.8 percent in vacated military barracks, 3.7 percent in
other shelters, 0.8 percent in tents, 13.5 percent in self-built
houses, 1.3 percent in houses built by HABITAT, 3.0 percent in
houses built by non-governmental organizations, and 17.4 percent were scattered in other localities.[17] HABITAT and non-
governmental organizations became involved in their affairs only
after the 1991 Persian Gulf war, when the safe haven zone was
created. Amenities and social services in these locations were
non-existent or sub-standard.

Prior to their expulsion, most of these people were very well
established financially in their communities and had accumulated considerable amounts of wealth. A recent study shows that
an average family had an accumulated wealth of ID 208,010 before expulsion. In contrast, average family assets were valued at
only ID 8,240 after displacement. Most of these people had to
sell whatever jewels they had saved in order to make ends meet.
Loss of wealth, jobs, and friends, and the disruption of children's
education and normal life have had a devastating impact on the
livelihood of these people. Helplessness and deterioration in

---

[16] *Ibid.*, Table 2.3.
[17] *Ibid.*, Table 2.1.

their emotional status added to their vulnerability and many health hazards. The losses of displaced Kurds turned into financial gains for many Arab settlers who came from other parts of the country. In addition to free houses and farmland, the government offered considerable financial incentives to entice Arabs to settle in Kurdistan.[18]

CPA And Internally Displaced Persons

Since the downfall of the Baath regime on April 9, 2003, the Coalition Provisional Authority (CPA) has kept its distance from the fallout of ethnic cleansing and Arabization of Kurdistan. The resolution of this important issue has been left to local authorities to tackle. Blanket statements made by the coalition authority suggest that the reality created by Saddam Hussein on the ground will be preserved in the foreseeable future. The CPA claims that the expulsion of Arab settlers from Kurdistan would mean another form of ethnic cleansing and that two wrongs will not make things right. The indifference shown by the coalition to the consequences of the ethnic cleansing has been a cause for deep concern among the Kurds. Members of the coalition claim that they have neither the tools nor expertise to handle this multidimensional issue. Constant delay in settling this problem has contributed to the increased tension between Arab settlers and the internally displaced Kurds.

The CPA might have been aware of the scale of ethnic cleansing and Arabization which had taken place in Kurdistan long before the Iraqi war. The report of a mission to Iraq launched during 2002 by the Brookings Institution on internal displacement must have been available to the Defense Department before the Iraqi war started.[19] The writer of these lines participated in a meeting at the Brookings Institution, attended by

---

[18] Mohammed M.A. Ahmed, "The Chronic Problem of Kurdish Refugees and Internally Displaced Kurds in Southern Kurdistan-Iraq," *Kurdish Exodus: From Internal Displacement to Diaspora*, eds. Mohammed Ahmed and Michael Gunter (Sharon, MA: Ahmed Foundation for Kurdish Studies, 2002), p. 34.

[19] Fawcett and Tanner, *The Internally Displaced People of Iraq*, pp. 48-49.

government representatives and non-governmental organizations, which reviewed the draft mission report before it was fi-
nalized and released. Though the report was prepared before the
downfall of the Baath regime, it made a number of useful recommendations for the return of the internally displaced persons
to their homes and farms. Among its recommendations was the
creation of "A Return Task Force" similar to that in Bosnia.[20]
However, no mention was made in the report of the political and
economic fallout of the problem.

In advance of the war, the U.S. Administration created 18
committees to address different reconstruction issues in the post-
Saddam Hussein era. The problem of the internally displaced
persons in Iraq was assigned to a committee headed by the
United States Institute of Peace in Washington, D.C. The committee debated procedural measures for the return of the internally displaced persons, including the Kurds, to their homes and
farms. The present writer attended one of several meetings held
at the Institute to discuss this topic. The committee consisted of
Kurds, Arabs, an Assyrian, a Turkman, US government officials
and non-governmental organizations. While the moderator drew
attention to technical procedures for an orderly return of the internally displaced Kurds to their homes and farms, representatives of the Iraqi ethnic groups were more concerned about the
future political status of their compatriots in Kurdistan. The representatives of non-Kurdish groups were agreeable to the return
of Kurds to their former homes and farms provided that it did not
adversely impact the status of their compatriots. The participants
avoided discussing either the political map of the Kurdish region
or the relocation of Arab settlers to their place of origin. It was
emphasized that an en masse return of displaced Kurds to their
homes and farms should be prevented at all costs.

On April 28, 2003, the United States Institute of Peace released a report on the Kirkuk property disputes.[21] It stated that
"as looting and disorder in Iraq abate, there remains a risk of

---

[20] *Ibid.*

[21] John Brinkley, *Avoidance of Violence in Kirkuk Requires Settling
Property Disputes Quickly* (Washington, D.C.: The United States Institute of Peace Newsbite, April 28, 2003).

violent conflict over real property claims, especially in Kirkuk and other areas the Saddam Hussein regime tried to Arabize."[22] The report also suggested that lessons learned from Bosnia, Kosovo, and elsewhere be used to deal with property claims disputes. The coalition is yet to take any initiative to address the displacement problem, let alone its political fallout. Though the CPA has so far halted the return of the displaced persons, it has mediated minor disputes over farm proceeds for 2003.

A strong campaign started before and during the Iraqi war against the return of the internally displaced Kurds to their homes and farms. Unwittingly, some non-governmental organizations joined the chorus by making inflammatory statements about the possibility that the internally displaced Kurds might take revenge against Arab settlers who are occupying their homes and farms. World Vision reported that 3,000 Arabs have been displaced in Mosul since the fall of Baghdad and that they were worried that this was only "the tip of the iceberg."[23] One wonders if the World Vision reporters were aware of the presence of some 800,000 internally displaced persons in Kurdistan, many of whom are from Kirkuk and Mosul. These Kurds, who want to go back to their homes and farms from which they were expelled, are now being branded as trouble makers and a source of instability in the region.

Without having a clue to the population mix of Kirkuk, Nermeen Al-Mufti tried to aggravate the situation by claiming that a Kurdification campaign is ongoing in the province of Kirkuk, and that Kirkuk is predominantly Turkman.[24] Abdul Bari Atwan of the London-based Arabic Daily *Al-Quds Al-Araby*, joined the chorus of disinformation by stating that Kurds are now occupying land owned by others.[25]

The Director of the London-based Human Rights Watch, Ha-

---

[22] *Ibid.*

[23] Danna Harman, "Kurds and Arabs Give Coexistence a Chance in Iraq," *Christian Science Monitor*, accessed over the Internet, May 23, 2003.

[24] Nermeen Al-Mufti, "Turkmans Under Threat," Report No. 24. (Institute for War and Peace), accessed over the Internet, June 25, 2003.

[25] Bryar Mariwani, KurdishMedia.com, accessed over the Internet, June 9, 2003.

nia Mufti, reported from Arbil, Iraq, that "Kirkuk is a disaster waiting to happen."[26] Hania Mufti predicted "widespread reprisal killings, retaliatory forced displacement, and other acts of violence against resettled families are possible once tens of thousands of forcibly displaced persons return to reclaim their homes."[27] Though these gloomy predictions did not materialize, they had a negative impact on decisions made by the CPA on the internally displaced Kurds.

CPA Blocks Return Of Internally Displaced Kurds

After having suffered so much emotional pain, financial losses, prolonged deprivation, loss of children's schooling and employment opportunities, the internally displaced Kurds were expecting a better reception from the CPA, non-governmental organizations, and media. Most of all, they expected the help and guidance of the coalition forces to regain what they had lost.

The pressure by media, neighboring countries, and US generals obliged the Kurdish leadership to block the flow of Kurdish returnees to Kirkuk and Mosul. For political expediency, Major General David Petraeus, Commander of the Army's 101st Airborne Division, must have placed considerable pressure on the Kurdistan Democratic Party (KDP) and the Patriotic Union of Kurdistan (PUK) to constrain the movement of their compatriot Kurds "until political decision-makers decreed otherwise."[28] The General stated that he "could not allow creation of a new refugee problem," by allowing the return of the displaced Kurds to their homes and farms.[29] It was reported that "everywhere a visitor goes in Kirkuk, angry Kurds wave documents in your face, the deeds of the homes they once legally owned and were taken by Hussein."[30]

---

[26] Hania Mufti, "Impending Interethnic Violence in Kirkuk," (Human Rights Watch), accessed over the the Internet, March 28, 2003.

[27] *Ibid.*

[28] Harman, "Kurds and Arabs Give Coexistence a Chance in Iraq."

[29] *Ibid.*

[30] Sharon Waxman, "For Iraqi Kurds Displacement by Arabs, Home is a Place in the Distant Past, Kirkuk," accessed over the Internet, June 24, 2003.

Petraeus forced many Kurdish returnees from their own land, on which Arab settlers had built houses. He told the returnee Kurds to go and find shelters elsewhere. Though the Arab settlers of the town of Dubiz openly acknowledged that the land on which they had built their houses does not belong to them, the CPA helped them to remain in homes they had illegally built on other people's land. In a civilized world, homes built on other people's land are demolished and their perpetrators are fined. However, in this case, the CPA expelled the rightful owners from their land and allowed the violators of the law, Arab settlers, to remain.

Arab settlers of the village of Hifa, 30 kilometers north of the city of Kirkuk, who have exploited Kurdish farmland since 1975, are also unwilling to vacate their homes in favor of their rightful owners without compensation.[31] Lieutenant Colonel Randy George, Deputy Commander of the 173rd Airborne Division, had informed the media that he had told the returnees not to come back again to the village until a decision has been reached regarding Kurdish rights to their old property.

After the collapse of Saddam Hussein's government on April 9, 2003, many Arab settlers packed their personal effects and vacated the houses and farms they had illegally occupied. Others had taken shelter in nearby Arab settlements awaiting relocation to other parts of the country. However, the expressed position of the coalition that the status quo will be maintained until further notice emboldened Arab settlers to return to homes and farms they had illegally occupied.

By postponing the resolution of property disputes, the CPA not only compromised the future of the internally displaced Kurds, but also endangered the safety of its own troops in the Kurdish region. Armed Arab settlers reacted violently to a few returnee Kurds, resulting in some 10 casualties on both sides. Some of the armed Arabs had come all the way from Haweija to join their brethren in the city of Kirkuk against the Kurds. Haweija is heavily settled by Al-Obeid tribal members, who are part of the Baath Arab nationalist network in Kurdistan. In view

---

[31] "Arab Homes on Kurdish Lands Fuel Rivalries in Northern Iraq," *Jordan Times*, accessed over the Internet, September 30, 2003.

of their strong nationalist stance, they quickly established check-points to block the advance of American troops to their town.[32] Some ten months after the downfall of the former Iraqi regime, the coalition forces are still facing strong resistance from these Arab settlers.

The indecision by the CPA regarding the displacement prob-lem has complicated the lives of the internally displaced Kurds. A certain Mrs. Barani is one of those who tried to reclaim her house in the Azadi district of Kirkuk. After seeing her deed, the Arab settler first agreed to vacate her house in two weeks, but later changed his mind when he learned that the CPA had de-clared that the status quo will be preserved.[33] For this reason, when Mrs. Barani returned to reclaim her house, the settler not only refused to vacate her house, but was also very rude to her. Many of those Kurds who had returned to their homes and farms were soon forced by the CPA to return to where they had come from and others were jailed by the coalition.[34] While American intervention staved off an immediate crisis, a future clash seems to be inevitable and could prove the most destabilizing factor in northern Iraq.[35]

The Turkmans, who are supported by Turkey, have joined Arab settlers in their campaign against the Kurds, wrongly ac-cusing them of looting their homes and shops and trying to change the reality created by the former government on the ground. They want the American troops to reinforce the outcome of the ethnic cleansing implemented by the former regime. While the Turkmans claim that they were ethnically cleansed from Kirkuk and Mosul in large numbers just like the Kurds, they have aligned themselves with the Arab settlers who supposedly have also occupied their homes and farms. The question is where these internally displaced Turkmans are and how many of them are there? If they are not pursuing Turkey's agenda, why should

---

[32] Daren Butler, "North Iraq Arabs Long for Saddam, Say US Favors Kurds," *Jordan Times*, accessed over the Internet, May 23, 2003.

[33] Saadulla Abdulla, "Another Unfinished Business of America in Iraq," The Kurdish Media, accessed over the Internet, July 15, 2003.

[34] Brian Mcquarrie, "A Test of New Freedom in Kirkuk," *Boston Globe*, August 17, 2003.

[35] Harman, "Kurds and Arabs Give Coexistence a Chance in Iraq."

the Turkmans join forces with Arab settlers against the Kurds? While the Turkmans have coexisted with the Kurds for centuries, why are they now turning their backs on their old neighbors? Why did Turkey not come to their rescue when Saddam Hussein was expelling them from Kirkuk and Mosul?[36] Though there are no statistics on the internally displaced Turkmans, it is likely that their number is not significant.

Though municipal councils and property claims commissions have been created by the CPA in both Kirkuk and Mosul since the fall of the regime, there is no sign of any serious effort to address the fallout of the Arabization and ethnic cleansing in Kurdistan. The coalition might have blocked the return of the Kurds to their homes and farms in order to appease Turkey and to gain the goodwill of Arabs, including Arab settlers. Having very limited options, the Kurds had to temporarily accept the new reality created by the CPA in order to help them create a semblance of normalcy in their region. However, it is unlikely that the Kurds will accept the outcome of Saddam Hussein's Arabization of their region.

Despite having been helped by the CPA, Arab settlers have intermittently attacked coalition forces and oil pipelines in the region. Sheikh Hatim Al-Obeid, an Arab Sunni of the Al-Obeid tribe of Haweija, was arrested by the coalition troops for allegedly sabotaging the Kirkuk-Yumurtalik oil pipeline on August 31, 2003.[37] The coalition had been paying $100 per month to 100 members of his tribe to protect the pipelines. However, he had failed to prevent attacks by the unemployed members of his tribe.

Municipal Councils and Property Claim Commissions

By sidelining the consequences of ethnic cleansing, the CPA has created false expectations among Arab settlers and Turkmans

---

[36] Nicholas Birch, "Turks Feel Betrayed by Detentions," *Daily Star*, accessed over the Internet, July 10, 2003.

[37] Welat Lazgin, "US Arrests Leader of Al-Obeid Tribe for Attacks on Pipeline," The Kurdish Media, accessed over the Internet, September 1, 2003.

and considerable uncertainty about the future of the internally displaced Kurds. The municipal elections in Kirkuk might clarify the case in point. In preparation for the elections of May 28, 2003, the military administrator of Kirkuk, General Ray Odierno, selected 300 electors equally drawn from the Kurdish, Arab, Turkman, and Assyrian communities.[38] Each community was allowed to elect 6 candidates for the city municipal council, and General Odierno gave himself the right to select 6 independents, 5 of whom were Kurds. A similar election was organized in the city of Mosul. These elections gave the presidency of the city council of Kirkuk to a Kurd and the deputy position to a Turkman. As for the city of Mosul, an Arab won the presidency of the council and a Kurd became his deputy. Though these elections gave the appearance of inter-ethnic harmony in the cities of Kirkuk and Mosul, they have not eliminated inter-communal tensions.

The membership of the council in Kirkuk was apportioned based on the assumption that 35 percent of Kirkuk city's population were Kurds, 35 percent Arabs, 20 percent Turkmans, and 5 percent Christians.[39] These estimates would have been quite different had the officials considered the actual population estimates of the city and its environs. While the Turkmans continue to claim that they are the majority of the city's population (60 percent), Arabs say no, they are the majority (65 percent) and that the Kurds and Turkmans each account for only 15 percent of its total population. Ayden Bayatli, a member of the executive council of the Iraqi Turkman Front, claimed that while the Turkmans represent 13 percent of the Iraqi population, they have been allotted only one seat on the Iraqi Governing Council. He said this is contrary to the principle of proportional distribution of positions on the council. Despite the inflated figures of the Turkman population in the 1957 census, the Turkmans actually constituted about 2.2 percent of Iraq's population, not 13 percent, as Bayatli claims.

---

[38] Louis Meixler, "Lawyer Becomes Mayor Amid Pleas Against Divisiveness," *Boston Globe*, May 29, 2003.
[39] *Ibid.*

While the situation in the Arabized areas calls for urgent action, Lieutenant Colonel Harry Schute, US Army civil affairs officer, says that any decision about the future of the city of Kirkuk has to be made by the local people and not the United States. In the absence of a third party, however, it will be impossible to settle these outstanding disputes amicably.

Choosing his independent candidates from among the Kurds gave the impression that Odierno was favoring the Kurds over the Arabs, Turkmans, and Assyrians. For this reason, they (non-Kurds) were about to withdraw from the municipal council. Apportioning political positions on the basis of the reality created by the former regime is unfair to the Kurds and misleading to other minorities. The coalition should have openly used the pre-Arabization statistics as a base for the municipal elections. How could the coalition claim that the exercise of selecting city council members was "a test case in pluralism?"[40]

Arab settlers are telling the Kurds that we are all Iraqis and let us forget the past. The Kurds are telling them, how can we forget the massacres committed against us, gassing of our people, raping of our wives and daughters, and robbing of our homes and farms? The Kurds consider Kirkuk to be part of their historical heritage and are demanding that Arab settlers be relocated to their place of origin. Turkmans and Arabs consider the Kirkuk municipal council to be neither democratic nor fair. They accuse the Kurds of having benefited disproportionately from their close association with the Americans and suspect them of having signed secret agreements with them. Both Arabs and Turkmans claim that there is a disproportionate number of Kurds in the city's police force, and that they are unhappy seeing the Kurdish flag flying everywhere and being spoken to in Kurdish. How could the US-backed CPA claim that they will be able to revive the so called "communal harmony that Saddam Hussein laid waste with his divide-and-conquer policy"?[41] The present population mix of Kirkuk has no resemblance to that which existed before Saddam Hussein started ethnically cleansing the city and its environs.

---

[40] Mcquarrie, "Test of New Freedom in Kirkuk."
[41] *Ibid.*

Turkman-Arab Alliance Against Kurds

The visit to Ankara in the fall of 2003 by an Al-Obeid tribal delegation to create an Arab-Turkman bloc against the Kurds should be viewed with grave concern. It is disturbing when one reads in newspapers that the Arabs of Mosul are agitated and uneasy about Kurds from the neighboring areas purchasing real estate property in the city proper. While historians know that the city of Mosul was an integral part of the Ottoman Mosul *Wilayat*, Southern Kurdistan, many Arabs accuse the Kurds of trying to Kurdify it and are "fearful that the ethnic balance" created by the Baath regime might shift against them.[42]

The comments made by Colonel Joe Anderson, commander of the 101st Airborne's 2nd Brigade and the one who is in charge of Mosul, are also unhelpful for inter-ethnic harmony in the city. He says it would be too much if 10 Kurdish families move at once into an Arab neighborhood which had had no Kurdish neighbors before.[43] It appears that Col. Anderson is arguing in favor of some form of social engineering, which would discriminate against the Kurds who were forced out of the city by the former regime. One wonders if he is aware that Saddam Hussein forcibly removed thousands of Kurds from their homes in the city and its environs and settled Arabs from other parts of the country in their place. The present population mix of Mosul, Kirkuk, Khanaqin and elsewhere in Arabized Kurdistan was engineered by the former regime to marginalize the Kurdish political power base. Though such statements might gain the colonel a few Arab "friends" in Mosul (who have resisted the occupation of his forces), they are likely to alienate the Kurds, who helped him free the city from Saddam Hussein's loyalists.

The Associated Press reported on August 28, 2003 that violent clashes between Kurds and Turkmans had erupted after a Turkman Shiite shrine in the town of Tuz Khormatu was damaged by a mortar shell from an unknown source. The town is located about 40 miles south of Kirkuk and 110 miles north of

---

[42] Faramari, "Kurds, Arabs Have Good Relations."

[43] *Ibid.*

Baghdad.[44] While some Turkmans pointed fingers at the Kurds, others suspected Saddam Hussein's loyalists were trying to inflame inter-ethnic tensions in the area. Yet others suspected the Sunni Turkman nationalists, the Turkman Front, were responsible for the incident in order to create a pretext for the Turkish army to occupy Iraqi Kurdistan. Turkey has repeatedly warned that any attack on its Turkman brethren by Kurds will provide the grounds for sending its troops to Southern Kurdistan.[45] Some five Turkmans and three Kurds were killed as a result of the confrontation. American troops also shot and killed two Turkmans after they had fired on them. This was followed by a large demonstration by Turkmans in the city of Kirkuk, protesting earlier clashes between Kurds and their brethren in Tuz Khurmatu, which is predominantly Kurdish. Three more Turkmans were shot in the city of Kirkuk by the security police after their station was attacked.[46]

This latest incident led the Turkman representative on the Iraqi Governing Council, Sangul Cepuk, to call for disarming the city's police force, which she accused of being dominated by Kurds.[47] While the Kurdish mayor, Abdul Rahman Mustafa, called for inter-ethnic harmony, his deputy, a Turkman, said that Turkmans demand their rights and called for punishing the perpetrators. This shows the depth of the mistrust which exists between Kirkuk's dwellers. Though no one knows who was responsible for the shelling of the Shiite shrine, the Turkmans continued to point a finger at members of the Patriotic Union of Kurdistan (PUK), which has denied the charges. The conflict

---

[44] Bryar Mariwani, "Clashes in Kirkuk Leave Several Dead," The Kurdish Media, accessed over the Internet, August 23, 2003.

[45] Justin Huggler, "Ethnic Clash in Oil City Spells More Trouble for US," accessed over the Internet, August 25, 2003.

[46] "Three Turkmans Shot Dead After Turkman-Kurd Fighting in Nearby Town," Associated Press, accessed over the Internet, August 23, 2003.

[47] "Turkman Representative on Iraqi Council Wants Kirkuk Police Disarmed," Associated Press, accessed over the Internet, August 24, 2003.

was settled by paying "blood money" to the families of those who lost their loved ones in the incident.[48]

Incidents such as that of Tuz Khurmatu tend to complicate and draw attention away from settling the consequences of the ethnic cleansing and the Arabization of Kurdistan. Arab settlers and Turkmans exploited this incident to strengthen their political positions against the Kurds. Under pressure from the CPA, the Kurds had to give up some of their seats on the city municipal council of Kirkuk to the Turkmans in order to bring the conflict under control.

The CPA has lately transferred the issue of internal displacement to the United Nations to handle. The United Nations Development Program announced that it has earmarked some $400 million to help return the displaced persons to Kirkuk.[49] The program, which is being financed by the World Bank, "will feature building homes for the returnees who have lost their former residences and giving them cash aid."[50] While the program contemplates helping displaced persons to return to Kirkuk, it makes no reference to the relocation of Arab settlers from Kurdistan to other parts of the country. This type of program is expected to prolong the agony of the displaced persons, since their return to Kirkuk has been made conditional upon building homes and finding jobs for them. In view of the broken Iraqi legal system and the unreliable United Nations bureaucracy, it might take years to implement such a program. This program has come to a halt since the United Nations withdrew its staff from Iraq after its headquarters was bombed on August 19, 2003.

While Arab settlers are allowed to build on their present gains, the living conditions of the displaced Kurds are expected to further deteriorate. Non-governmental humanitarian organizations contend "that Iraq's judiciary has been so disfigured by 35 years of totalitarian injustice that it lacks enough experienced

---

[48] Pamela Hess, "Town Agrees to Repair Shrine, Pay Victims," United Press International, accessed over the Internet, August 25, 2003.

[49] "UNDP Allocating 400 Million Dollars to Return Displaced to Kirkuk," Agence France Presse, accessed over the Internet, August 18, 2003.

[50] Ibid.

and untainted professionals to conduct the many complex investigations and trials that will be required to achieve justice."[51]

In the absence of specific guidelines, members of the coalition have in the interim resorted to their personal judgment to settle real estate and related disputes. They have often imposed settlements on the basis of what they had perceived to be fair, but not necessarily just or legal. Those who have profited from the Baath party's Arabization policy and practices have been equated with those who have suffered from it.[52] Although the Kurds have been oppressed, gassed, tortured, and dispossessed of their homes, they still have been treated with "our nonsense about being even-handed in Iraq."[53]

While the Kurds were the first to lend a helping hand to American troops against Saddam Hussein's regime, Kurdish grievances have yet to receive the serious attention of the United States. By aligning themselves with the Americans, the Kurds have antagonized their Arab, Turkish, and Persian neighbors. In the absence of international protection, these unfriendly neighbors are expected to level harsh punishment on the Kurds once their American friends depart the country. So far, the Kurds have been treated just like the Sunni Arabs, who are still battling American troops, and the Shiites, who have so far maintained a degree of neutrality in the Iraq war. The Shiites have thanked the Americans for ridding the country of Saddam Hussein, but are telling them that they have already overstayed their welcome. While Sunni Arabs take pride in resisting American occupation, the Kurds are still awaiting American assurances about their uncertain future. Wittingly or unwittingly, the Americans are punishing their Kurdish friends, rewarding their enemies, and alienating the neutral.[54]

The inter-ethnic tensions resulting from the former regime's ethnic cleansing and Arabization policy have created serious tensions between Kurds, Arabs and Turkmans, which could not be

---

[51] Editorial Page, *Boston Globe*, July 18, 2003.

[52] Ralph Peters, "Unfinished Business," *New York Post*, accessed over the Internet, June 1, 2003.

[53] *Ibid.*

[54] Ralph Peters, "Break Up Iraq Now," *New York Post*, accessed over the Internet, July 10, 2003.

remedied by the occasional statements made by the coalition military generals. Unless the fallout of the ethnic cleansing is addressed fairly and justly, inter-ethnic tensions will remain high and could erupt into violence at any time.

External Meddling and Inter-Ethnic Tension

Turkey's continued meddling in the internal affairs of Kurdistan-Iraq has complicated the resolution of the issue of ethnic cleansing and inflamed the inter-ethnic tensions created by the former Iraqi regime. Aside from laying numerous legal and historical claims on Southern Kurdistan-Iraq, Turkey has sent thousands of troops across its border to intimidate and discourage its population from seeking greater political autonomy. Turkey has also trained and armed its Turkman proxies in order to destabilize the region and undermine the achievements of the Kurdistan Regional Government (KRG). Prior to the recent Iraqi war, Turkey had threatened the Kurds with a war of its own if they announced independence or sought greater local autonomy. Turkey considers that any political gain by Iraqi Kurds will embolden Turkey's own Kurdish population to demand the same. Thus, Turkey set a number of red lines for the Kurds not to cross. The Turkish government declared that "it would not tolerate the seizure of the northern Iraqi cities of Mosul and Kirkuk; that it would oppose Kurdish control of Iraq's rich northern oil fields; that it would oppose Kurdish domination of its Turkman allies; and, finally, that it would oppose the founding of any sort of independent Kurdish entity, including a federal arrangement, in northern Iraq."[55] Turkey's attitude towards its Kurdish neighbors and its stance on their future destiny is a disaster in the making.

Turkey has adamantly opposed the return of the internally displaced Kurds to their homes and farms in the oil-rich provinces of Kirkuk and Mosul with a view to improving the numerical advantage of its Turkman brethren in the region. Turkey has ignored the fact that about 200,000 of the 800,000 internally displaced people in Iraqi Kurdistan are from the province of Kirkuk

---

[55] Mohammad Noureddine, "Turkey's Iraq Odyssey Ends in Tragedy," *Beirut Daily Star*, accessed over the Internet, April 18, 2003.

and that they want to return to their homes and farms from which they were forcibly expelled. It is only natural for the Kurds to be a dominant political force in their own backyard. Instead of such threats, Turkey should help the KRG to strengthen its democratic institutions with a view to according their Turkman brethren a greater role in administering Iraqi Kurdistan. Though the Turkmans account for a small portion of the total population, Turkey wants the political power shared equally between the Turkmans and the Kurds.

In view of its deteriorated relationship with the United States, Turkey passively watched Kurdish fighters enter the cities of Kirkuk and Mosul immediately after the fall of Baghdad. Since its parliament turned down the U.S. demand for bases, Turkey was deprived of the opportunity to enter the war and prevent Kurdish fighters from entering Kirkuk and Mosul. In order to mend fences, the US unwisely agreed to allow Turkey to dispatch a group of military advisors to Kurdistan to keep a close eye on the Kurds.

Since the end of the Iraqi war, Turkey has tried at least twice to destabilize the Kurdish region. Once during April 2003, American troops captured 12 Turkish soldiers, dressed in civilian clothing, in a humanitarian aid convoy to Turkmans in Kirkuk. The infiltrators had carried propaganda material, ammunitions, and military weapons to be delivered to their Turkman allies. The second attempt was on July 4, 2003, when American troops raided the office of Turkey's special forces in Sulaymaniya and detained 11 Turkish special forces and 24 of their Turkman allies. They were accused of plotting to assassinate the newly-appointed Kurdish governor of Kirkuk.[56] Turkey has used "Iraqi Turkmans as a bargaining chip to stifle Kurdish ambitions" in their homeland.[57]

Since the Tuz Khurmatu inter-ethnic incident, it appears that the moderate Turkman political parties have consolidated their positions and aligned themselves with the radical Iraqi Turkman Front (ITC) with a view to hardening their opposition to the in-

---

[56] Esra Aygin, "US Frees Some of Turkish Special Forces," Associated Press, accessed over the Internet, July 5, 2003.
[57] Noureddine, "Turkey's Iraq Odyssey Ends in Tragedy."

creased Kurdish political power in city of Kirkuk. During its recent convention, the Iraqi Turkman Front replaced Sanan Ahmed Agha with Faruk Abdullah Abdurrahman as its leader in order to confront the Kurds more vigorously.[58] The new leader, who opposes the Kurdish demand for a federal system of government, has asked Turkey to send troops to Iraq not so much for keeping peace in the country but for preventing any change in the status quo created by the former regime in Kurdistan. The Al-Obeid tribal leader, who was invited to the Turkman convention, delivered an emotional speech calling for unity between Arabs and Turkmans against the Kurds.

The Turkman and Arab settlers have sought the help of the radical Shiite leader, Muqtada Sadr in Najaf with a view to preventing the Kurds from regaining the majority status in the city of Kirkuk and its environs. His representative, Abdul Fattah Musawi, has vowed to set up a coalition force consisting of Sunni Arabs, Shiite Arabs and Turkmans against Kurds.[59] These people seem to consider the return of Kurds to their homes as a provocation. Though some efforts have been made by some community leaders to maintain the peace, many people fear that the simmering tensions between ethnic groups could boil over at any time. The virulent sermons of Musawi, an Arab Shiite cleric, and his calls for sacking Kurdish policemen, the removal of their flags from public places, and unveiling of plaques in the memory of Shiite dignitaries have stirred considerable fear and emotions among the Kurds.

Though the Arabs realize that the claims of the Kurds are legitimate, they feel threatened by the Kurds' return to their homes and farms. As for the Kurds, they are frustrated by the absence of a neutral legal body to quickly help them return to their homes and feel that their rights have been compromised by the CPA.

While the radical Turkmans are helping Turkey to find a role for itself in reshaping the future of Iraq, some Turkmans are

---

[58] Murat Unlu, "New Leader of Turkmans Say Turkey Won't Intervene in ITC's Policy," *Turkish Daily News*, accessed over the Internet, September 17, 2003.

[59] "Community Powder Keg Ready to Explode in Kirkuk Despite Official Cool," *Agence France Presse*, accessed over the Internet, September 22, 2003.

calling on Turkey to stop meddling in their affairs. The moderate Turkmans are asking where Turkey was when Saddam was repeatedly suppressing them.[60]

The Turkish writer, Mehmet Ali Birand, states that Turkey must abandon its grand schemes and should reconcile with the idea that "an independent Kurdistan must be founded and that Turkey cannot prevent that."[61] At a time Turkey is trying to create a Turkish state for about 200,000 Cypriot Turks in Cyprus, it opposes the creation of any entity for some 5 million Kurds in Iraqi Kurdistan. It is time that the United States asks Turkey to stop threatening the Iraqi Kurds and start learning how to live with them in peace and harmony.

Political Map of Kurdistan

Some have asserted that the rising tensions between Arabs, Kurds, and Turkmans in the Arabized areas of Kurdistan are caused by land disputes and not inter-ethnic struggle for power and domination. In reality, the heightened tension is rooted in both inter-ethnic power struggles and land disputes. Unless the political aspects of ethnic cleansing and Arabization are addressed in a holistic manner, an orderly return of the internally displaced Kurds to their homes and farms will ensure neither justice nor long-term peace and stability in the region.

While ownership disputes may require a set of procedural and legal yardsticks, the resolution of the political aspects of ethnic cleansing demand the restoration of the administrative boundaries of Kurdistan which existed before 1963, when the Baathists first came to power. Redistricting the Kurdish region was done by the former regime for the sole purpose of marginalizing the political power base of the Kurdish people. Therefore, unless the political fallout of the ethnic cleansing is tackled in a holistic

---

[60] Ilnur Cevik, "Kurdistan Observer," accessed over the Internet, July 21, 2003.
[61] Mehmet Ali Birand, "Are We Going to Differentiate Between Ideas and Weapons?" *Turkish Daily News,* accessed over the Internet, June 5, 2003.

manner, inter-communal tensions are expected to erupt into further violence in Arabized Kurdistan.

In addressing this problem one must answer a number of
questions of direct concern to the internally displaced persons.
For example, how long should the internally displaced Kurds
wait until they are allowed to return to their homes and farms?
What should be the destiny of Arab settlers who came to settle in
Kurdistan for financial gains or ideological reasons? Should the
Kurds accept the reality created by the former Iraqi regime in
their region just to create the semblance of normalcy in Arabized
Kurdistan? If not, what should they do to redress the problem?
Would the future Iraqi government agree to help relocate Arab
settlers to their place of origin? Should settlers on public lands
be treated the same way as those who occupied the houses and
farms of the forcibly relocated Kurds?

Arab settlers, who were an integral part of Saddam Hussein's
ethnic cleansing apparatus to Arabize the Kurdish region, are
now accusing the Kurds of being traitors for helping the coalition
troops to bring down their "benevolent" Baath regime. Likewise,
the Turkmans and their patron, Turkey, are deeply distrustful of
the American designs and those of their new Kurdish allies.

Ironically, though the Kurds have been the most reliable
American allies, they have been used to bring other Iraqi groups
in line with the American agenda, as Britain did to their parents
and grandparents during and after World War I. Though the
Kurds have received no explicit assurance from their American
friends about their future status, they have continued to closely
cooperate with them in the creation of the Iraqi Governing
Council and its ministerial cabinet. In the process, the attention
of the Kurdish leadership has been diverted from the priority
needs of the Kurdistan Regional Government to the creation of a
national Iraqi government in Baghdad. This change in focus has
had a direct bearing not only on the fate of the internally displaced Kurds, but also on the future status of Kurdistan.

The mounting US casualties, inter-ethnic violence in Kirkuk,
persistent Sunni Arab resistance in the center, the attack on UN
headquarters in Baghdad, the ambush of British forces in Basra,
the death of the Shiite leader, Mohammed Baqir al-Hakim, in a
car-bomb attack, the double suicide bombers attacks on the KDP

and PUK centers in Arbil on February 1, 2004, and continued violence first by the Sunni Arabs and then by radical Shiites have increased uncertainties about the future status of Iraq as well as that of the Kurdistan Regional Government.

The United States had initially foreseen a longer term occupation of Iraq, but for domestic reasons it later decided to transfer power back to the Iraqis as early as June 30, 2004.[62] The strenuous efforts made by the United States to increase participation of the international community in the peacekeeping force in Iraq have not fully succeeded. However, transferring power back to the Iraqis during such a short span of time would create considerable uncertainty about the future status of Kurdistan and the fate of the internally displaced persons in the region.

Since the overthrow of the former Iraqi regime, the Kurds have been used by the CPA to neutralize internal dissent and silence external rumors that Iraq is on the verge of being fragmented and that a Kurdish state might soon emerge. In support of the CPA, the Kurdish politicians delivered speeches inside and outside Iraq claiming that they were all Iraqis before being Kurds and that Kurds and Arabs were brothers and that their main goal was to preserve the unity and the territorial integrity of the country. In one of her speeches, Nasreen Sideek Barwari, a Kurdish member of the appointed Iraqi ministerial cabinet, stated that she "looks forward to being a full-fledged, equal, and integral part of a new, better Iraq."[63] She called for Arbil and Sulaymaniya to be treated just like Baghdad and Basra.

The wisdom of such statements by Kurdish politicians is questionable on the grounds that they might compromise their future negotiating position. Was Barwari talking about the provinces of Arbil and Sulaymaniya within or without any official boundaries of Kurdistan? If she was talking about Iraqi provinces without a separate Kurdish entity, Kurdistan, then there will be no ground for the relocation of Arab settlers from Kirkuk and Mosul to their place of origin in the center and south.

---

[62] Stephen J. Gain, "Slaying of a Key Figure Steps Up Pressure on US Search for Allies,"*Boston Globe*, August 30, 2003, p. A8.
[63] Nesreen Sideek Barwari, "Iraq Through Iraqi Kurdistan," The Kurdish Media, accessed over the Internet, July 22, 2003.

In the absence of Kurdistan as a separate administrative unit, all Iraqis will be entitled to settle and live freely wherever they wish. Aside from returning the internally displaced Kurds to their homes and farms, there will be no remedy for addressing the political fallout of the ethnic cleansing. The United States has taken not only a neutral position on the issue of a federal system of government for Iraq, but has also opposed creation of an independent Kurdistan, which is being supported by many intellectuals and writers. The United States has also opposed the "longstanding Kurdish claims that the provinces of Kirkuk and Mosul be included in a federal Kurdish entity, as well as their claim that a share of Iraq's oil wealth be earmarked for them."[64]

The Kurds were more optimistic about their own future when the former regime was overthrown than now. They have put their own future at risk by pinning all their hopes on the American coalition which is facing considerable uncertainties in Iraq. The cordial relationship which existed between the Kurds and Arabs immediately after the war seems to be gradually fading; Kurds are being attacked physically and in the media for not being true Iraqis and for not submitting to the whims of the Arab majority. The Arab members of the Iraqi Governing Council have gradually turned their backs on the concept of a federal system of government which offers the Kurds greater regional autonomy.[65]

It is also disturbing to learn that the discovery of a 1997 Iraqi census, which was kept secret by the former regime, has prompted the CPA to advance the perceived elections for a representative government in Baghdad. Colonel Allen Irish, a US Army officer working with the provisional authority in Baghdad, had stated that "the figures compiled by geographical subdivision could be the basis of an electoral apportionment and so a building block of the democratic elections promised to Iraqis by the provisional authority."[66] This statement sheds further doubt

---

[64] Charles Oliver, "Kurds Fear for Role of Political Movements," *Financial Times*, accessed over the Internet, May 23, 2003.

[65] Patrick E. Tyler, "Iraqi Groups Badly Divided Over How To Draft a Charter," *New York Times*, accessed over the Internet, September 30, 2003.

[66] Felicity Berringer, "Where, the Census Asks, Did Those Iraqi Men Go?" *New York Times*, accessed over the Internet, August 8, 2003.

on the CPA's intentions regarding the Kurdish question and the administrative boundaries of Southern Kurdistan. So far, there has been no serious discussion of the consequences of the ethnic cleansing carried out by the former regime and ways and means to address them.

The statements made by Paul Bremer, the CPA administrator, at Congress that the creation of a Kurdish state is against American interests is unhelpful for maintaining Kurdish-American solidarity against tyranny and terrorism in the Middle East.[67] Furthermore, despite the opposition of the Iraqi Governing Council, including the Kurdish bloc, Washington sought Turkey's military assistance in Iraq in exchange for an US $8.5 billion loan. However, after some thought, the United States reversed its plan to invite Turkey's military participation in the Iraqi peacekeeping force. Participation of Turkish troops in the peacekeeping force, which was approved by the Turkish Parliament on October 7, 2003, would have been a further blow to the hopes and aspirations of the Kurds of Southern Kurdistan.[68] The CPA was well aware that Turkey stands against anything called Kurd or Kurdish, not only in Turkey but also in the neighboring countries.

Though Turkey's military presence in Iraq might have reduced American casualties, it would have certainly jeopardized the future of some 5 million Kurds, who have suffered considerable abuse in the hands of successive Iraqi governments and have been betrayed several times before by the United States. It would have been unworthy of the United States to deliver the Kurds, as a sweetener to Turkey in exchange for "10,000 Turkish troops—who will act solely in Ankara's interests, not in the interests of Washington or the people of Iraq."[69]

With almost total "unanimity, analysts, scholars and veterans from across the political spectrum" said that moral issues aside, the presence of Turkish soldiers would exacerbate "the volatile

---

[67] "Bremer Says Kurdish State Is Against U.S. Interests," *Turkish Daily News,* accessed over the Internet, September 26, 2003.

[68] Louis Meixler, "Turkey Votes to Send Peacekeepers to Iraq," *Boston Globe,* October, 8, 2003.

[69] Ralph Peters, "Bush's Betrayal of Kurds," *New York Post,* accessed over the Internet, October 9, 2003.

ethnic and sectarian situation" in Iraq.[70]   While Turkey denied
the United States a second corridor through its territories against
Saddam Hussein and Arabs put up strong resistance in the center
and south, Kurdish women, children, and men received U.S. soldiers with open arms and flowers in Southern Kurdistan. The
Kurds thought that the United States had finally become their
savior.

The United States might have mistakenly believed that Turkey's close ties with the former Baathist regime would have enabled it to restore stability in the Sunni Arab triangle. More
likely, however, Turkey's alignment with the residuals of the
former regime could have antagonized not only the Kurds and
Shiites, but also Arab nationalists who opposed the Baathists.
The presence of Turkish soldiers in the country would have certainly led to further chaos and bloodshed in the country.

Turkey is now trying through the back door to influence
events inside Iraq. Turkey has played an active role in influenc-
ing the position of the neighboring countries regarding the future
shape of Iraq. Several inter-governmental meetings have been
held in Ankara, Damascus, Cairo and recently (February 14-15,
2004) in Kuwait to discuss the future of Iraq. These countries
consider that the creation of a federal system of government, as
proposed by the Kurds, would threaten the unity of Iraq and the
stability of the neighboring countries. Turkey is adamantly opposed to any plan which might grant the Iraqi Kurds more freedom than Turkey permits its own Kurdish population.

The generous political posture demonstrated by the Kurds
could squander their past sacrifices, recent gains, and future
prospects. The Kurds have already made too many concessions
to their new friends and to their neighbors. It seems that the hon-
eymoon for the Kurds is over and that they have to face the hard
reality that their national aspirations differ from those of the Arabs and Turkmans. Their survival as a nation is at stake at this
critical juncture of their history. Aside from the Turkish factor,
strong forces within Iraq and in the neighboring Persian Gulf
countries, as reflected in the Al-Jazeera Television Broadcasting

---

[70] Michelle Goldberg, "Betraying the Kurds Again," accessed over the
Internet, October 14, 2003.

program, are once again projecting the Kurds as villains and separatists who are trying to create another Israel in the north of Iraq.[71] The recent anti-Kurd articles in *Al-Quds Al-Araby*, which welcomes the deployment of Turkish troops in Southern Kurdistan-Iraq, are most disturbing.[72] Unless the Kurds are able to maintain the momentum of defending the legitimacy of their demands, they will emerge from the recent Iraqi war empty handed.

The Kurds must expand and intensify contacts with the members of the United Nations Security Council who legitimized the occupation of Iraq by approving Resolution 1511. Faced with serious opposition from Arabs and Turkmans to a federal system of government, the Kurds would have no choice but to seek independence from Iraq. Why should the Kurds defend the territorial integrity of Iraq unless their rights could be protected from future abuses? Many intellectuals and writers have lately called for the creation of a separate state for the Kurds. Ralph Peters states that "after the Jews and Armenians, they [the Kurds] have been the most persecuted ethnic group of the last hundred years, always denied an independent homeland, shot, gassed, driven from their homes—and even victimized for the use of their native dialects."[73] The unity of Iraq, which has been maintained by sheer force ever since World War I, cannot be continued unless a conducive environment can soon be created for coexistence between Kurds, Arabs, and Turkmans. Faced with the present opposing interests, it is unlikely that peace and stability can be restored to the region without giving the Kurdish people the opportunity to determine their own future.

Recommendations

To address the consequences of ethnic cleansing in Kurdistan fairly and judiciously, one must restore the situation to the pre-

---

[71] "Kurds and the Future of Iraq," Al Jazeera TV Channel, October 7, 2003.
[72] See, for example, Kurda Amin, "Do We Really Need Those Savages To Maintain Security and Rebuilt Iraq?" accessed over the Internet, October 18, 2003.
[73] Peters, "Break Up Iraq Now."

Baathist rule of 1963 to the greatest extent possible. This should be done as quickly as possible in order to minimize the suffering of the displaced Kurds and to restore their political and civil rights as a distinct ethnic group.

The life, liberty, and the pursuit of happiness of the Kurds should become the guiding principles for all quarters concerned with the Kurdish question. Appeasing Turkey and the Arab community might serve the short-term American interests, but would jeopardize the long-term peace and stability in the region. The cost of maintaining the so-called territorial integrity of Iraq has been too high in terms of Kurdish human lives and suffering. For this reason, many intellectuals and political practitioners have come to the conclusion that the time is ripe for the creation of a Kurdish state in the Middle East.

While ethnic cleansing created opportunities for Arab settlers to accumulate wealth and build their political fortunes, the displaced Kurds have endured deprivation in squalor, makeshift shelters, and tent cities. Arab settlers took over not only the homes and farms of displaced Kurds, but also their former jobs. Unless all signs of ethnic cleansing and Arabization are removed from Kurdistan, including the relocation of Arab settlers, interethnic tensions are expected to remain high. Any delay in the relocation of Arab settlers would certainly compromise the outcome of any future elections at the local and national levels.

The displaced Kurds should be entitled not only to recover their lost homes and farms, but should also be compensated for lost incomes from their confiscated assets, as well as lost jobs, education, and employment opportunities of their children. Short of such efforts, most of the burden of the ethnic cleansing and Arabization will unfairly and unjustly fall on the internally displaced Kurds and their descendants.

The lost opportunities of the displaced Kurds should be used as a yardstick to measure the overall losses sustained by them as individuals and as a group. As already partially mentioned, this formula should include variables ranging from lost jobs and real estate incomes, foregone education and employment opportunities of children, emotional distress, isolation and separation from relatives and friends, to hardships endured in refugee camps.

Maximum efforts should be made to quantify these variables for compensation purposes.

In order to tackle the root causes of the problem, it is recommended that three committees be created to address different aspects of the ethnic cleansing and Arabization in Kurdistan. The first committee is to address the issue of the administrative boundaries of Kurdistan, the second is to handle the grievances of the internally displaced Kurds, and the third is to plan the relocation of Arab settlers to other locations in the center and south of Iraq.

The restoration of the administrative boundaries of Southern Kurdistan should be based on the original borders of the Ottoman Mosul Wilayat before it was annexed to Iraq. This task would require a team of cadastral surveyors and cartographers to redraw the political map of Southern Kurdistan and to restore the historic names of its towns and villages. Saddam Hussein not only detached five counties from the original province of Kirkuk and attached them to adjacent provinces, but he also changed Kirkuk's name to Al-Tamim. The acceptance of the present reality by the Kurds means that they will condemn themselves to gradual assimilation and extinction as a nation. Therefore, the restoration of the political map of Southern Kurdistan should be the top and urgent priority of the Kurds since it has a direct bearing on the outcome of future censuses and apportionment of political positions at the local, provincial and central levels.

A committee, equipped with the necessary technical and financial resources, should also be created to help the victims of ethnic cleansing return to their homes and farms in an orderly fashion and be compensated for their losses based on foregone opportunities. A sub-committee should also be formed to collect detailed data and information about the displaced families and individuals with a view to verifying their claims to a given piece of property or their place of origin. Those with clear titles of ownership to specific properties should be granted immediate permission to return to their homes and farms. Disputes concerning properties kept within families without property deeds, should be settled through neighborhood committees. Registries and cadastral maps for townships, cities, and villages should be created for updating land ownership records. In addition, a compensation subcommittee should be established with a view to estimating the foregone opportunities and losses sustained by displaced Kurds and others. Another subcommittee should provide the means of transport to help these people return to their homes and farms.

A third committee should handle the relocation of Arab settlers to their place of origin or elsewhere in the center and south. Subcommittees should be created to help these settlers financially and provide them with means of transport to relocate elsewhere in the country. A list of Arabs who have settled in Kurdistan after 1963 should be made available to this committee as soon as possible in order to make preparatory arrangements for their relocation. Since it is difficult to separate those who moved to the region under the Arabization program from those who have settled for ideological and commercial reasons, the planners might consider grouping all of them under one category for relocation purposes.

CHAPTER 4

Kurdish Prospects in Post-Saddam Iraq

Michael M. Gunter

On March 19, 2003, the United States finally launched a war against Iraq, which quickly drove Saddam Hussein from power. Winning the peace, of course, will prove more difficult than winning the war. An artificial state cobbled together by British imperialism following World War I,[1] Iraq has truly proven to be a failed state. Its future has now become even more uncertain. Within this uncertainty, however, lies renewed opportunities for the different people who live in Iraq. The purpose of this article is to analyze the future prospects of one of these groups, the Kurds.

Into the first half of the 19th century, the traditional decentralized Ottoman state and millet system of religious communities, in effect, offered the various nations of the Ottoman Empire autonomy.[2] Beginning in the 1830s, however, the Ottoman Em-

---

[1] On this point, see Toby Dodge, *Inventing Iraq: The Failure of Nation Building and a History Denied* (New York: Columbia University Press, 2003). Portions of this article were originally published as "Kurdish Future in a Post-Saddam Iraq," *Journal of Muslim Minority Affairs* 23 (April 2003), pp. 9-23.

[2] In general, see Kemal Karpat, *An Enquiry into the Social Foundations of Nationalism in the Ottoman State: From Social Estates to Classes, from Millets to Nations* (Princeton: Center of International Studies, 1973); Halil Inalcik, *The Ottoman Empire: The Classical Age, 1300-*

pire began to centralize in an attempt to modernize itself and stave off the Western onslaught.[3] This process of centralization eliminated the autonomy long enjoyed by the Kurdish emirates.[4]

Following World War I, modernization policies continued with the demise of the Ottoman Empire and the development of modern states in Turkey, Iran, Iraq,[5] and Syria. The price to be paid for a modernized state, however, was a highly centralized government that sought to assimilate its minorities.[6] Such a vision of modernity had no place for a Kurdish identity. Indeed, in Iraq the Baathist state of Saddam Hussein eventually unleashed a genocidal assault on its Kurdish minority in the guise of its so-called Anfal campaign of chemical warfare and mass murder.[7] In

---

1600 (London: Weidenfeld & Nicolson, 1973); Stanford Shaw and Ezel Shaw, *History of the Ottoman Empire and Modern Turkey.* Vol. II: *Reform, Revolution, and Republic: The Rise of Modern Turkey, 1805-1917* (Cambridge: Cambridge University Press, 1977); and more specifically, see Paul White, *Primitive Rebels or Revolutionary Modernizers? The Kurdish National Movement in Turkey* (London; Zed Books, 2000), pp. 56-57.

[3] Bernard Lewis, *The Emergence of Modern Turkey* (2nd ed.; London: Oxford University Press, 1968).

[4] David McDowall, *A Modern History of the Kurds* (London: I.B. Tauris, 1996), pp. 38-65.

[5] For a detailed history of modern Iraq's earlier decades, see Stephen H. Longrigg, *Iraq, 1900 to 1950: A Political, Social, and Economic History* (London: Oxford University Press, 1953). More recently, see Phebe Marr, *The Modern History of Iraq* (Boulder, Colo.: Westview Press, 1985); and Charles Tripp, *A History of Iraq* (2nd ed.; Cambridge: Cambridge University Press, 2000). For further background, see Majid Khadduri, *Socialist Iraq: A Study in Iraqi Politics Since 1968* (Washington: The Middle East Institute, 1978); and Marion Farouk-Sluglett and Peter Sluglett, *Iraq Since 1958: From Revolution to Dictatorship* (London: Kegan Paul International, 1987).

[6] For an excellent discussion of this point, see Andreas Wimmer, *Nationalist Exclusion and Ethnic Conflict: Shadows of Modernity* (Cambridge: Cambridge University Press, 2002), pp. 156-95.

[7] Human Rights Watch/Middle East, *Iraq's Crime of Genocide; The Anfal Campaign against the Kurds* (New Haven: Yale University Press, 1995); and Kanan Makiya, *Cruelty and Silence: War, Tyranny, Uprising and the Arab World* (New York: W.W. Norton & Company, 1993), pp. 151-99. Also see Samir al-Khalil (Kanan Makiya), *Republic of*

Turkey, the Kurds were targeted to lose their identity as "mountain Turks" in need of assimilation.[8] The modernization policies in Iran of Reza Shah Pahlavi and his son, Mohammad Reza Shah Pahlavi, ended the Kurdish tribes' nomadism and thus much of their identity.[9] Even more, the Ayatollah Ruhollah Khomeini's Islamic Revolution had no place for a separate Kurdish identity in its Islamic Republic.[10] Finally, in Syria, the government denied much of its Kurdish population citizenship in its dictatorial modern state.[11]

Only Saddam Hussein's monumental miscalculation in bringing down upon himself the United States-led attack during the Gulf War in 1991 and the subsequent safe haven protected by a no-fly zone, enabled a de facto Kurdish state to emerge in northern Iraq.[12] No one, however, recognized this state because it threatened to destabilize the existing regional state system.[13] Despite the relative prosperity it began to enjoy after 1997 from its 13 percent of Iraq's renewed oil sales, the future of this de facto Kurdish state ironically depended upon Saddam Hussein's remaining in power. Once he was gone, it was unlikely the United

---

Fear: The Politics of Modern Iraq (Berkeley: University of California Press, 1989)

[8] Michael M. Gunter, *The Kurds and the Future of Turkey* (New York: St. Martin's Press, 1997), p. 6.

[9] McDowall, *Modern History of the Kurds*, pp. 66-86, and 214-83.

[10] Farideh Koohi-Kamali, *The Political Development of the Kurds in Iran: Pastoral Nationalism* (New York: Palgrave Macmillan, 2003); and Nader Entessar, *Kurdish Ethnonationalism* (Boulder, Colo.: Lynne Rienner Publishers, 1992), pp. 29-48.

[11] Mustafa Nazdar (Ismet Cheriff Vanly), "The Kurds in Syria," in *A People without a Country: The Kurds and Kurdistan*, ed. Gerard Chaliand (New York: Olive Branch Press, 1993), pp. 194-201; and Ismet Cheriff Vanly, "The Kurds in Syria and Lebanon," in *The Kurds: A Contemporary Overview*, eds. Philip G. Kreyenbroek and Stefan Sperl (London: Routledge, 1992), pp. 143-64.

[12] For a discussion see Michael M. Gunter, *The Kurds of Iraq: Tragedy and Hope* (New York: St. Martin's Press, 1992), pp. 49-95.

[13] Michael M. Gunter, *The Kurdish Predicament in Iraq: A Political Analysis* (New York: St. Martin's Press, 1999), pp. 111-26; and Gareth R.V. Stansfield, *Iraqi Kurdistan: Political Development and Emergent Democracy* (London and New York: RoutledgeCurzon, 2003).

States would continue to protect it from a post-Saddam Iraqi government.[14] Indeed, the United States and the regional states all insisted that Iraq's territorial integrity be protected. There would be no independent Kurdish state. Turkey even declared that any attempt to implement such a state would be a *casus belli.*

Faced with such harsh realities, the Iraqi Kurds turned to federalism as their best realistic hope in a post-Saddam Iraq. Turkey, however, saw federalism as simply another step toward the Kurdish independence it feared and would not accept. Moreover, continuing advocates of a modern centralized state viewed federalism as a divisive future based on a return to the failed past of a decentralized state. It little impressed such opponents of federalism that such post-modern Western states as the United States, Germany, and Switzerland actually based part of their success on a federalism that provided a national unity while allowing necessary regional differences. Even the movement of such time-honored unitary systems as Great Britain, France, and Spain to implement far reaching decentralization schemes to loosen their overly centralized states, failed to impress these critics of putative Iraqi federalism.

Thus, if the Iraqi Kurds were going to establish a successful federalist solution in a post-Saddam Iraq, they were going to have to convince the rest of the Iraqis that decentralized schemes such as federalism were not incompatible with successful modernity.

Even more, the Iraqi Kurds and their fellow Iraqi citizens were going to have to learn how to implement a system of federalism—which would have to depend on a deeply imbued democratic ethos Iraqis lacked—to implement what by definition would be a complicated and sophisticated division and sharing of powers between a central (national or federal) government and its regional (state) components. Despite the democratic edifice they had built after 1991, for example, even the Iraqi Kurds had fallen into internecine conflict between 1994 and 1998. Given Iraq's historical lack of a democratic ethos, therefore, this prob-

---

[14] Michael M. Gunter, "United States Foreign Policy toward the Kurds," *Orient* 40 (September 1999), p. 433.

lem would seem even more challenging than the one involving the belief that only centralization could lead to a modern state.

Visionary Future

Federalism was first seriously broached as a solution to the Kurdish problem in Iraq following the Gulf War in 1991. On October 4, 1992, the parliament of the de facto Kurdish state in northern Iraq declared Iraqi Kurdistan a constituent state in a federal Iraq. Both of the two main Iraqi Kurdish leaders endorsed the concept. Queried over the meaning of what had been declared, Massoud Barzani, the leader of the Kurdistan Democratic Party (KDP), declared that a federation "is a more advanced concept than autonomy but is not outside the framework of Iraq."[15] Jalal Talabani, the leader of the Patriotic Union of Kurdistan (PUK), elaborated: "The federal state will be like the State of California in the United States."[16] Iraqi opposition conferences at Vienna, Austria (June 16-19, 1992) and Salah al-Din in northern Iraq (late October 1992) also adopted the principle of federalism as a solution for the Kurdish problem, but without implementing any specific constitutional formulas.[17]

---

[15] Cited in "KDP's Barzani Interviewed on Federation Plans," *Al-Akbar* (Cairo), Nov. 22, 1992, p. 4; as cited in *Foreign Broadcast Information Service—Near East & South Asia*, Dec. 1, 1992, p. 25. "Autonomy" had been the official, earlier goal of most Iraqi Kurdish parties, but given its results, most now felt that it had been a terrible failure. For analyses of this earlier period, see Edmund Ghareeb, *The Kurdish Question in Iraq* (Syracuse: Syracuse University Press, 1981); Sa'ad Jawad, *Iraq and the Kurdish Question, 1958-1970* (London: Ithaca Press, 1981); Edgar O'Ballance, *The Kurdish Revolt, 1961-1970* (Hamden: Archon Books, 1973); and Ismet Cheriff Vanly, "Kurdistan in Iraq," in *A People without a Country: The Kurds and Kurdistan*, ed. Gerard Chaliand (New York: Olive Branch Press, 1993), pp. 139-93.

[16] Cited in "Kurdish Officials Interviewed," Ankara Kanal-6 Television Network in Turkish, 1730 GMT, Oct. 19, 1992; as cited in *Foreign Broadcast Information Service—West Europe*, Oct. 22, 1992, p. 72.

[17] For analyses of these earlier Iraqi opposition conferences, see Michael M. Gunter, "The Iraqi National Congress (INC) and the Future of the Iraqi Opposition," *Journal of South Asian and Middle Eastern Studies* 19 (Spring 1996), pp. 1-20; Michael M. Gunter, "The Iraqi Op-

Over the years Baathist Iraq had supposedly countenanced a wide range of attitudes toward the Iraqi Kurds' relationship with the rest of Iraq.[18] Yet even when the Baathists spoke about the Kurds as a nation (*qawm*) possessing national rights and aspirations, they were careful to declare that these rights were given to a people, not to the territory because rights to the territory implied secession. In addition, these rights were given by proclamation (*bayan*), rather than agreement (*ittifaq*). This choice of terms meant that the Baathist state was the sole sovereign power unilaterally awarding certain privileges to the Kurds and thus, of course, could withdraw them at any time.

Finally, the designation Kurdistan (usually employed by the Kurds when referring to their geographical homeland) has seldom been used by the Baathists. Instead, the Baathists used such terms as the region, zone, northern region, our north, or the autonomous area. For their part, the Kurds have strongly objected to the concept of Iraq being part of a pan-Arab union because this would reduce them to being an obscure minority. The proper way to visualize Iraq would be as consisting of two parts, Iraqi Kurdistan and Arab Iraq. Only the latter would be part of the Arab union or homeland.

As Barham Salih, the prime minister of the Kurdistan Regional Government in Sulaymaniya (PUK) recently explained in reference to the accomplishments made by the Kurds over the past decade: "These achievements should be celebrated as a model for the rest of Iraq. Indeed, we Kurds are willing to give up our dreams of an independent Kurdistan in order to bring our expertise in governing to a new democratic Iraq."[19] To examine this future, the remainder of this article will analyze the draft

---

position and the Failure of U.S. Intelligence," *International Journal of Intelligence and CounterIntelligence* 12 (Summer 1999), pp. 135-67; and Robert G. Rabil, "The Iraqi Opposition's Evolution: From Conflict to Unity?" *Middle East Review of International Affairs (MERIA) Journal* 6 (December 2002), 17 pp., on-line journal, <http://meria.idc.ac.il>.

[18] The following discussion is largely based on Ofra Bengio, *Saddam's World: Political Discourse in Iraq* (Oxford: Oxford University Press, 1998), pp. 109-20.

[19] Barham A. Salih, "Give Us a Chance to Build a Democratic Iraq," *New York Times*, Feb. 5, 2002.

constitutions prepared by the Iraqi Kurds in 2002 for the Iraqi Kurdistan Region and the Federal Republic of Iraq, the results of the Iraqi opposition conference held in London from December 14-17, 2002, and the all important roles of the United States and Turkey.

Draft Constitution[20]

Preamble.
The draft "Constitution of the Iraqi Kurdistan Region" opens with a preamble that attempts to justify what the Kurds seek to accomplish: "The Kurds are an ancient people who have lived in their homeland of Kurdistan for thousands of years, a nation with all the attributes that entitle it to practice the right of self-determination similar to other nations and peoples of the world." United States president Woodrow Wilson's Fourteen Points issued during World War I, the relevant provisions of the Treaty of Sevres in 1920, and British promises that "officials of Kurdish origin should be appointed to the administration of their own land and that Kurdish should be the language of education, the courts and for all services rendered" are also mentioned. Nevertheless, "Southern [Iraqi] Kurdistan was annexed in 1925 to the newly created state of Iraq."

The preamble continues by noting that when Iraq was admitted to the League of Nations, it made a statement on May 30, 1932 that "includes a number of international obligations and sets out guarantees for the rights of the Kurds that Iraq is not allowed to amend or abolish. . . . These obligations have been transferred to the United Nations organization and are still in effect to this day." The preamble also mentions the interim Constitution for the Republic of Iraq issued in 1958 which "stated in

---

[20] The following citations are taken from the draft obtained by the present author from the authorities of the Kurdistan Regional Government. Nouri Talabany, an Iraqi Kurdish jurist living in London, also drew up a useful draft Constitution for the Iraqi Kurdistan Region in 1992. See *The Kurdish View on the Constitutional Future of Iraq* (London, 1999). Also of interest is the stillborn "Autonomy Draft Law" that resulted from Barzani's and Talabani's negotiations with the Iraqi government in the spring of 1991. See Gunter, *Kurds of Iraq*, pp. 63-70.

Article 3 that Arabs and Kurds are partners in the Iraqi state," as well as the agreement reached on March 11, 1970 between the Kurds and the Iraqi government that "recognized autonomy for the people of Kurdistan within the Iraqi Kurdistan Region."

Having listed these constitutional and legal precedents, the preamble concludes that "in spite of this, successive Iraqi governments have turned their backs on these obligations to the Kurds and instead have practiced a racist and chauvinistic policy of ethnic cleansing and destruction by all political and military means." The Anfal campaign, Halabja, and the Faili Kurds, among others, are specifically mentioned.[21]

The preamble then goes on to detail United Nations Security Council Resolution 688 of April 5, 1991 which established the Safe Haven for the Kurds and gave the Kurds the "opportunity to elect their first parliament on May 19, 1992 and to establish the Kurdistan Regional Government." The Kurdish parliament then chose "the federalism formula . . . as an ideal solution for the ethnically pluralistic Iraqi society that would safeguard its unity and would . . . satisfy the legitimate aspirations of the people of Iraqi Kurdistan as this formula will guarantee their participation in the making of decisions while protecting the integrity and unity of Iraq." Finally, the preamble also broaches the necessity for "sufficient international guarantees" for the proposed draft Constitution "so that all sides to the agreement will abide by it and respect its terms."

General Matters.

The draft Constitutions for the Iraqi Kurdistan Region and the Federal Republic of Iraq would set up a form of federalism in which the Kurds and Arabs each establish their own regional governments and then delegate specific limited powers to a central government. The Kurdistan Regional Government would have its own elected assembly and president, write its own laws, control the budget for the region, raise taxes, have its own police and defense forces, run the region's schools and universities, own the region's natural resources, and receive a proportionate

---

[21] For details on these specific events, see Gunter, *Kurds of Iraq*, pp. 17, 43-45, and 87-88.

share of Iraq's vast oil wealth. The Federal Republic of Iraq would control foreign affairs, collect customs duties, and issue a currency.

The draft Constitution foresees "a multiparty, democratic, parliamentarian, republican political system" for the Kurdistan Region which would consist "of the provinces of Kirkuk, Sulaymaniya and Erbil in their administrative boundaries prior to 1970 and the Province of Duhok along with the districts of Aqra, Sheikhan, Sinjar and the sub-district of Zimar in the province of Ninevah, the districts of Khanaqin and Mandali in the Province of Diyala, and the district of Badra in the Province of Al-Wasit." The region's people would "consist of the Kurds and the national minorities of Turkmen, Assyrians, Chaldeans, and Arabs," while Kirkuk[22] would be the capital of the Kurdistan Region. "Kurdish shall be the official language," and "official correspondence with the federal and regional authorities shall be in both Arabic and Kurdish." It would be "compulsory" to teach Arabic in the region, while "Turkman shall be considered the language of education . . . for the Turkmans . . . [and] Syriac shall be the language of education and culture for those who speak it in addition to the Kurdish language."

Basic Rights.

An entire part or section of the draft constitution guarantees that "citizens of the Kurdistan Region are equal before the law in their rights and responsibilities without discrimination due to race, color, sex, language, ethnic origin, religion, or economic status." In addition, "women shall have equal rights with men."

---

[22] Until the second Gulf War began in March 2003, it seemed unlikely that Kirkuk would become the capital of the Kurdistan Region because the Kurds were not a majority there. Substantial numbers of Turkmans and Arabs also lived there. In addition, given its Turkman population and rich oil reserves, Turkey had made it clear that Kirkuk was unacceptable as the capital. Thus, Arbil (Irbil/Erbil), the current capital of the region, seemed more likely to continue in this role. Now that the Iraqi Kurds have stepped into the former Turkish role as the main U.S. ally on the northern front and Saddam Hussein's policy of Arabizing Kirkuk seems likely to be reversed, however, Kirkuk may yet become the capital. See below.

Another specific article guarantees "freedom of expression, pub-lication, printing, press, assembly, demonstration, and forming of political parties, union and associations." In addition, "freedom of religion . . . is guaranteed."

This part of the draft constitution also declares that "all types of torture, physical or psychological, are prohibited." In addition, "the privacy of postal, cable and telephone communications is guaranteed" and similarly "the right of ownership." Finally, the draft speaks to the rights of education, work, social security benefits, public health, and political refugees.

Governmental Institutions.
Part III of the draft constitution would establish a regional As-sembly,[23] President,[24] and Judiciary. The Assembly would be "elected through direct secret, general ballot" and "fair repre-sentation of national minorities shall be observed." Parliament's term would run for five years or less if it "does not give a vote of confidence to the Council of Ministers in three successive votes."

---

[23] Multiparty elections were held for the Kurdistan Regional Parliament (Assembly) on May 19, 1992, but only the KDP and the PUK received more than the required 7 percent of the vote necessary to enter the leg-islature. After the votes of the smaller parties were proportionately dis-tributed, the KDP won 50.22 percent and the PUK won 49.78 percent. Following lengthy negotiations, the two main parties agreed to split 50 seats apiece. The remaining 5 seats were given to the Christian minor-ity. The Turkmans had chosen not to participate.

During the KDP-PUK civil war from 1994-1998, the entire assem-bly was unable to meet, and rival KDP and PUK governments existed in Arbil and Sulaymaniya. In October 2002, as plans began to materi-alize for a post-Saddam Iraq, the full assembly finally reassembled. As of this writing (April 2004), however, the two separate governments still exist.

[24] During the elections for a parliament on May 19, 1992, the Kurds also voted for a supreme leader (president). Barzani won 466,819 votes, while Talabani tallied 441,057. Two other candidates won much smaller numbers. Since no one won a majority, however, a run-off election was necessary. Given Kurdish divisions, such an election was never held and no president was chosen.

The draft constitution states that "the President of the Kurdistan Region . . . is the highest executive authority and . . . represents the President of the Federal Republic of Iraq in the region and substitutes for him/her on state occasions and coordinates between the federal and regional authorities." The President "is elected by direct, secret, general ballot by the people of the region" in a manner that "shall be regulated by law" for a term of "five years." If the office of the President falls vacant, "the President of the Kurdistan Regional Assembly shall assume responsibilities of the President until such time as a new President is elected."

In addition to the President, "the Kurdistan Region Council of Ministers is the highest executive and administrative authority in the region; it carries out its executive responsibilities under the supervision and guidance of the Kurdistan Regional President." The Council of Ministers or Cabinet is to consist of the Prime Minister and no more than 15 ministers. While the Prime Minister must be a member of the Regional Assembly, his ministers may be members or need only "meet the necessary qualifications for membership in the Assembly." The Cabinet shall include "representation of the national minorities, Turkmans, Assyrians, and Chaldeans" and meet with the approval of both the President and Assembly.

The draft constitution also speaks of "the region's court system in all its levels" as being "independent with no power above it except the law itself." It is to possess "general jurisdiction over all public and private entities and individuals except those stipulated in a law." This exception pertains to "the non-Muslim communities [which] have the right to establish religious, 'spiritual,' legal bodies in accordance with a special law." In a manner suggestive of the former Ottoman millet system, "these bodies shall have the right to look into all personal matters of citizens belonging to those communities, matters which are not included in the competence and responsibility of the 'Muslim' religious courts."

Administrative and Fiscal.
Part IV of the draft constitution provides for various local governmental institutions, while Part V deals with fiscal matters.

The Regional Government "can levy and collect taxes and duties within the region," but "export and import duties (customs) are the responsibility of the federal authority." Special attention should be noted to the provision that the "Kurdistan Region's share of natural resources, in particular, oil, and revenue from the sale of its products in and outside the country, as well as grants, aid, [and] foreign loans made to the Federal Republic of Iraq [shall be] in a proportion based on the relation of the region's population to the total population of Iraq."

Ultimate Matters.

Disputes among the Kurdistan regional authorities over the interpretation of the draft constitution "shall be referred to the Cassation Court of the Kurdistan Region." The Federal Constitutional Court shall adjudicate constitutional conflicts that might arise between the Kurdistan region and the Arab region or the Federal Republic of Iraq. Finally, given the past Kurdish history of unfilled rights, the draft constitution declares near its end that if it is "changed without the consent of the Kurdistan Regional Assembly . . . this shall afford the people of the Kurdistan Region the right of self-determination." This, of course, means the right to become an independent state.

Draft Constitution of the Federal Republic of Iraq[25]

Preamble.
The preamble of the draft constitution of the Federal Republic of Iraq declares in its opening section that Iraq "has not enjoyed peace and security" because it has been "characterized by a high degree of centralization." This centralization and "the indifference of decision makers . . . are the basic reasons for the Kurds being deprived of their legitimate rights under the successive Iraqi governments." Federalism "would be more consistent with the pluralist nature of the Iraqi community made up of the two primary nationalities, Arabs and Kurds, in addition to other na-

---

[25] The following citations are taken from the draft constitution obtained by the present author from the authorities of the Kurdistan Regional Government.

tional minorities present among the population . . . and is a suitable basis for solving the Kurdish problem in Iraq." In addition,
federalism "affords the Kurdish people the enjoyment of their
legitimate national rights and internal independence within the
region of Kurdistan and within the framework of a single Iraqi
state and without disrupting the unity of that state."

The preamble also mentions the necessity of "giving women
their full rights . . . of their equality with men under the law, . . .
national religious tolerance, . . . and human rights . . . in accordance with the provisions of the Universal Declaration of Human
Rights and other related international treaties and conventions."
Finally, the new Iraqi state is to be "founded on a democratic,
parliamentarian, federal system."

Basic Rights.

Many democratic guarantees of the proposed draft constitution
of the Federal Republic of Iraq are virtually verbatim repetitions
of the draft constitution for the Iraqi Kurdistan Region cited
above and, therefore, need not be repeated here.

The Federal Republic of Iraq will consist of two territorial regions that are constitutionally defined: an Arabic region and a
Kurdish region. "Power is inherent in the people as they are the
source of its legitimacy." The draft constitution establishes
Baghdad as the capital, declares that Iraq "shall have a flag, an
emblem, and a national anthem that shall reflect the union between the Kurds and the Arabs," states that "the state religion is
Islam," and that "Arabic is the official language of the federal
state and the Arab region. Kurdish shall be the official language
of the Kurdistan Region." The draft also specifically declares
that "citizens are equal under the law without discrimination due
to sex, race, color, language, religion, or ethnic origin."

Institutions.

The federal parliament will consist of two chambers: the National Assembly (Chamber of Deputies) and the Assembly of the
Regions. Although not specifically detailed, it would seem that
the National Assembly would represent the people of Iraq according to their population, while the Assembly of the Regions
would represent the two regions on an equal basis despite the

differences in population. It also should be noted that each chamber "participates on an equal footing" with the other. The federal parliament would serve a five-year term, and no individual could hold a position in more than one federal, regional, or local legislative body at the same time.

The President of the Federal Republic of Iraq would "be elected through direct ballot for a period of five years and may stand for re-election once." In an attempt to insure an ethnic balance between the two regions, the draft constitution provides that the President and the Prime Minister must be from different regions. Furthermore, the Council of Ministers (Cabinet) "shall represent both regions in proportion to the region's populations."

The membership of the High (Constitutional) Court shall be evenly divided between members from each region. It shall have the duty of interpreting the federal constitution, conflicts over its meaning between the federal and regional levels, and conflicts between the regions.

Responsibilities.
The draft constitution specifically declares that the federal government shall assume the following responsibilities: declaring war and concluding peace; setting out foreign policy and diplomatic and consular representations; concluding international treaties and agreements; defending the country; issuing currency and planning monetary and banking policy; defining standards for weights and measures and designating salary policy; drafting general economic planning aimed at development in the regions in the areas of industry, commerce and agriculture; ordering federal general audits; overseeing federal security affairs; and concerning itself with citizenship, residency and foreigners' affairs, oil resources, and nuclear power.

The draft constitution also specifically states that "each region shall have a share of the revenues from the oil wealth, grants, and foreign aid and loans in proportion to their population in relation to that of the total population of the country." In addition, each region shall have the authority to levy taxes on income, inheritance, agricultural land and property taxes, property registration fees, court fees, license fees, and water and electricity charges.

Ultimate matters.

The final part of the federal draft constitution seeks to guarantee the rights and powers of the Kurds and the Kurdistan Region. "Citizens of the Kurdistan Region shall be appointed to the various positions in the federal ministries and other bodies both inside and outside the country and in particular in the deputy minister, director general, or other high level positions according to the ratio of the regional population to the total population of the Federal Republic of Iraq." This proportionality principle applies even to student fellowships and student admissions to all schools both inside and outside the country.

Another specific article seeks to "redress the effects of Arabization and deportations that took place in some parts of the Kurdistan Region" in such areas as Kirkuk and several other places. Kurds "should return to their previous homes in those areas," while "the Arab citizens who were brought by the authorities into those areas at any time since 1957 should return to their original homes." In addition, Kurdish "peshmerga forces and their various divisions shall constitute a part of the Armed Forces of the Federal Republic of Iraq."

The federal draft guarantees that the borders of the Kurdistan Region cannot be altered "except with the approval of the Assembly of the region concerned." The Kurds are given a veto over amendments to the Federal constitution by the provision that "the terms of this [Federal] Constitution cannot be amended unless through a 2/3 majority vote by members of both the Federal and Regional Assemblies." Another article of the draft constitution declares that the new Federal Republic of Iraq "shall be accountable to the United Nations organization for guaranteeing the rights, the boundaries, and powers of the two regions designated in this Constitution and the Regional Constitutions."

Mirroring the draft constitution of the Kurdistan Region, the Federal draft ends by granting the Kurds "the right of self-determination" if either the Regional or Federal constitutions are unconstitutionally altered. This final provision clearly implies the right of the Kurds to become independent. Yet as Dr. Barham Salih, the prime minister of the Kurdistan Regional Government in Sulaymaniya (PUK) recently concluded: "We Kurds are championing a federal, pluralist democratic Iraq that cannot again brutalize its citizens and threaten its neighbors. The final irony may be that the Kurds, the perennial victims of the Iraqi state, will turn out to be its savior."[26]

Will It Work?

The best laid plans, of course, can fail to materialize. The Kurdish future in post-Saddam Iraq also will depend on the willingness of the Arab majority in Iraq to accept federalism, as well as the position of the United States and such neighboring states as Turkey and Iran. Viewed from these perspectives, the Kurdish future in post-Saddam Iraq becomes much more problematic.

On August 9, 2002, senior U.S. officials met in Washington, D.C. with the so-called Group of Six Iraqi opposition groups.[27] Here it was decided to initiate a "Future of Iraq" project for separate discussions on some 16 different topics including public health, economics, law, political structure, and other topics that would be vital to rebuilding a post-Saddam Iraq. In addition, a group of 32 expatriate Iraqis calling themselves the "Democratic Principles Workshop"[28] began drawing up a 79-page document entitled "The Transition to Democracy in Iraq,"[29] and discussing its principles with such senior U.S. officials as Condoleezza Rice, the national security adviser.

---

[26] Barham Salih, "A Kurdish Model for Iraq," *Washington Post*, Dec. 9, 2002.

[27] In addition to Barzani's KDP <http://www.kdp.pp.se> and Talabani's PUK <http://www.puk.org>, these included Ahmad Chalabi's Iraqi National Congress (INC) <http://www.inc.org.uk>, Ayad Allawi's Iraqi National Accord (INA) <http:// www.wifaq.com>, Muhammad Baqir al-Hakim's Supreme Council for the Islamic Revolution in Iraq (SCIRI) <http://sciri.org>, and Sharif Ali bin al-Hussein's Constitutional Monarchy Movement <http://www.iraqcmm.org>.

[28] This group consisted of Iraqi intellectuals in exile such as the author Kanan Makiya cited above, and representatives of Iraqi opposition and human rights groups. See Judith Miller, "Iraqi Opposition Circulates Plan for Post-Hussein Era," *New York Times*, Nov. 26, 2002.

[29] The following citations are taken from Mustapha Karkouti, "Exclusive: Post-Saddam Roadmap Envisions Federal State," *Gulf News Online*, Dec. 5, 2002.

This document dealt with all aspects of life in Iraq and called for a "democratic and federally structured Iraq based on the principle of separation of powers, and principle of protection of individual human rights and group rights." The document noted that the Kurdish experience had been the driving force behind the new idea of federalism and declared bluntly that "federalism has become the sine qua non for staying inside a new Iraq and [not] trying to secede from it." The declaration questioned, however, whether the new federal Iraq should be simply based on two separate (Arab and Kurdish) national regions or some type of territorial bases consisting of multiple national and ethnic groups that would blunt ethnic conflicts.[30] U.S. officials opposed any effort to establish a government in exile that might "disenfranchise" possible opponents in Iraq of Saddam Hussein.

Finally, the meeting held in Washington, D.C. on August 9, 2002 agreed that a large opposition conference would be held before any U.S. or U.N. action to unseat Saddam Hussein. A few days before the London conference convened, the United States appointed Zalmay Khalilzad as its special envoy to the Iraqi opposition. Previously, Khalilzad had served in a similar role as the chief U.S. advisor to Hamid Karzai, the interim president of Afghanistan. He also had been an adviser to Unocal, a U.S. oil company and a senior adviser on the Middle East on the U.S. National Security Council. Although an able interlocutor, Khalilzad's tardy appointment illustrated how the United States

---

[30] Brendan O'Leary has suggested yet another alternative, which he termed federacy. Under such a system, Iraqi Kurdistan could enter a federal arrangement with the central Iraqi government, while the rest of the country would **not** be federally organized. Such an arrangement might better satisfy the Kurds' desire for federalism, while accommodating the Arabs' wish to maintain elements of a unitary state if that is what they want. Brendan O'Leary, "Right-sizing and Right-peopling the State: Regulating National and Ethnic Differences," keynote speech given at an international conference on "Iraqi Kurdistan—Ten Years of Self-Rule and Future Prospects," University of Southern Denmark, Odense, Denmark, Nov. 30, 2002. For further background, see Brendan O'Leary, Ian S. Lustick, and Thomas Callaghy, eds., *Right-Sizing the State: The Politics of Moving Borders* (New York: Oxford University Press, 2001).

viewed the Iraqi opposition as less than a major player or potential future government.

In addition, the United States freed some $92 million that had
been held up from the 1998 Iraq Liberation Act to help train
some 3,000 Iraqi dissidents screened by the INC for possible use
in any war against Saddam Hussein. These Iraqis began training
at an air base in Taszar, Hungary to act as military police, inter-
preters, spotters and guides for U.S. forces if they invaded Iraq.

London Opposition Conference

After much discussion and hesitation, more than 400 delegates
met at the London opposition conference from December 14-17,
2002.The conference itself fell short of establishing a definitive
and unified Iraqi equivalent of a government in exile that would
serve as the partner of the United States in a post-Saddam Iraq.
Such, however, was not its goal as envisioned by the United
States, which instead wanted a mere show of support for whatever the United States would finally and largely unilaterally decide to do.

The conference's closing political statement[31] rejected any
form of foreign occupation in a post-Saddam Iraq, stated that a
post-Saddam government should respect the present autonomous
arrangements in Iraqi Kurdistan pending the enactment of a new
Iraqi constitution, and argued that the transitional period should
be run by a three-member "sovereignty council" and a civilian
coalition government. In addition, an interim "national council"
with legislative powers would name a committee of experts to
draft a permanent constitution, which would subsequently be put
to a referendum. None of these principles met with the approval
of the United States.

In addition, it became clear that the Iraqi opposition would
have great trouble being accepted by the Iraqi population itself
because most Iraqis viewed the opposition as out of touch with

---

[31] The following discussion is based on "Political Statement of the Iraqi
Opposition Conference in London," *Brayati* (Arbil), Dec. 19, 2002; as
accessed over the Internet, Dec. 20, 2002.

events in Iraq. Finally, the opposition itself was able to achieve only partial unity in what it wanted and who would belong to it.

Nevertheless, the London conference did achieve much that seemed supportive of what the Kurds were seeking. Its concluding political statement declared that "Iraq will be a democratic parliamentary, pluralist, federal (for all Iraq) state and will accordingly enact a humane and civilized concept of citizenship based on equality and elimination of discrimination against all people, religions, races and sects." Specifically, the conference condemned "all the racial injustice, oppression and ethnic cleansing which the Iraqi regime has carried out premeditatively on the people of Iraqi Kurdistan, particularly genocide and Anfal operations which . . . moved the conscience of people all over the world." The statement even mentioned "the need to . . . prosecute those who committed these crimes in international courts."

In addition, "the conference condemns . . . especially the changing of the [largely Kurdish] national character of Kirkuk, Makhmur, Khanaqin, Sinjar, Shekhan, Zimar and Mandali, and so on." The Faili Kurds, "whom the [Iraqi] regime deported outside Iraq under the pretext that they were of Iranian origin" should also have their Iraqi citizenship and property returned.

Specifically detailing "the adoption in the National Assembly of Iraqi Kurdistan of a complete federalism bill in its session on 7 October 2002, the conference debated the experiences of federal systems and concluded that is an appropriate system of government for Iraq, which must be taken cognizance of as a basis for the resolution of the Kurdish problem . . . after the end of the dictatorial Saddam regime and anticipated changes in Iraq." The conference also "highly appreciates the experience in Iraqi Kurdistan in areas of freedom, democracy and reconstruction," and "believes that it is possible to benefit from this experience as an advanced step on the path of the anticipated democratic transformation in Iraq."

In his keynote address to the London conference Jalal Talabani again endorsed federalism for the Kurdish future in a post-Saddam Iraq by arguing that it represented "a democratic framework within which to solidify ties among Arabs, Kurds,

Turkomen and Assyrians in a free and united state."[32] Massoud Barzani told the conference that he agreed with this judgment regarding federalism "because it represents a civilized and balanced solution that guarantees everyone's rights."

The United States

At first, the United States seemed to be supporting the Kurdish position with talk about regime change leading to a new democratic Iraq that would even be a model for the rest of the authoritarian Middle East. By February 2003, however, such talk had obviously taken its toll on such U.S. allies as Turkey, Saudi Arabia, and the various Gulf states who all feared the advent of destabilizing change in Iraq. To win their support against Saddam Hussein and prevent what it too saw as the destabilization of the Middle East, the United States began to contemplate having an American general run post-Saddam Iraq for as much as two years. This U.S. general would call upon the pre-existing Iraqi, even Baathist, infrastructure once it had been shorn of its top leadership in each ministry.[33]

Under this scenario, what was to become of the de facto Kurdish administrations which had been successfully running things since 1991? Would there be two separate governments in post-Saddam Iraq, the U.S. general in Baghdad and the preexisting Kurdish administrations in the north? Since this was doubtful, the new U.S. position smacked of a betrayal of the

---

[32] This and the following citation were taken from Kurdistan Newsline, "Talabani and Barzani Remarks at Opposition Meeting," Dec. 18, 2002; as accessed over the Internet, Dec. 18, 2002.

[33] Zalmay Khalilzad, the U.S. contact with the Iraqi opposition, revealed the details of this plan to Jalal Talabani, Nechirvan Idris Barzani (the KDP prime minister), and other members of the Iraqi opposition at a meeting in Ankara, Turkey early in February 2003. Karl Vick, "Exile Group Leaders Fault U.S. Plan for Postwar Iraq," *Washington Post*, Feb. 12, 2003. Fouad Ajami, a leading Arab-American authority on the Middle East, recently argued that post-Saddam "Iraq could do worse than having the interim stewardship of a modern-day high commissioner." See "Iraq and the Arabs' Future," *Foreign Affairs* 82 (January/February 2003), p. 15.

Kurds on the level of Nixon and Kissinger's actions in 1975 when the latter justified the U.S. actions by simply observing that "covert action should not be confused with missionary work."[34]

Sami Abdulrahman, a longtime leading KDP official who was tragically killed in the Irbil bombing on February 1, 2004, declared that the U.S. plan was "very disappointing,"[35] and would "give the government on a platter to the second line of Ba'athists." Hoshyar Zebari, another important KDP official who also became the interim Iraqi foreign minister in the summer of 2003, predicted that "there is going to be a backlash." Kanan Makiya, the prominent Iraqi dissident cited above, wrote that "it is a plan designed to humiliate the Kurdish people of Iraq and their experiment of self-rule," and then added that "the plan reverses a decade-long moral and financial commitment by the US to the Iraqi opposition, and is guaranteed to turn that opposition from the close ally it has always been during the 1990s into an opponent."[36]

To appease its ally Turkey, the United States also agreed to let Turkish forces enter Iraqi Kurdistan to help establish order and told the Iraqi Kurds not to oppose the Turks. This proposal also brought a strong condemnation from the Iraqi Kurds. Hoshyar Zebari declared that "we oppose any Turkish unilateral military intervention, whatever the pretext," and predicted that "Turkish intervention would prompt intervention from Iran."[37]

---

[34] "The CIA Report the President Doesn't Want You to Read," *Village Voice*, Feb. 16, 1976.

[35] This and the following two citations were taken from Patrick Cockburn, "Kurdish Leaders Enraged by 'Undemocratic' American Plan to Occupy Iraq," *Independent*, Feb. 17, 2003.

[36] Kanan Makiya, "Our Hopes Betrayed: How a US Blueprint for Post-Saddam Government Quashed the Hopes of Democratic Iraqis," *Observer*, Feb. 16, 2003.

[37] Cited in Gareth Smyth, "Presence of Turkish Troops Unsettles Iraqi Kurds," *Financial Times*, Feb. 13, 2003. For background to the Turkish-Iranian rivalry over northern Iraq, see Michael M. Gunter, "Turkey and Iran Face Off in Kurdistan," *Middle East Quarterly* 5 (March 1998), pp. 33-40.

At this point, however, Turkey shot itself in the foot by not letting U.S. troops use Turkey as a base to open up a real northern front in the second Gulf War. As a result, the Iraqi Kurds were suddenly thrust into the role with ultimate consequences only time can completely reveal. The conclusion of this article will offer some speculation concerning these consequences.

Conclusion

Turkey's almost paranoid opposition to Kurdish nationalism, and Turkey's strong strategic alliance with the United States since the days of the Truman Doctrine in 1947, have arguably been two of the main reasons for the inability of the Kurds to create any type of an independent state in the modern Middle East that began to develop after World War I. The Treaty of Sevres (1920) and initial U.S. support for a Kurdish state foundered on the rock of Turkish resurgence under Mustafa Kemal Ataturk. To some extent, the modern Turkish nation-state was constructed over the prostrate body of Kurdish nationalism.

Although the United States paid lip service to the idea of Kurdish rights, when the chips were down, again and again the United States backed its strategic NATO ally Turkey when it came to the Kurdish issue. Thus, from the point of view of American foreign policy, rebelling Turkish Kurds (the PKK for example) were bad Kurds, while rebelling Iraqi Kurds (the KDP and the PUK for example) were **good** Kurds. This seemingly illogical Manichaean dichotomy, however, made immediate sense in terms of American foreign policy opposition to Saddam Hussein, but support for Turkey. Indeed, the U.S. role went so far as to hand deliver Abdullah Ocalan, the PKK president, to Turkey in February 1999.[38]

Now in return, of course, the United States expected Turkey to support important American foreign policy positions. This Turkey failed to do when it rejected the U.S. request for Turkish bases to establish a northern front in the war against Iraq that

---

[38] Michael M. Gunter, "The Continuing Kurdish Problem in Turkey after Ocalan's Capture," *Third World Quarterly* 21 (October 2000), p. 850.

began in March 2003. This Turkish action may prove to be a turning point in history, leading the United States no longer to consider Turkey its major strategic ally and instead look more favorably upon the Iraqi Kurds who militarily supported the U.S. war effort against Saddam Hussein. What good is Turkey's strategic location if it does not support the United States on such important military matters? Indeed, new U.S. bases have been developed in the former communist states of Bulgaria and Romania, and may also become available in a future pro-Western Iraq, especially in the Kurdish area.

The supreme irony of Turkey's refusal to grant bases to the U.S. war effort, however, is that Turkey allowed the Iraqi Kurds to assume the role as the northern front against Saddam Hussein. Suddenly, Turkey shut itself out from a major role in the future of northern Iraq and allowed some of Turkey's worst fears to take shape with the Iraqi Kurds becoming the main U.S. ally on the northern front. Quickly, the Iraqi Kurds occupied the oil-rich Kirkuk and Mosul areas which would have been unthinkable had Turkey anchored the northern front. What is more, Turkey had no choice but to acquiesce in the Iraqi Kurdish moves.

The reversal in roles became all the more obvious when the United States arrested 11 Turkish special forces troops operating in northern Iraq early in July 2003 and reportedly accused them of planning to assassinate the newly elected Kurdish mayor of Kirkuk. In the past, Turkish forces had operated with impunity and indeed the U.S. blessing in northern Iraq. Now the implied U.S. message was that the Turks could no longer function in northern Iraq as they had been. The affair caused an unprecedented crisis in U.S.-Turkish relations and presented their longtime strategic relationship with possibly its biggest crisis of confidence ever.[39]

In addition, powerful Iraqi Kurdish opposition to the deployment of 10,000 Turkish troops to even areas in Iraq south of the Kurdish area—a decision the Turkish parliament took in October

---

[39] "Ozkok: Biggest Crisis of Trust with US," *Turkish Daily News*, July 7, 2003, accessed over the Internet; and Nicholas Kralev, "U.S. Warns Turkey against Operations in Northern Iraq," *Washington Times*, July 8, 2003, accessed over the Internet.

2003 in an effort to revive its failing fortunes with the United States and control over evolving events in Iraq—helped force Turkey to rescind its offer to provide these troops shortly after it was issued. Osman Faruk Logoglu, the Turkish ambassador to the United States, complained that the United States was giving "excessive favors" to the Iraqi Kurds and thus encouraging future civil war and Kurdish secession.[40]

Now, of course, the permanently operating factors of Turkey's geographical location and relative military superiority over the Kurds remain. Given time, therefore, it is likely that Turkey will partially reassert its strategic relationship with the United States. For the moment, however, there is an historic opportunity for the Iraqi Kurds, to step forward, with U.S. support, to achieve what Turkey has always opposed with U.S. support: an autonomous federal state within Iraq or even an independent Kurdish state.[41]

And why not a Kurdish state? What is so sacred about the territorial integrity of a failed state like Iraq?[42] Indeed, within the past decade, both the Soviet Union and Yugoslavia broke up into numerous new states. Earlier, Singapore split off from Malaysia, Bangladesh from Pakistan, and, more recently, Eritrea broke away from Ethiopia and East Timor from Indonesia. The United Nations also has in the past officially approved self-

---

[40] Jonathan Wright, "Turkey Accuses U.S. of 'Favoritism' in Iraq," Reuters, Nov. 4, 2003, accessed over the Internet; and Howard LaFranchi, "Bound to Iraq, Kurds Eye Options," *Christian Science Monitor*, Nov. 24, 2003, accessed over the Internet. The most Turkey was willing begrudgingly to grant the Iraqi Kurds was some form of geographical federalism within possibly the pre-existing 18 Iraqi governorates. Such geographical federalism would dilute concentrated Kurdish power. The Kurds, however, continued to insist on ethnic federalism that would focus their power as an ethnic group.

[41] Sabrina Tavernise, "Returning to Iraq, Few Kurds Want to be Part of It," *New York Times*, May 25, 2003, accessed over the Internet.

[42] See, for example, Ralph Peters, "Break Up Iraq Now!" *New York Post*, July 10, 2003, accessed over the Internet.

determination for the Palestinians[43] and black South African majority.[44]

Why do the Arabs so rightfully demand a state for the Palestinians, but so hypocritically deny one for the Kurds? Why do the Turks demand self-determination for the Turkish Cypriots, but so hypocritically deny the same for the Kurds? It is not logical; it is not fair, and until there is real justice for the Kurds, we will have this great instability in the Middle East.[45]

The Iraqi Kurds, however, would be well advised to proceed with caution and the consent of both their Arab compatriots within Iraq and their neighbors in Turkey because in the long run the United States will leave Iraq. The Kurds then will have to live with the Arabs and the Turks who always will remain next door. Thus, the Iraqi Kurds should be rather modest and from their new found position of relative strength try to cut the best deal possible with Turkey to show Ankara that the Kurds are not the enemies of Turkey, that the two can cooperate to the mutual advantage of both. This will take extraordinary skill and imagination on the part of both parties, but given the past tragedies failed earlier policies have entailed, both the Kurds and Turkey deserve better in the post-Saddam world.

In the meanwhile, as the various ethnic and sectarian groups in post-Saddam Iraq struggle to hammer out the specifics of a new Iraqi constitution and to regain Iraqi sovereignty on June 30,

---

[43] See, for example, U.N. General Assembly Resolutions 2672 C (XXV), in *UN Chronicle*, 1971, no. 1, p. 46; 3236 (XXIX), in *UN Chronicle*, 1974, no. 11, pp. 36-74; and 33/23, in *UN Chronicle*, 1978, no, 11, p. 80.

[44] See, for example, U.N. General Assembly Resolutions 2396 (XXIII), in *UN Chronicle*, 1969, no. 1, p. 94; and 31/61, in *UN Chronicle*, 1976, no. 1, p. 79.

[45] For further recent background on these points, see Tim Judah, "In Iraqi Kurdistan," *Survival* 44 (Winter 2002-3), pp. 38-51; Carole A. O'Leary, "The Kurds of Iraq: Recent History, Future Prospects," *Middle East Review of International Affairs (MERIA)*, 6 (December 2002), accessed over the Internet; and Bill Park, "Strategic Location, Political Dislocation: Turkey, the United States, and Northern Iraq," *Middle East Review of International Affairs (MERIA)*, 7 (June 2003), accessed over the Internet.

2004, the very definition of what federalism should mean hangs in the balance. The majority Shiites seek a definition that would allow the central government to impose national standards on any Kurdish federal state. Otherwise, the Shiites fear that federalism would simply be the final step before Kurdish independence that would truncate the Iraqi state. Given their tortured historical existence in Iraq, however, the Kurds insist that they must have the right to maintain a Kurdish militia, expand their boundaries to include Kirkuk and a guaranteed right to its oil resources, and the right not to accept *Shariah* [Islamic law] as the basis of the constitution and law.[46] Failure to solve these dilemmas threatens to lead to more violence and even civil war that may either crush the Kurds or lead to their independence.

---

[46] Dexter Filkins, "Iraqi Kurdish Leaders Resist As the U.S. Presses Them To Moderate Their Demands," *New York Times*, Feb. 21, 2004, accessed over the Internet.

CHAPTER 5

Turkey and Kurdistan-Iraq Relations: The Consolidation of Iraqi Kurdish Nationalism: 2003-2004

Robert Olson

Introduction

This article addresses the further consolidation of Kurdish nationalism in Kurdistan-Iraq from 1 March 2003 to 1 April 2004. It emphasizes the consolidation of Iraqi Kurdish nationalism—as reflected in the relations of the Kurdistan Democratic Party (KDP) and the Patriotic Union of Kurdistan (PUK)—with Turkey and the Kurds' reactions to perceived Turkish policies toward Kurdistan-Iraq and Arab Iraq. It uses the term Kurdistan-Iraq with a hyphen to denote what it considers the semi-sovereignty that the KDP and PUK had achieved in the decade of the 1990s, especially after the establishment of the Kurdistan Regional Government (KRG) in 1992. It argues further that the Iraqi Interim Constitution announced on 8 March 2004 further consolidates Kurdish nationalism in Kurdistan-Iraq. The hyphen represents the degree of governmental control that the KDP and PUK exercised over the territories they control. The hyphen distinguishes these territories from similar regions such as Kurdistan Turkey, Azerbaijan Iran, Baluchi Iran or Baluchi Pakistan to name a few such regions.[1] The hyphen also indicates that this article recognizes that the regions controlled by the KDP and PUK are not sovereign in that sovereignty demands international and legal recognition by states and international institutions.

Turkish Role

This article commences its analysis and argument with the failure of Turkey's parliament to pass the 1 March 2003 resolution that would have allowed some 62,000 U.S. troops to transit (and some to be stationed in) Turkey on their way to invade Iraq. The resolution also provided that Turkish troops, estimated to be around 45,000, would participate with the Americans in the invasion.

This article assumes that the development and growth of Kurdish nationalism in Turkey and in Kurdistan-Iraq, as well as in Iran and Syria, grew significantly during the decades of the 1980s and 1990s. The commencement of armed conflict in 1984 between the Turkish Armed Forces (TAF) and the *Partia Karkaren Kurdistan* (PKK) and the nearly two decades of war that followed strengthened enormously Kurdish nationalism in Turkey. In the case of Iraq, the Iraq-Iran war (1980-1988), the consequences of the first Gulf war in 1991, the subsequent creation of a "safe haven" for the Kurds in northern Iraq and the establishment of a Kurdistan Regional Government (KRG) in Arbil in 1992 contributed fundamentally to the consolidation of Kurdish nationalism in the region that this author now calls Kurdistan-Iraq.

This article also argues that from 1 March 2003 to 1 April 2004, Turkey was impelled to enter into a policy of state-to-government(s) relations with the KDP and PUK which differed in substance and nuance from the status of mere state-to-region

---

[1] In previous works this author has detailed more thoroughly why he defined the Kurdish-controlled region of northern Iraq as Kurdistan-Iraq. See Robert Olson, *Turkey-Iran Relations, 1979-2004: Revolution, Ideology, War, Coups and Geopolitics* (Costa Mesa, CA: Mazda Publications, 2004), pp. 207-13; and "Turkey and Kurdistan-Iraq, 2003," *Middle East Policy*, 11 (Winter 2004), pp. 115-19.

relations that had existed previously.[2] While Turkey did not have official Foreign Ministry representation in Kurdistan-Iraq during this period, it did have a plethora of officially sanctioned trade delegations, business delegations and a number of Turkish companies that were operating in Kurdistan-Iraq that needed the cooperation of Kurdish officials to carry out their work. In addition, both the KDP and PUK had representatives in Ankara that almost acted like ambassadors.[3] There were scores of meetings between Turkish officials and KDP and PUK representatives throughout the 1990s and early 2000s. Indeed, in one well-known incident, the PUK had even allowed a Turkish oil and gas company to drill and lift oil in the PUK-controlled region.[4]

The importance of this issue to Turkey was made clear during Prime Minister Recep Tayyip Erdoğan's visit to Washington on 25-30 January 2004. In conversations with President George W. Bush and Vice-President Dick Cheney (and many others), Erdoğan noted that Turkish Petroleum, Inc. (TPAO) and other Turkish firms held licenses to drill and lift oil in northern Iraq. In order to facilitate the work of the Turkish companies, however, Erdoğan requested the White House to instruct Paul Bremer, the U.S. chief administrator of the Coalition Provisional Authority (CPA), to tell the Iraqi Governing Council (IGC) to give the necessary approvals for the Turkish companies to operate. Bush and Cheney responded, "We will take notice of the topic."[5]

During the 1990s, some 500 to 1500 trucks crossed the border post of Habur/Ibrahim al-Khalil almost on a daily basis. After the U.S. invasion of Iraq in March 2003, the truck traffic rose to some 2000 trucks a day. Throughout this period, oil was sent, when not interrupted by sabotage, from the Kirkuk fields via two pipelines through Turkey to terminals at Ceyhan on the Mediterranean coast. All of these developments required cooperation

---

[2] For more details see Olson, *Turkey-Iran Relations...*, pp. 234-37.

[3] The KDP representative in Ankara is Safain Dizai and the PUK representative is Bahroz Galaly.

[4] The PUK had granted permission to the Turkish owned Pet-Oil and General Energy Company to drill, lift and market oil in territories it controlled. For more on this topic see Olson, *Turkey-Iran Relations...*, pp. 161-2.

[5] *Hürriyet*, 2 February 2004.

between Turkish and Kurdistan-Iraq officials. What this article argues below is that after 1 March 2003, much of the trade and interaction between Turkey and Kurdistan-Iraq continued, but the U.S. war against Iraq allowed the Kurdistan-Iraqis to strengthen their position vis-à-vis Turkey, at least up to 1 April 2004 where this study ends.

It is important to note that before 1 March 2003 and prior to the assumption of power by the Justice and Development Party (AKP) on 3 November 2002, Turkey's previous governments— the Democratic Socialist Party (DSP), Motherland Party (MP) and National Action Party (NAP) that were in power from the overthrow of the Welfare Party (WP) in 1997 to November 2002—were confronted with the consolidation of Kurdish nationalism in northern Iraq. Each leader of these three parties— Bülent Ecevit, Mesut Yılmaz and Devlet Bahçeli—had to deal with the consolidation of Kurdish nationalism in northern Iraq. It was during the tenure of the above parties that the Kurdish entities in northern Iraq developed more strongly into the entity that this article calls Kurdistan-Iraq. A crucial period for this evolution was from the establishment of the KRG in 1992 to the signing of the Washington Accords in September 1998, which brought closure to the internecine fighting between the KDP and PUK that flared intermittently from 1994 to 1998.

In February 1998, Mesut Yılmaz, then prime minister, charged repeatedly that the U.S. intended to "create an independent Kurdish state in northern Iraq and to control the oil fields of Iraq." Bülent Ecevit, then leader of the DSP and subsequently prime minister declared, "The U.S. has no Iraq policy."[6] The statements of Yılmaz and Ecevit in February 1998 characterized the attitude and position of Ankara toward U.S. policy in Iraq, especially toward the KDP and PUK: the U.S. had no policy toward Iraq and, if they did, they would not be able to implement it.

From 1998 to early March 2003, it seems that Ankara thought differences between the KDP and PUK would probably be strong enough that Ankara could continue to pursue a policy of division and a state-to-region relationship, which meant that a

---

[6] *Hürriyet*, 4 February 1998.

greater measure of recognition of Kurdistan-Iraq's semi-sovereignty would not have to be accepted. However, the rejection of the 1 March 2003 resolution impelled Turkey, unwillingly to be sure, to pursue a different policy, which was characterized as more of a state-to-government(s) relationship than a state-to-region one. The evolution of this change was a consequence of developments that occurred in the wake of the failed resolution.

Several developments occurred from 1 March 2003 to the bombings of the KDP and PUK office buildings in Arbil on 1 February 2004, which contributed to the consolidation of Kurdish nationalism in Kurdistan-Iraq, as reflected in Kurdistan-Iraqi relations with Turkey. The Turkish parliament's failure to pass the 1 March resolution, for example, contributed to the strengthening of Kurdistan-Iraqi nationalism and the KRG's consolidation of power by allowing the Kurdistan-Iraqi Kurds to maintain the self-government they had been exercising since 1992. If Turkish troops had joined U.S. forces in the invasion of Iraq, it is highly unlikely this would have been the case. Second, the participation of KDP and PUK forces with U.S. forces, especially in the U.S. conquest of Kirkuk, Tikrit and Mosul, strengthened the Kurds. The KDP and PUK capture of Iraqi army and resistance forces' weapons and vehicles, including tanks, and the arms supplied to them by U.S. forces also contributed to the Kurdish confidence in their self-government.[7] In addition, the Kurdish region suffered little damage as compared to other parts of Iraq which meant the Kurds could spend what resources they had on building infrastructure and security, rather than on simply rebuilding. The U.S. occupational forces' acceptance of the Kurdish retention of captured weapons and supplies was in flagrant violation of the 28 February 2003 agreement between the U.S. and Turkey in which the Americans promised to provide Kurdish peshmergas with only light weapons that were to be collected after the fighting was over.[8]

---

[7] For an inventory of the weapons captured by the KDP and PUK up to 23 April, see Anadolu Agency, 23 April 2003.

[8] For details of the 28 February agreement see, Olson, *Turkey-Iran Relations...*, pp. 185-87.

The retention of captured weapons and supplies by the KDP and PUK was just one of many "red lines" that the Turks had established that were deleted by the U.S. after its 20 March 2003 invasion of Iraq. The lack of response by Turkey to the erasure of these red lines reduced the Kurds' fear of the Turkish threat from the north. The fall of Kirkuk to U.S. and Kurdish forces on 10 and 11 April 2003 and the failure of the TAF to come to the aid of the Turkmans, as they had stressed again and again they would, was another boost to Kurdish self-confidence and self-government. When U.S. forces expelled a dozen Turkish Special Forces on the outskirts of Kirkuk on 23 April 2003—Turkish commandos who claimed they were on a humanitarian mission but which no one believed—the Kurds seemed further assured that the likelihood of substantial Turkish intervention had diminished.

The expulsion of the 12 Turkish Special Forces troops did not, however, deter Turkey from trying to influence the course of unfavorable developments in northern Iraq, especially in the multiethnic cities of Kirkuk and Mosul. It was, however, in Sulaymaniya on 4 July 2003 that U.S. forces captured 11 Turkish Special Forces personnel along with 19 Turkman members of the Iraq Turkman Front (ITF) who were in the ITF headquarters building in PUK-controlled Sulaymaniya. The U.S. occupational command alleged that the Special Forces and Turkmans were planning to assassinate Abdul Rahman Mustafa, the newly elected mayor of Kirkuk.

Ankara vehemently denied all such charges, but many harsh words were spoken between it and Washington. The U.S. emphasized that the operation was carried out against the Turks and Turkmans who were suspected of involvement in activities not only unauthorized by the U.S., but also directed against civilian leaders endorsed by the U.S. occupational authorities. A senior U.S. State Department official said, "The United States had substantial intelligence that the Turks were engaged in activities against local leadership."[9]

The TAF and the Turkish public were particularly offended that the U.S. troops had placed bags over the heads of the cap-

---

[9] *Washington Times*, 8 July 2003.

tured Turkish soldiers reminiscent of captured terrorists or alleged al-Qaeda members. The "bag affair" led Turkey's TAF Chief-of-Staff Hilmi Özkök to declare, "This incident has unfortunately led to the biggest crisis of confidence ever between the U.S. and Turkish armed forces." Özkök added, "But there is something as important as these relations. That is our national honor and the honor of the Turkish Armed Forces."[10]

The Iraqi Kurds were probably delighted with the bruising of TAF honor and the implication of American actions that the U. S. occupational forces would not tolerate Turkey's jeopardizing further the already shaky balance of ethnic groups in northern Iraq, especially in Kirkuk and Mosul. The detainment and expulsion of the Turkish Special Forces from Sulaymaniya had several consequences: 1) it reduced Turkey's presence in Sulaymaniya and Kirkuk (at least non-clandestine presence) and in other towns in northern Iraq, and restricted Turkish armed forces, with the exception of its "peacekeeping" troops (which is discussed below) to the area they occupied inside Iraq along the Turkish-Iraqi international border; 2) it decreased further, at least for the time being, the strategic and tactical cooperation between Turkey and the U.S. in Kurdistan-Iraq and in Arab Iraq; 3) it lessened Turkey's presence to unofficial representation, trade delegations, and its "peacekeeping" forces in Kurdistan-Iraq, especially in Arbil; and 4) Ankara perceived that Washington was not too concerned about the effects of Iraqi Kurdish nationalism on Kurdish nationalist movements in Turkey.

Another consequence of the 4 July 2003 expulsion was that it impelled Ankara to further recognition of the new status of the Kurds in Kurdistan-Iraq. After 4 July 2003, with the exception of the areas they occupied along the Turkish-Iraqi border, Turkish troops would be in Iraq only at U.S., NATO or UN invitation. Kurdish armed forces, under the aegis of U.S. occupational forces, and with the exception of some heavily armed U.S. units in Kurdistan-Iraq, especially along Kurdistan-Iraq's borders with Iran and Syria, would be in control of most of Kurdistan-Iraq. By January 2004, KDP and PUK officials were fond of saying, in

---

[10] *The New York Times*, 7 July 2003.

order to emphasize the stability of their region as compared to Arab Iraq, that only 200 CPA troops were in Kurdistan-Iraq.

The 4 July affair and its consequences seemed to strengthen the confidence of the Kurds not to allow Turkish troops to enter Iraq, even regions of northern Iraq not controlled by them. However, during the mid-June 2003 visit of Uğur Ziyal, the principal adviser to the Turkish Foreign Ministry, the U.S. requested that Turkey send up to 10,000 "peacekeeping" troops to aid U.S. and coalition forces in the pacification of Iraq and to combat Iraqi resistance forces.[11] The U.S. attitude regarding Turkish troops in Iraq had changed dramatically within a few months due to the U.S. occupational forces inabilities to squash the resisting forces. The U.S. now needed Turkish forces to legitimize its occupation of Iraq and to eventually reduce its presence there.

The decision on whether or not Turkey would send troops to Iraq dragged on through the summer and early autumn of 2003. On 7 October, Turkey's parliament passed a resolution that Turkey would be willing to send up to 10,000 troops to Iraq. But after strong objections from Kurdish leaders and from the Iraq Governing Council (IGC), on which five Kurds sat, on 7 November Turkey announced that it would not be sending troops to Iraq. The decision not to send troops was a result of pressure from the KDP, PUK and IGC on L. Paul Bremer, the chief administrator of the CPA. Massoud Barzani, the head of the KDP and a member of the IGC, declared that he would resign from the IGC if Turkish troops entered Iraq. Most of the members of the IGC, including the 20 who were not Kurds, agreed with Barzani. Even though Kurds held only five of the 25 seats on the IGC, it was clear that the non-Kurds also did not want Turkish troops in Iraq. In addition, the non-Kurds had to have the cooperation of the Kurds on a host of other problems confronting Iraq and how it was to be governed that were more important than whether Turkish troops were to be in Iraq. Ankara also had to consider that Hoshyar Zebari, the foreign minister representing the IGC, was the former foreign affairs spokesman for the KDP. Not only were the KDP, PUK, and other Kurdish organizations in control

---

[11] *Radikal*, 25 June 2003.

of Kurdistan-Iraq, but they also were a force to be reckoned with in the IGC and the CPA.

The above mentioned developments contributed to Ankara's need to strengthen relations with officials and citizens of Kurdistan-Iraq. After all, the flow of trade and trucks picked up considerably in 2003 as a result of the U.S. invasion and the necessity of supplying the peoples of Iraq, as well as coalition forces, with electricity, food and shelter. By late 2003, there were reportedly some 2000 trucks a day crossing the border port at Habur/Ibrahim al-Khalil. Oil flowed intermittently through Turkey from the Kirkuk fields to the port of Ceyhan on the Mediterranean. If Turkish businessmen and companies wanted to do business in Kurdistan-Iraq, they would have to obtain the support and cooperation of Kurdish officials. Indeed, Ankara had to consider that Kurdish officials in the IGC had considerable influence in allowing Turkish companies to operate in Arab Iraq as well as in Kurdistan-Iraq. These developments necessitated movement toward a state-to-government(s) relationship between Turkey and Kurdistan-Iraq. On 18-19 November 2003, when Jalal Talabani visited Ankara, he did so not as just the leader of the PUK and as a Kurdish politician, but as the Interim President of the IGC with the trappings of a state-to-state visit.

Another difference between the U.S. and Turkey concerned the U.S. heeding the advice or demands of the KDP and PUK not to attack and disarm the remnants of the PKK /KADEK/ *KONGRA-GEL* guerrilla forces, estimated to be between 2000 and 5000, and ensconced in the Kandil Mountains in the far northeastern corner of Iraq.[12]

The U.S. continued to stonewall the Turks as to the reasons why they and/or the KDP and PUK peshmergas would not move against the PKK. It was a particularly sore point with the Turks

---

[12] Henceforth, this author will refer to these forces as the PKK. The forces in the Kandil mountains were known as the Kurdistan Workers Party (*Partia Kakaren Kurdistan* or PKK) until 2002. They then changed their name to the Kurdistan Freedom and Democracy Party (KADEK). In November 2003, KADEK announced that it was dissolving and would be replaced by a broader body, called *KONGRA-GEL* or Kurdistan Peoples Congress that would seek a peaceful solution with Turkey.

that U.S. forces, with or without the participation of the Kurds, did not move against the "terrorist" PKK throughout 2003, especially since the U.S. was waging war, both overtly and covertly against "terrorism" around the world. On 19 May 2003, the Turkish daily, *Cumhuriyet*, reported that the Bush administration had told Turkish officials, "in a frank manner, that fighting against or disarming the PKK was not a top priority of the U.S. government at the current time, insisting that it needed all of its forces to secure the safety of American troops in Iraq."[13] It struck many in Turkey as odd that it was one of the U.S.' top priorities to disarm (which had been accomplished in April 2003) the *Mojahedin-e Khalq*, an organization that was a self-proclaimed enemy of the Islamic Republic of Iran and the U.S., but the U.S. refused to move against, disarm or expel the PKK, who were a self-proclaimed enemy of the U.S.' ally, Turkey. It must have seemed to some Turks that, in certain circumstances, it was better to be an enemy rather than a friend of the U.S. At the time, Ankara may also have thought the U.S. inaction was more punishment for failure to pass the 1 March 2003 resolution.

It was only during Prime Minister Erdoğan's 25-30 January 2004 visit to Washington that Paul Wolfowitz—Deputy Secretary of Defense and one of the U.S.' main policy makers with regard to Turkey as well as one of the main architects of the war against Iraq—stated in an interview with Mehmet Ali Briand and Cengiz Çandar, two of Turkey's foremost political journalists, that the PKK had no place in Iraq and that U.S. forces would move against them in a timely fashion.[14] The U.S. State Department had actually added the *KONGRA-GEL* (the new name for the PKK/KADEK) to its list of terrorist organizations on 13 January 2004 and had informed the U.S. Embassy in Ankara of this fact on that date. The White House apparently wanted to wait until Erdoğan was in town to announce the addition. Adding the *KONGRA-GEL* to its list of terrorist organizations meant that any group, fund, service or charity found to be contributing to it would be prosecuted.

---

[13] *Cumhuriyet*, 19 May 2003.

[14] The complete interview can be found at www.defenselink.mil/, 29 January 2004.

By January 2004, the U.S. administration obviously thought, due to their difficulties in pacifying Iraq, they would have to be more responsive to Turkey's demands for U.S. action against the PKK. The U.S. had been instrumental in coercing Turkey to declare an amnesty for the PKK forces in Iraq, at least for the rank and file and those who had not killed Turkish military personnel or other high level officials in Turkey (including Kurds). On 29 July 2003, Turkey's parliament passed an amnesty law, but in the subsequent months only a few hundred PKK members took advantage of it.[15] The repentance laws were to expire on 6 February 2004. Only about 700 members of Hezbullah (Kurdish militants from Turkey) and 650 PKK militants took advantage of this amnesty.[16]

There are several possible reasons why the U.S. did not attack, disarm or expel the PKK from Iraq: 1) it may well have been that, as the U.S. occupational forces declared, they were too busy pacifying Iraq and fighting the Iraqi resistance to spare the necessary troops to attack the PKK; 2) the U.S. may not have moved against the PKK because it would be an action opposed by the KDP and PUK who favored a "full amnesty" for the returning PKK with no restrictions on participation in political life; 3) the KDP and PUK did not want the U.S. to attack the PKK and be perceived by the Kurds in Turkey that they (the KDP and PUK) were simply the lackeys of the U.S.; 4) the KDP and PUK certainly did not want to participate with U.S. troops in an attack which would worsen further their positions with the Kurdish nationalist movements in Turkey; and 5) given the above, the U.S. hardly wanted to irritate the KDP and PUK upon whose cooperation they depended for pacifying and organizing Arab Iraq.

Mahmud Osman—a prominent Kurdish politician, former high-ranking KDP official and a member of the IGC—probably spoke for much of Kurdish leadership when he stated: "These people [PKK] are not terrorists. They are simply requesting their rights in Turkey. The United States took this step [declaring

---

[15] *Hürriyet*, 30 July 2003. The parliamentary vote was 361 in favor and 68 against.
[16] *Cumhuriyet*, 10 February 2004.

them a terrorist organization] simply to satisfy Turkey."[17] The *Financial Times,* which reported the story, editorialized that Osman's remarks suggested that if coalition forces moved against the PKK, it would anger the Kurds.

The issue of the PKK forces in Iraq indicated that the KDP and PUK had considerable influence in opposing any U.S. military action against the PKK. The KDP and PUK especially did not want the Kurds of Turkey to perceive them as doing the work of Turkey for the sake of Turkish-U.S. relations. The PKK issue is another illustration of the growth of Kurdish nationalism in terms of Iraqi Kurdish relations with Turkey and within the context of Kurdish nationalism itself.

The issue of Turkey's "peacekeeping" military personnel in Iraq and the attempts of the KRG to remove them in early January 2004 is yet another example, much like the PKK issue, in which the Kurdistan-Iraqi Kurds attempted to consolidate their nationalist movements. On 27 January 2004, Nechirvan Idris Barzani, Prime Minister of the KDP-controlled region, demanded that Turkish military personnel in the Peace Monitoring Force (PMF)—consisting of some 400 troops comprised mostly of Turkmans and Assyrians, but commanded by Turkish officers—be dismantled as it was no longer needed in the wake of the collapse of Saddam Hussein's regime and his subsequent capture. The PMF had been put in place after the September 1998 Washington Accord to secure the cease-fire between the quarreling KDP and PUK.

Barzani stated, "the offices of the PMF would be closed and if that did not work, we will do what is necessary." Ankara re-

---

[17] *Financial Times*, 29 January 2004. Mahmud Osman was the personal physician to Mulla Mustafa Barzani. He broke with Barzani after his collapse in 1975 and went to Europe where he formed the Kurdistan Democratic Party-Preparatory Committee. In 1978 he returned to northern Iraq and a year later he joined with Rasul Mamand to form the Socialist Party of Kurdistan (SPK). Osman went into exile in the United Kingdom and essentially became an independent elder statesman. After the United States war against Iraq in 2003, Osman returned to Iraq and became a member of the Iraq Governing Council (IGC). I want to thank Michael Gunter and Mohammed Ahmed for the above information.

sponded to Barzani's challenge by stating that, if the PMF were attacked, Ankara would not stand by silently doing nothing and would use requisite military measures, if necessary."[18] Lieutenant-Colonel James Bullion of the U.S. Civil Affairs Battalion in Arbil was quoted as saying that it was "unlikely" that the Kurds would use force to expel the Turkish troops in Arbil. "If they do, it will create a very very big international problem."[19] It is notable that Nechirvan Idris Barzani's threat came only two weeks after the U.S. State Department added *KONGRA-GEL* to its terrorist list, one day before Prime Minister Erdoğan met with President George W. Bush in the White House and just four days before the KDP and PUK office buildings were blown up in Arbil.[20]

Iraqi Kurdish Nationalism Strengthens

The 1 February 2004 bombings of the KDP and PUK offices in Arbil, the capital of the Kurdistan Regional Government (KRG)—in which more than 100 people were killed and scores injured including top officials of the KDP and PUK—also contributed to a strengthening of Kurdish nationalism. The consequences of the bombings reinforced opinions among not only the KDP and PUK leadership, but also the Kurdish public that Kurds would have to take matters into their own hands. The Kurds certainly would see no reason for placing more of their affairs in the hands of non-Kurds or even of Kurds under the authority of some kind of Iraqi government, which itself was under the authority of the CPA. The bombings in Arbil strengthened those KDP and PUK officials who favored a two-region Kurd and Arab federation, instead of the 18 governorate scheme that was meant to reduce Kurdish control in northern Iraq.[21] In the wake

---

[18] Associated Press, 27 January 2004; and *Hürriyet*, 28 January 2004.

[19] *Hürriyet*, 28 January 2004; and *Asian Times*, 30 January 2004.

[20] Erdoğan and Bush met on 28 January 2004.

[21]It is interesting that Kurdish officials, especially Massoud Barzani, stated that the 18 governorates scheme offered by the CPA was less than what Saddam Hussein had offered in 1970 and in negotiations up to 1974. In 1974, Saddam Hussein had reportedly offered the Kurds a share in the administration and the oil revenues of Kirkuk. (Whether

this offer was genuine, of course, is questionable.) This last attempt of the Baathist government and the Kurds to negotiate occurred in mid-1973 and continued until the outbreak of war in March 1974. It seems, however, that Saddam Hussein's government did make earnest offerings to negotiate an autonomy settlement based on the 1970 agreement. Baghdad thought obviously that its position vis-à-vis the Kurds had been strengthened by its 1972 Friendship Treaty with the Soviet Union. Mulla Mustafa Barzani's alliance with Iran and his "belief" that the U.S. (and Israel) would support him in any renewed conflict with Baghdad impelled him not to negotiate in good faith with Baghdad. When Barzani showed little interest in negotiating, the Iraqi government "reduced the scope of the 1970 autonomy agreement." Hostilities subsequently broke out. In July 1973, Barzani had sent his son, Idris, and Mahmud Osman, Barzani's "foreign minister" and closest collaborator outside of the family, to Washington. Osman subsequently told Jonathan Randal, "I didn't think it was a very serious relationship for us, because I knew the key for the Americans was the Shah."

Throughout the latter part of 1973 and the first two months of 1974, the situation between the Kurds and Baghdad deteriorated. On 23 March, just prior to the outbreak of fighting, General Andrei Grechko, the Soviet Defense Minister, who had known Barzani while he was in exile in the Soviet Union (1947-1958), flew to Baghdad in an attempt to prevent armed conflict. (See Oles Smolansky, *The USSR and Iraq: The Soviet Quest for Influence* (Durham and London: Duke University Press, 1991), p. 89. (I thank Michael Gunter for the above reference.) Again, according to Randal, "at the prompting of Tehran and Washington, Barzani refused." On the virtual eve (one has to assume very late March) of renewed hostilities, Saddam Hussein again offered to share Kirkuk and its oil. (One has to assume here that Randal is referring to the governorate of Kirkuk, not just the city.) However, Barzani's son, Idris, turned him down: "We're stronger than you believe," he said, "and will oblige you to accept all our demands." Hussein replied, "If there is war, we will win." The material in this footnote is taken from Jonathan Randal, *After Such Knowledge, What Forgiveness? My Encounters with Kurdistan* (New York: Farrar, Straus and Giroux, 1997), pp. 153-58.

The administrative map of Iraq was changed in 1976. Parts of the former Kirkuk governorate were attached to the governorate of Sulaymaniya, other parts to the Diyala governorate and yet additional parts to the Tikrit governorate. The Tikrit governorate's name was changed to Salah ad-Din. Arbil, which was part of the Kirkuk governorate, was turned into a new governorate. Duhok, which had been part of the Moof the bombings, the KDP and PUK leadership also had to consider more seriously the grass-roots nationalist movements among Kurds to bring the issue of independence to referendum. By 1 February 2004, some 1.5 million signatures had been gathered to support a referendum.[22]

It did not take long for the repercussions of the 1 February 2004 bombings to be felt in the KRG's parliament. On 5 February, the Kurdish parliament convened and called for quicker unification of the KDP and PUK governments. This was obviously opposed to the federation schemes offered by the CPA and a setback to the 28 February deadline for the IGC to draft a "Basic Law" to govern the country until elections and the writing of a full constitution in 2005.[23] One of the parliament's first actions was not to recognize an IGC decision to change rules on divorce and other family issues. In December 2003, while a Shiite leader, Abdul Aziz al-Hakim, occupied the rotating presidency of the IGC, the council had voted to abolish the law regulating marriage, divorce, child custody and inheritance, instead allowing different religious groups to apply their own laws and traditions. The KRG parliament stated that it would enforce a family law passed in 1959 and the amendments that the Kurdish administration introduced into it.[24]

Public opinion also began to play an even stronger role in Kurdistan-Iraq after the 1 February 2004 bombings. This development meant that the KDP and PUK leadership would have to consider growing Kurdish nationalism in their decision-making, especially with regard to the 18 governorate scheme that the

---

sul governorate, also became another governorate. For these changes, see Nouri Talabani, *Arabization of the Kirkuk Region* (Sweden: Kurdistan Studies Press, 1991), pp. 66-77. I thank Mohammed Ahmed for directing me to the above two sources.

[22] Peter Galbraith, "Kurds Show Their Grit," *Los Angeles Times*, 11 February 2004.

[23] Reuters, 5 February 2004.

[24] Mahmud Osman, a member of the IGC and a Sunni Kurd, said that the council's decision had been hasty and it should have deliberated with experts and women's organizations. The decision passed by a slight majority instead of the necessary two-thirds vote. Associated Press, 5 February 2004.

CPA was pushing. There was a host of stories in the Kurdish media after the bombings calling for the independence of Kurdistan-Iraq for a plethora of reasons.

On 9 February 2004, Kurdish journalist, Khasraw Saleh Koyi, supported such reasoning when he wrote: 1) the Kurds should "discourage unknown Arabs from visiting and/or residing in Kurdistan. Such Arabs must provide proof of authorization from recognized authorities for their presence in Kurdistan; 2) all hotels, motels, as well as households in Kurdistan should inform local authorities of their Arab and/or other suspected guests; 3) eliminate Islamic religious studies in elementary, secondary and high schools, as well as the studies that glorify Arab history and culture in all Kurdish schools; 4) highlight the fact that Kurdish ethnicity is a constant factor, which predated Islam and will outlive all religions; that the Islamic religion was imposed on the Kurds by violence; that Arabs used Islam to loot Kurdistan and wipe out the Kurds; that this Arab mentality is here now and will be here indefinitely; 5) neither trust Arabs nor be fooled by their sweet talks and deceptive promises; 6) view every Arab stranger in Kurdistan as a suspect and a potential time bomb; 7) when encountering Arabs in Kurdistan, don't think of them in terms of Iraqism, Islam and brotherhood. Instead, think of what their nation has done to the Kurds in the past and what they are capable of doing to them today and tomorrow; 8) remember, 'An Arab trusting Kurd is a naïve, and doomed Kurd'"[25]

Koyi went on to state, "It is predictable that if Arab, Islamist and nationalist terrorist organizations (enjoy the backing of various regional states), [and] don't cease their hostilities against the Kurds, the following may be some of the imminent consequences: 1) it will generate anti-Islam emotions, as well as nationalist antipathy against the Arabs and their culture; 2) it will encourage many Kurds to abandon Islam, go back to Zoroastrianism and/or embrace Christianity or Judaism; and 3) make it

---

[25] Khasraw Saleh Koyi, "How to Deal with Arab 'Islamist and Nationalist' Terrorism in Kurdistan," KurdishMedia.com, 9 February 2004.

impossible for the Kurds to co-exist with Arabs in the same states: the already thin faith is thinner now.[26]

Public opinion for independence continued to grow throughout February 2004. Popular resistance to the 18 governorate scheme and the attempts by the IGC and the drafters of the Basic Law (Interim Constitution) to demand the dismantling of the KDP and PUK peshmerga forces and have them incorporated under the authority of the government to be established in Baghdad also grew. On 14 February, some 10,000 students, teachers, engineers and activists marched in Sulaymaniya in remembrance of Saddam Hussein's Anfal campaign carried out in 1987-88 in which some 200,000 Kurds died. "We are asking for independence," said Nawroza al-Khaffat, chairman of the Kurdistan Contractors' Union.[27] The organizers of the march claimed they had gathered 1.5 million signatures, 85 percent of whom wanted full independence, on a petition to ask Massoud Barzani and Jalal Talabani, leaders of the KDP and PUK, to submit any constitutional agreement they negotiated in Baghdad to a referendum in the north. The referendum drive indicated strongly that many Kurds thought that the KDP and PUK leadership might settle for less than independence.

By 25 February, the signatures for the referendum swelled to 1.7 million. Halkaut Abdullah, a member of the Reform Movement for Kurdistan and one of the organizers of the petition drive, declared: "We expect the majority to support independence. This is their ambition, although they are not necessarily realistic."[28] These February marches indicated, perhaps for the first time in the history of the Kurds of Iraq, that their major leaders would very seriously have to consider public demands for whatever form of government they negotiated. Failure to do so would result in a serious lack of legitimacy and confidence in their leadership.

From 20 to 25 February 2004, there were sustained efforts in Kurdistan-Iraq and in the international Kurdish diaspora to ob-

---

[26] *Ibid.* In addition to Koyi's piece, also see Dr. Rashid Karadaghi, "The Price of Friendship," KurdishMedia, 10 February 2004.

[27] *The Financial Times*, 16 February 2004.

[28] *The New York Times*, 25 February 2004.

tain as many signatures as possible on the referendum to vote for Kurdish independence. Even as the referendum drives were taking place, another bombing occurred on 23 February in Kirkuk killing at least 10 people and wounding some 50.[29] Along with the much more deadly bombing of 1 February, these two terrorist bombing attacks coming a little over three weeks apart spurred further public demands that Kurds take care of their own security.

New Problems

Even as Kurdish public opinion was galvanizing demands for independence, the actions of Ankara and Washington made it clear that the Kurdish struggle and demands for federated autonomy, let alone independence, would be difficult. On 8 February, Rifat Hisarcıkoğlu, the chairman of Turkey's Union of Chamber of Commerce, headed a large delegation of Turkish businessmen to Baghdad to request of Paul Bremer that Turkish companies be given a larger share in the building of Iraq's infrastructure. One of the ironies of the meeting was that the Turkish delegation was addressed by Colonel William Mayville, the commander of the 173rd airborne brigade in Kirkuk. This was the same Mayville who had commanded the unit that had captured the 12 Turkish Special Forces officers in the famous "4 July Affair" which, as discussed above, "led to the biggest crisis of confidence ever between the U.S. and Turkish armed forces."[30] Now, eight months later, Colonel Mayville was brought to Baghdad by Paul Bremer to tell the Turkish businessmen that Turkish investment and participation in the building of Iraq's infrastructure and economy were welcome. "We [the U.S.] invite you to make investments in Kirkuk. Kirkuk has a strong Turkmans business community and since you show such an interest in Kirkuk you should contribute to its economic wealth."[31]

---

[29] *The New York Times International*, 23 February 2004.

[30] See footnote 10 above.

[31] *Hürriyet*, 15 February 2004. On the 14 February, Sedat Ergin received from Turkey's Newspaper Association the award for the best journalist story and reporting in the category of political-social news 2003 for his articles on the 4 July "bag affair."

Sedat Ergin, the main political writer for *Hürriyet,* interpreted the changed U.S. position to mean that the federation of Iraq would not be based on religion or ethnicity and, hence, opposed to a separate Kurdish region in the federation. Ergin opined that Washington's changed position was stated to Prime Minister Erdoğan during his visit to Washington on 25-30 January 2004. This meant, wrote Ergin, that in the new U.S. policy Turkey would play a major role in Iraq's integration into the world economy.[32] After all, the large Turkish Chamber of Commerce delegation left for Baghdad only two weeks after Erdoğan's departure from Washington. Ergin speculated that the green light from Washington meant that Turkish businessmen could hope to receive contacts of up to $2 billion from the $18.6 billion that the U.S. allocated for the "reconstruction" of Iraq in 2004.

Ergin also thought that the new U.S. policy would demand that Ankara no longer "index" all of its policies toward Iraq with reference to northern Iraq, but rather adopt multifaceted policies based on economic cooperation with U.S. occupational forces and whatever government was in power in Baghdad.[33] The attempts to implement such policies by Washington and Ankara would provide serious challenges to growing Kurdish nationalism in Kurdistan-Iraq. How the Kurds would deal with such challenges would strongly affect the future directions of Kurdish nationalism in Iraq.

A big challenge to the Kurds occurred during the negotiations to draft the interim constitution of Iraq. When the draft constitution was announced on 1 March 2004, the Kurds were left in control of the three governorates—Duhok, Arbil, Sulaymaniya—that they already controlled. "We wanted areas in other governorates that are Kurdish to be under the control of Kurds. However, the Americans didn't want us to change the existing borders. I think Turkey played a role in this because the Americans began claiming this only after Recep Tayyip Erdoğan's visit [to Washington from 25-30 January]. The Americans are listening to

---

[32] "Iraq'in dünya ekonomisiyle entergrasyonunun Türkiye üzerinden gerçekleşmesi teması Amerikan tarafınca sıkça vurgulanıyor," *Hürriyet,* 15 February 2004.
[33] *Ibid.*

Turks in general and this is a disadvantage to Kurds. The U.S. administration began to increase opposition to our demands after Erdoğan's visit."[34]

Mahmud Osman also declared that the issue of borders and the role of the Kurdish pershmerga in the future armed forces of Iraq would be left to future negotiations: "These two points, mainly the peshmerga and the territory's borders, remain because these are the security points and [they] cannot be solved. You know, security totally lies with the American coalition forces. They have their own policy. They can't change it for us. That's why these things will remain." Osman added that the Kurds retained the right to keep their militias until a final solution was reached. He said the peshmerga is "not just a militia but a force of the whole nation. They are like an army of the Kurdish people. These forces have existed already for 50 years, and they cannot just be disbanded and sent home." He did think that the peshmerga might be transformed into regular Iraqi forces. Some of them could become part of a police force. Others might become border guards or national guards in the Kurdish region or join the new Iraqi army.[35]

Osman also thought that the referendum campaign greatly strengthened the Kurdish bargaining position: "This pressure from the Kurdish street, from the Kurdish population, it is there, always it is there, including [among] the Kurdish leadership. And I think the Kurds, they have the right to self-determination, and they have the right to have a real say in what goes on in Iraq in the future. So it is within that—that question of a referendum—and obviously it creates a constant pressure on everybody who deals with the Kurdish question. The best solution now is to be included in a federation in a democratic Iraq, at least for this period of time."[36] Thus, in a little over one year after the U.S. invasion of Iraq, the Iraqi Kurds, both leaders and populace had been able to position themselves to negotiate in the future with an elective Iraqi government the terms of their own self-determination. This would pose the biggest challenge to the

---

[34] Reuters, 1 March 2004.
[35] *Asian Times*, 3 March 2004.
[36] *Ibid.*

Kurds in the 21st century and test the strength of their growing nationalism and its eventual configuration.

The announcement of the signing of the interim constitution on 1 March 2004 was delayed when five Shiite members of the IGC decided not to sign it because of a clause that stipulated that if two-thirds of the voters of any three provinces rejected the permanent constitution in a country-wide referendum, it would not go into effect. This seemed to indicate that if the Kurds, who controlled three provinces, voted against the permanent constitution, it would not go into effect. Shiite members were also unhappy with an article that established a single president with two deputies; the Shiite members thought this diminished their power too severely. The draft of the interim constitution was finally passed on 8 March 2004 after the Kurdish leaders threatened to leave the negotiations: "We already have our own government," said one Kurdish official, "if the Shiites try to make us obey, we won't ask for anything. We will just keep what we have."[37]

The negotiations over the drafting of the interim constitution demonstrated clearly the clout that Kurds would exercise in any forthcoming constitutional arrangements for the federated state of Iraq. The fact that they possessed territory which they could defend with considerable armed forces reinforced their constitutional and legal bargaining position. The negotiations over the drafting of the interim constitution demonstrated clearly for the first time the strength of Kurdish nationalism as expressed in legal and jurisprudential law relevant to a national state and legitimated in international law. After the signing of the interim constitution on 8 March 2004, growing Kurdish nationalism was clearly evident, especially among young people, most of whom when asked said they wanted an independent state: "We never want to mix with Arabs again; they [the Arabs] were raised on fighting and cruelty; we have a different skin color, etc."

Many Kurds under 20 did not speak Arabic, although some acknowledged they would have to learn it, if they wanted to attend college in Arab Iraq. While many young Kurds wanted independence, most of their longtime political leaders were happy with the autonomy they had gained in three provinces. Nechir-

---

[37] *New York Times*, 8 March 2004.

wan Mustafa Amin, an important adviser to PUK leader Jalal Talabani, said he was overjoyed with the interim constitution. Farid Asasard, Director of the Kurdish Strategic Studies Center, stated, "What the Kurdish street doesn't understand is that there's a big difference between declaring and sustaining a state; they [the young people] would like such state, but no one would recognize or back up such a state."

Asasard's position was seconded by Barham Salih, the Prime Minister of the PUK-controlled region of Kurdistan-Iraq, who emphasized that, rather than the declaration of an independent state, Kurdistan-Iraq should strive to become part of a global economic and cultural community. In support of this vision, Salih announced that his PUK government had hired a Turkish firm to build Sulaymaniya's airport for commercial air traffic.[38] Despite the different and seemingly contradictory positions between the younger generation and Kurdistan-Iraqi political leaders regarding the appropriateness of an independent Kurdish state in current political and geopolitical circumstances, both are expressions of a consolidating and confidence building Kurdish nationalism.

Repercussions in Iran and Syria

The Kurds of Kurdistan-Iraq, especially the younger generation, found some assurance in the strength of their nationalist feelings when there were extensive demonstrations and riots in Kurdistan-Iran in support of the Iraqi interim constitution and demands for more autonomy of the Kurds in Iran. The Kurdistan Democratic Party of Iran (DPKI) reported that up to 50,000 people had demonstrated in Mahabad and 10,000 in Mariwan with additional large demonstrations in Sanandaj, Bana and Sardasht; demonstrators shouted slogans demanding "democracy in Iran and autonomy for Iranian Kurdistan."[39]

---

[38] www.Flash-bulletin.de 16 March 2004. The above quotes are all from this source.
[39] www.pdki.org, 11, 15 March 2004; and kurdishmedia.com, 11 March 2004.

Demonstrations supporting the interim constitution were larger and more violent in Syria where demonstrations and riots following a soccer match on 12 March 2004 continued for several days with reports of up to 40 killed, over 100 wounded and thousands detained. Riots continued from 11 to 16 March in predominantly Kurdish cities throughout Syria's "Duck Beak," as the triangular region in eastern Syria adjoining Turkey and Iraq is known. Demonstrations and riots, including the attacking and burning of police stations and Baath Party offices, were especially widespread in Qamishli, Hasaka, and the towns along Syria's border with Turkey such as Raas al-Ayn, Amudah, Malikiya, Ayn Diwar, Jawadiyah, Tal Birak, and Tal Tamir. There were also large demonstrations in Syria's second largest city, Aleppo, as well as Afrin, a city 65 km. north of Aleppo and in other towns.[40]

Suspected Kurdish nationalists were detained in Damascus. One report estimated that up to 2,000 Kurds, including men between the ages of 14 and 50 in the Kurdish Zorawa neighborhood of Damascus, were detained. There were even reports that a Kurdish nationalist and tribal leader had died or been killed in a Syrian hospital. Other accounts reported that Kurds had killed nine Syrian officers, and that in Amuda, a town near Qamishli, Kurds had killed a judge and four soldiers.[41] The unrest grew to the point that it was reported in the Kurdish media that on 16 March, two U.S. Sikorsky helicopters had arrived in Qamishli and that Americans met with Kurdish and Syrian government, intelligence and military officials. The Americans reportedly demanded that the Syrian regime cease its harsh responses to the Kurdish demonstrations in eastern and other parts of Syria, including Damascus.[42]

The simultaneous demonstrations among the Kurds in Iran and Syria, as well as strong support from Kurds in Turkey, no

---

[40] KurdishMedia, *The Christan Science, Monitor, The New York Times, Turkish Daily News, Hürriyet, Cumhuriyet, Yeni Şafak,* and Reuters among others, provided extensive coverage of the demonstrations and riots.

[41] Kurdistan Observer, 15 March 2003; and KurdishMedia.com 16 March 2004.

[42] KurdishMedia.com 16 March 2004.

doubt strengthened considerably the feeling of nationalism among the Kurds of Kurdistan-Iraq. Of course, as leaders of Kurdistan-Iraq were well aware, this increasing tide of Kurdish nationalism in Iran, Syria and Turkey also posed serious challenges to their autonomous federal state. There were demonstrations in Sulaymaniya in support of Kurdish brethren in Syria. Thus, as a result of their legal and by extension internationally recognized status within the interim constitution of federated Iraq and the support shown to that status by Kurds in Iran, Syria and Turkey, the leaders and people of Kurdistan-Iraq faced the challenge of defending and extending their new status even as it was challenged by the governments in Ankara, Damascus, Tehran and Baghdad.

One of Kurdistan-Iraq's prominent leaders, Prime Minister Barham Salih of the PUK-controlled region of Kurdistan-Iraq, stated: "We have our own problems to deal with and we do not want to be involved in the domestic affairs of our neighbors." In a telephone interview with *The Turkish Daily News*, Salih said it was "embarrassing for the Iraqi Kurds as they are caught in an awkward situation between a friendly administration in Damascus and the local Kurds."[43] Reports from Syrian Arab sources said that the unrest was fanned by the U.S., but Iraqi Kurdish leaders said they did not "believe the Americans have a finger in the unrest in Syria . . . because this is not the way the Americans operate."[44]

Other observers stated that "if similar incidents start in the Kurdish areas of Iran this could be an indicator that Washington is now involved in efforts to show the stick to Damascus and Tehran through the Kurds. There is talk that the Americans are in close contact with Iranian Kurdish groups."[45] Despite Turkey's concern regarding the increasing growth and militancy of Kurdish nationalism in Syria, Cengiz Çandar, one of Turkey's most prominent journalists of political affairs, stressed that the PKK had found shelter and backing in Syria for two decades and during this time it had recruited hundreds of Syrian Kurds to fight

---

[43] *Turkish Daily News*, 19 March 2004.
[44] *Ibid.*
[45] *Ibid.*

with the PKK in Turkey against the Turkish Armed Forces: "Now the militants who served for the Kurdish separatist cause in Turkey may well be stirring trouble in Syria."[46]

Conclusion

The argument that relations between Turkey and the Iraqi Kurds proceeded from a state-to-region to a state-to-government(s) relationship does not mean, as indicated above, there is or will be an inevitable movement to a state-to-state relationship. Indeed, the relationship could return to a state-to-region relationship or even to a relationship in which the relations between the two parties would be conducted largely through the government in Baghdad along the lines envisioned in the 18 governorate scheme—a relationship in which the Iraqi Kurds would have less autonomy than they exercised in the state-to-region relationship that existed from 1992 to 1 March 2003. The Iraqi Kurds, however, will resist this development.

In changed circumstances, of course, the existing relationship could alter quickly. For example: 1) Turkey might find it necessary to invade Kurdistan-Iraq. This could occur if the Iraqi Kurds declared an independent state. 2) Another case might be if the U.S., because of increased resistance from Arab Iraqis, decided to reduce significantly its presence (withdrawing to military enclaves), which could lead to civil war. 3) Still another scenario for Turkey's intervention would be if the Kurds, Arabs and Turkmans of Kurdistan-Iraq were to engage in internecine fighting. 4) A fourth situation could arise if the Kurds of Iran sought more autonomy in the event of the weakening or toppling of the Islamic Republic, leading to closer relations between the Kurds of Iran and Kurdistan-Iraq. 5) Yet another case could arise if Turkey thought that Iran was beginning to exercise too much influence in Arab Iraq, and it looked like a Shiite-dominated Arab Iraq had possibilities of emerging . 6) Finally, yet another possibility would be if the government of Kurdistan-Iraq decided to support the Kurdish nationalist movements or organizations in Turkey to the point that Ankara thought they jeopardized Tur-

---

[46] *Ibid.*

key's national security, threatened governing institutions, or would lead to actions that would destabilize or significantly weaken Turkey's government or challenge its armed forces.

In conclusion, therefore, developments from the Turkish parliament's rejection of the 1 March 2003 resolution (that would have approved Turkey's joining the U.S. attack against Iraq) to 1 April 2004 represented efforts by the Kurdistan-Iraqi Kurds to consolidate their nationalist movement in Kurdistan-Iraq. These efforts by the Iraqi Kurds proceeded against what they rightfully perceived to be attempts to diminish their hard-won semi-sovereignty. The Iraqi Kurds also realized by the end of 2003, and certainly by 1 April 2004, that their policies were in contradiction to efforts and policies by the U.S. to give greater attention and sway to Turkey's concerns regarding Kurdistan-Iraq and Arab Iraq. Kurdish leadership had to be concerned by presentations of myriad U.S. officials during Erdoğan's Washington visit in January 2004 that the U.S. would not allow an independent Kurdish state to exist in Iraq, or even as a geographically autonomous region within a federated Iraq given the difficult circumstances in which Washington found itself in 2004. Such statements by U.S. officials must have further impelled Kurdish officials to realize that in order to maintain the control and semi-sovereignty they exercised in Kurdistan-Iraq and the influence they had in Arab Iraq, especially in the IGC, they would have to tolerate some Turkish presence, largely business activities, in Kurdistan-Iraq and in Arab Iraq. The extent to which Kurdistan-Iraqis tolerated this presence would play an important role in the future dimensions of nationalism in Kurdistan-Iraq.

CHAPTER 6

The Kurdish Issue in Turkey Following the 2003 Iraqi War

Hamit Bozarslan

Introduction

Writing on the evolution of the Kurdish issue in the Middle East and in Turkey at the end of 2003 is quite a difficult task. On one hand, the subjectivities and material constraints which determined this issue in the past have disappeared or radically changed. On the other hand, like many other burning Middle Eastern issues, the Kurdish issue also continues to evolve in a very uncertain environment. Thus, at times, one can only note how fragile the current balances and equations are without being able to make projections for more than a couple of days at a time. Although the "landmarks" proposed to understand a given current situation may still make sense a couple of years later, they might also become totally irrelevant within a couple of weeks.

In spite of this unpleasant situation and the related methodological difficulties, this article shall try to shed light on some regional and domestic factors which have contributed to the evolution of the Kurdish issue in Turkey. The starting hypothesis is that Ankara's inability to resolve its Kurdish issue or even to envisage a different policy than the one adopted since the foundation of the Turkish Republic in 1923 is a result of this Republic's very power structures. Unless the country's political authorities decide to change profoundly these power structures, which will require radical reforms, Turkey will be condemned to pass through heavy regional and domestic political crises. Although a central issue, the Kurdish issue is not the only one which attests to this cold-blooded conclusion.

"Red Lines" and "Internal Enemies": The Crisis of the Turkish Republic

In the past couple of years, Turkey has experienced a rather peaceful domestic situation, which sharply contrasts with the violence and deep political crisis which occurred earlier. The reason for this apparent calm, however, lies in the very crisis of the Turkish Republic, whose policies came to an undeniable dead-end by the beginning of the third millennium. The years 2000-2003 have in fact attested to the inability of the country's military and civil establishment to continue to conduct Turkish foreign and domestic affairs by the ultimatums, coercive measures and "hegemonic syntax"[1] instruments that in the past required the mobilization of the society against the so-called "external and internal enemies." The "power engineering" of the Republic, which has been widely "modernized" throughout the 1980s and 1990s, and which was rather successful in justifying a scorched-earth policy in Kurdistan-Turkey and the use of massive symbolic violence against the Islamists, appeared by the turn of 2000, all of a sudden, inefficient.

A brief return to the period before the November 2002 elections will illustrate this fact. In spite of the Turkish candidacy to the European Union and a long-standing "strategic partnership" with Washington, Turkish foreign policy was then obsessed by two "Red Lines." According to Ankara, crossing these "Red Lines" would ipso facto constitute a *casus belli*. These famous "Red Lines" were officially fixed in order to respond to the

---

[1] The civil "establishment" is constituted by the very conservative Constitutional Court and the Court of Appeals, some segments of bureaucracy, the Commission for Higher Education, the High Commission for Radio and Television, as well as the Kemalist intelligentsia. In the Turkish political language, the concept "deep state" describes the military and civil establishment together.

country's "security concerns." At the same time, they were sup-
posed to insure the supremacy of Turkey in the Middle East and
the supremacy of Turkishness as a nation or as a meta-historical
entity against the other ethnic or national entities. Ultimately,
their sole justification was a social-Darwinian one: the Turkish
nation had to win by its strength the "struggle for life" engaged
between the nations and any concession to the "enemies" would
mean a sign of external or internal weakness.[2]

The first "Red Line" was linked to the Cyprus issue. The
admission of Cyprus to the European Union, which obviously
would mean the non-recognition of the "Turkish Republic of
North Cyprus" by the international community, was considered
as a deadly threat to the "Turkish nation" and was presented as a
casus belli. The second "Red Line" aimed at preventing the formation of any viable Kurdish entity in Iraq, as well as the entry
of the Kurdish forces into Kirkuk. Ankara tirelessly explained
that even the return of civilian Kurds, massively expelled by
Saddam Hussein's regime, to their hometown would be considered as a *casus belli*. Turkey first argued that the city was the
"historical capital" of Iraq's "three million Turkmans."[3] When it
appeared that such an argument had no sociological or demographic accuracy, Ankara was obliged to acknowledge that the
idea of a Kurdish entity constituted per se a "threat" to Turkey
and to its Turkishness. The contrast and similarities between the
arguments were sharp: the Turks of Cyprus had the right to have
their own state because they were *Turks*, the Kurds of Iraq had
no right to have a viable entity—not to say a state— because
they were *Kurds*.

Similar "Red Lines" also existed domestically. In fact, two
groups were designated as "internal enemies": The Kurdish
movement and the Islamists both qualified as strategic threats
either to the country's national integrity or to its secular regime.
Media organs were massively mobilized to show the degree of

---

[2] For this notion, see M. Billig, *Banal Nationalism* (London: Sage
Publications), 1995.
[3] The exact number of the Turkmans in Iraq is not known. Based on
censuses going back to the 1920s, however, one can estimate that they
constitute around 5 percent of Iraq's total population

immediate threat that those enemies represented. The Turkish society was totally dumbfounded, without being able to know which one of these enemies, equally defined by the military as mortal, was the most mortal and the most immediate one. Throughout the 1990's in fact, the Turkish state has functioned as a *"fabrique* of production of internal enemies" and bore the main responsibility for the internal instability through which the country went. The entire Turkish political culture, in fact, evolved during this decade within the framework of the "Red Lines" marking the political syntax not only of the military and civil establishment, but also the political parties.

The Pulverization of the External "Red Lines"

A year after the November 2002, elections, one can make only three remarks. First, in spite of the lack of any radical change in Turkish foreign policy, the two external "Red Lines" have been largely pulverized. More strongly put, the entire foreign policy culture, based on military strength, "national security" and Turkishness' right to superiority, came to a dead-end. Second, the impossibility of preserving these "Red Lines" in foreign policy may well push the power holders to reinforcing the internal "Red Lines. The third remark is that a public opinion ready to support this very definition of politics as a "war" or as a "battlefield" is, for the time being at least, dramatically missing in Turkey.

In the field of foreign policy, the first "Red Line" was destroyed by Europe's acceptance of Cyprus' membership as a unified country in the European Union (EU). By May 2004, the government of Nicosia will become the sole legitimate representative of the island. Moreover, the EU's report issued on November 5, 2003,[4] clearly subordinated Turkey's accession to EU membership to her willingness and ability to find a solution to the Cyprus crisis. Even if no juridical text expresses it explicitly,

---

[4] European Commission, "Continuing Enlargement Strategy: Paper and Report of the European Commission on the Progress towards Accession by Bulgaria, Romania and Turkey," Brussels, 2003.

by May 1, 2004, Turkey will de facto be considered as a foreign country which occupies a part of the European Union. Similarly, Turkey will find herself in the very odd position of a candidate member which wants to adhere to the EU, but does not diplomatically recognize one of its full members.

Turkey, of course, can resolve this question by accepting U.N. General Secretary Kofi Annan's proposal presented in 2002. This proposal aimed at joining the two federal entities of Cyprus within one unified country. While allowing the presence of the Turkish troops in the island, it would reduce their number to only a couple of thousand (currently some 30,000 Turkish troops "protect" a Turkish population estimated at the most to be some 180,000), and would permit the Greek refugees to return to their homes from where they had been expelled during the 1974 Turkish invasion.

The new AKP (Justice and Development Party) government elected in November 2002 was at first quite sympathetic to the Kofi Annan Plan. The majority of the Turkish Cypriots, including the Anatolian Turks who have been settled in the island after 1974, have also warmly welcomed the Plan. Some 80,000 Turkish Cypriots demonstrated in favor of the Plan. The opposition of Rauf Denktas, the president of the "Turkish Republic of North Cyprus" and that of the Turkish army, however, obliged the AKP government to accept a more conservative, or rather a status-quo-based policy.[5]

Turkey, of course, had no margin to prevent Cyprus' access to the EU, and even less to deal with this new situation as one deals with a *casus belli*. Even Turkish public opinion was quite

---

[5] Both Denktas and the Turkish army insisted on the fact that the Cyprus issue was not restricted solely to the presence of the Turkish troops in the island, but to the very future of Turkishness as such. According to Denktas, the Kofi Annan Plan, the first stage of a longer project "aiming at the dismantlement of Turkey," constitutes a mortal threat for the Turkish nation. He also accused the European Union of aiming at the "imprisonment of the Turkishness in Anatolia." For a more diplomatic, but nevertheless similar reading of these foreign policy problems, see the interview with Chief of the General Staff General Hilmi Özkök in *Radikal*, November 9, 2003.

reluctant to accept Denktas' arguments. The pro-Denktas meetings gathered hardly a couple of thousand nationalists in Istanbul. The outcome, therefore, was the pulverization of this first "Red Line."

The second "Red Line," which concerned Iraqi Kurdistan, had an even more dramatic downfall. After months of negotiations, Turkey had promised Washington to allow it to open a "second front" in the coming second Gulf War. In return, Ankara would have obtained some $6 billion of foreign aid (instead of some $90 billion demanded) and also would have been allowed to send up to 60,000 Turkish troops, together with the American ones, into Iraqi Kurdistan. Ankara had made no mystery about its ambitions: these troops would have prevented the entry of Kurdish forces, and if necessary, the Kurdish civilian population into Kirkuk. They also would have had the task of disarming the Iraqi Kurdish military forces. Such a military excursion would have certainly created serious clashes and would have transformed a rather violence-free Kurdish zone into an explosive one.

However, on March 1, 2003, the Turkish Parliament decided for many reasons not to allow the American troops to use Turkish territory to open a second front. Probably, many Parliament members believed that the Americans would not be able to start the war against Saddam Hussein with only one single front. Some of them, as well as the members of the civil and military establishment, were almost openly anti-American. General Tuncer Kilinç, the secretary general of the National Security Council, which is the main non-elected organ dealing with national security issues in Turkey, for instance, clearly explained that the Turks should turn their back to the "West" (Europe and America) and turn their face to the other "Asian" powers, namely Iran (which was blacklisted by President Bush as a member of "the Axis of Evil") and Russia.[6] Others believed in a genuine "Muslim solidarity" which forbade them to contract any alliance with the non-Muslim countries against Muslim ones.

---

[6] See the Turkish newspapers of March 8, 2003.

Finally, some were sensitive to the reactions of a massively anti-American Turkish public opinion.

Whatever the reasons for the Turkish Parliament refusing the American request, the outcome was that the Kurds replaced the Turkish troops and became themselves the main forces of the famous "Second Front." Given the rapid evolution of the war, the Kurds then entered Kirkuk and Mosul without serious fights with the Iraqi army. Turkey, which had been almost openly accused by Washington of having betrayed their historical alliance, has been thus marginalized.

Ankara's attempt to use the Turkman card against the Kurds and even to organize an act of sabotage against the Kurdish governor of Kirkuk further deepened the crises between the two allies. When in October 2003, the Turkish Parliament finally authorized the government to send some 10,000 troops for a one-year period to some areas in Iraq designated by Washington, the Iraqi political forces were unanimous in their opposition. The declaration of the Turkish general staff, who hardly disguised the threat of using force against the Iraqi Kurds, did not improve the situation. Finally, Washington was obliged to decide not to accept any Turkish troops, thus pulverizing Turkish foreign policy's second "Red Line" Once again, Ankara could not deal with the new situation as one deals with a *casus belli*.

The Future of the Internal "Red Lines"

The end of these external "red lines," which considerably weakens the official state-advocated "national security" doctrine, may well contribute to increasing the problems at the domestic level. The military and civil establishments can be tempted thus by strengthening their position at the domestic level. At the same time, however, the domestic level politics appear, more and more, to be the Achilles' heel of this very establishment.

To understand this fact, one should remember that throughout the 1980s and 1990s, the regime's survival depended mainly on its ability to use a technique of enmity which was successful enough to mobilize some sections of the society either against the Kurdish nationalists or against the Islamist movement. Only the existence of an "enemy," which represented an "immediate and mortal threat" to the country's "integrity" or to the regime's "secular character," allowed the military and civil establishment to impose its hegemony in the political space, to marginalize or subordinate the political class, and to fix internal "red lines."

One should acknowledge that by the end of 2003, these internal "Red Lines" have not disappeared and that, in the future, the civil and military establishment will fight hard to save its domination in the political sphere. One should also recognize, however, that the "hegemonic bloc," which enabled the military and civil establishment to insure its durability, has considerably weakened.

The decision in 2000 of Abdullah Öcalan (largely followed by his fighters) to stop the armed struggle was one of the main factors which weakened this "hegemonic bloc." Although no concrete measure has yet been taken to satisfy the Kurds' minimal demands and claims, the Kurds won since then a de facto legitimate existence, or at least, are henceforth accepted as a quite banal fact. The evolution of the Kurdish issue in Iraq will probably also contribute to the further legitimization of the Kurdish issue in Turkey, and therefore, also the Kurdish political actors in Turkey.

A second factor which narrowed the military and civil establishment's margins, was the choice of one-third of Turkey's voters to bring the AKP, an offspring of the former Islamist movement, to power. The establishment's repeated attacks against the AKP government and elected deputies since the November 2002 elections—for example, boycotting their "veiled" wives during the official 2003 ceremonies celebrating the 80th anniversary of the foundation of the Turkish Republic—only brought even more popularity to the new government. The AKP, which obtained some 35 per cent of the votes during the 2002 elections, is credited by the opinion polls with some 44 per cent today.

We can thus legitimately think that the two "enemies" against whom the Turkish Republic had been founded,—namely, the Kurdish nationalists and Islamists (who are today largely converted to a neo-liberal or conservative right-wing party)—are stronger than ever before. Through their de facto legitimization, in fact, the Kemalist ideology as such becomes socially anachronistic. The Republic, whose legitimization depended on its ability to protect the nation against these "enemies,"[7] is henceforth unable to find new and "convincing" enemies.

Two examples illustrate this crucial lack of new "enemies." In 2001, Fethullah Gülen, the leader of a very respected and incredibly pro-state religious community, was presented as the most important new strategic threat to the Republic and was accused of "terrorism," a serious charge. The entire affair, however, ended in a fiasco. A second trial then charged some well-respected German foundations—which generously funded social research in Turkey (Konrad Adenauer, Fredrich Ebert, and Heinrich Böll)—of having constituted an underground "cartel" trying to destroy the "indivisibility" of the Turkish Republic. Once again, the trial ended in a fiasco.

These scandals, however, did not bring a substantial change in the power structures of the Turkish Republic. The National Security Council, whose secretary general remains a high-ranking military official in spite of a change in its status, is still the main power organ in the country. The most important political decisions are still made by the military and civil establishment; the army commanders are still allowed to "convoke" the presidents of the universities and dictate to them the conduct they must adopt in their academic *and* political life.

The government's reform policy is either very timorous or its application is blocked by the bureaucracy which possesses the real power within the state. As the decision of President Sezer not to invite the "veiled" wives of the cabinet members and AKP deputies to an official ceremony shows clearly, the members of the government and Parliament are seen as the de jure or de facto

---

[7] After the capture of the PKK's leader, Abdullah Öcalan, in Kenya in 1999, Turkish prime minister Bülent Ecevit made the following statement, which summarizes the main lines of the country's political culture: "It is by now obvious that Turkey is a powerful country. This does not worry only the regional [i.e. neighboring] countries, but also our Western allies who want to keep Turkey under their control. That's why we will always face problems originating from the [Middle Eastern] region or from the non-regional countries. We will dismantle PKK. But they will find other instruments and other pretexts. This is the price that Turkey has to pay for her strength and her power." "Ecevit: PKK Biter Baska Araç Bulurlar," *Hürriyet*, March 29, 1999.

"enemies" of the Republic. These "enemies" are simply tolerated by the state and not accepted as the country's political authority.

At this point, one can draw a paradoxical parallel between the Turkish and Iranian situations. In both countries the elected bodies can gain access to the official government offices, but the real power is held by a non-elected body, the clerical one in Iran and the military one in Turkey. While both countries recognize a kind of legitimacy to the popular sovereignty, ultimately, this sovereignty is subordinated to, and restricted by, another one: that of God in Iran, which is exerted by the clerics, and that of the "Nation" in Turkey, which is exerted by the military and civil establishment.

The Current Situation of the Kurdish Issue

For the Kurds in Turkey this evolution means, at once, both hope and a source of serious concerns. One should in fact admit that, since the end of the armed struggle announced by Öcalan in 2000, the situation in Kurdistan has notably improved. It is true that still many Kurdish politicians are arrested, massive human rights violations are committed,[8] and the Kurdish municipalities suffer from a deliberate policy of financial "suffocation." Still, one should also add that an embryonic civil society has emerged during these years, and both Kurdistan and the Kurdish communities in the country's main cities have given birth to important popular initiatives coming from below.

These initiatives are largely independent from any kind of political control, including that of the PKK/KADEK. In many places, informal cultural forums have also come to life. One should also emphasize the fact that through the dozens of municipalities controlled by HADEP/DEHAP, the Kurdish population experiences today a real local democracy. Finally, and probably more importantly, during the past few years, the Kurds have won a kind of self-esteem and dignity. The end of the internal conflicts between the PUK and the KDP in Iraqi Kurdistan,

---

[8] In a recent statement, Fethullah Gülen advocates openly the virtues of "militarism." See K. Bumin, "Fethullah Gülen ve Militarizm," *Yeni Safak*, November 8, 2003.

and between these two Iraqi Kurdish actors and the PKK/KADEK (renamed Kurdistan Peoples Congress in November 2003), has largely contributed to the improvement of the Kurdish self image. The recent development in Iraq, where the Kurdish region has been mostly free of violence and has become a model for the rest of the country, also contributes to this fact.

But one should also be aware of the fact that the current "no-war, no-peace" situation is also a source of serious concern. In fact, as Gülistan Gürbey shows in her essay published in this volume, no real reforms other than very cosmetic ones have become the reality in Turkey. The government's policy towards Kurdish demands, including those concerning the Kurdish language, still remains very repressive. The PKK/KADEK's fighters still are sporadically targets of Turkish military attacks. More importantly, the very existence of the Kurdish issue is still denied. The Kurds are, at best, assimilated to the country's "many ethnic groups speaking local dialects and languages." The "concessions" made to the Kurds, such as the right of having their "private language courses," are far below the degree of their awareness, tradition of militancy, political mobilization, and widespread nationalist discourse.

It is obvious that these "concessions," which could have satisfied the minimal Kurdish demands as they were formulated at the beginning of the 1960s, are far from answering the demands of cultural and political autonomy formulated today. In addition, the systematic non-application of these "concessions" deepens the feeling of humiliation; no private teaching institution, for example, has yet obtained the right to teach in Kurdish. In Batman, for instance, the courses could not start for one technical reason; the outside door was 85 cm. large, instead of the 90 demanded by the authorities.

One should also pay attention to the growing impatience and frustration among the young Kurds. Although no survey is available on this issue, one can easily observe the emergence of a new social and political generational actor among the Kurdish population in Turkey. As were the former generations, namely those who gave birth to the PKK and constituted its guerrilla army for more than 15 years, this generation is a very young one. The boys and girls who were only 12 years old when the PKK halted armed struggle in 2000 and are by now 15, constitute the members of this new generation. In the Kurdish (and Middle Eastern) environment, this age group is certainly approaching adulthood and self-responsibility. As the Second Palestinian *intifada* has shown, the frustrations of the very young but politicized generations and the feelings of fidelity towards their sacred cause can give birth to an unprecedented culture of radicalism and violence.

One fears that if no real reform policy is adopted and if the Turkish authorities continue to offer only the possibility of "repentance" to the PKK/KADEK fighters instead of starting a genuine process of reconciliation—the only one which can legitimize the existence of the Kurdish issue and the Kurdish political actors—this generation might be tempted once again to resort to violence. This generation, in fact, subjectively combines a recognition of the failure of the older ones (which evokes in them the duty of vengeance for the fallen "martyrs") and a recovered "self-esteem," which means the refusal to submit to further subordination or, in their own words, "slavery."

The PKK's leadership itself will probably be unable to control this new generation, which has not experienced the previous forms of socialization imposed by the PKK upon the elder generations. The September 2003 statements of the PKK/KADEK, which declared the cessation of the cease-fire by the end of the year and promised to answer militarily to any future Turkish attacks, can be read as a clear awareness of the frustrations of this new political generation.

Conclusion: The Military and Civil Establishment or the Strategy of Survival

Finally, one may well fear that the military and civil establishment, which is more than ever isolated from society, might itself be tempted to resort to violence in order to insure its own existence. In fact, either the AKP government will dare to marginalize the military and civil establishment, which, for the time being at least does not seem to be the case, or some sections of this establishment once again will try to play the game of domestic tensions, as they have done repeatedly during the 1980s and

1990s. One cannot determine which category might be targeted if such a scenario were to occur: Islamists, who are accused of having a strategy of *takiyya* and who are already under constant pressure from the military and judiciary; liberal intellectuals, who are accused of being in the pay of "countries which prepare a new Sevres treaty" in order to "divide the Eternal Turkish fatherland"; the Alevis and the radical-left opposition; or, once again, the Kurdish movement? In any case, one cannot exclude the hypothesis that the military and civil establishment might well decide to rescue itself by turning to such a suicidal policy.

As with the Cypriot case, the Kurdish issue constitutes the crossroads between foreign and domestic politics. A Turkish military expedition into Iraqi Kurdistan under the pretext of fighting "separatist terrorism" or a dramatic conflict between the Kurds and Turkmans, as Ankara almost openly tried to provoke immediately after the 2003 Iraqi War, might well be used in order to escalate the Kurdish conflict in Turkey itself, mobilize Turkish public opinion, and reinforce the army's place in the political sphere. Similarly, American problems in Iraq might also create an unforeseeable situation.

As stated at the beginning of this article, the horizon of visibility for Middle Eastern and Turkish affairs remains rather limited. The current situation in Turkey, both in regard to the Kurdish issue and the country's other main problems, can continue for quite a long period, but can also change unexpectedly and dramatically for the best or for the worst. For the best, because the AKP government might at one moment be obliged or feel strong enough to impose the radical transformations the country needs, including the recognition of the Kurdish issue and integration of the Kurdish actors, as was the case with the Catalans and Basques in Spain after the death of General Franco. Or for the worst, because the country's main power holders may be tempted by a policy of strengthened status quo or even a policy of increased repression, which might provoke new waves of struggle and violence.

CHAPTER 7

Implications of Turkey's Constitutional Reforms for the Kurds

Gulistan Gurbey

Turkey initiated constitutional reforms some 22 months after its candidature was approved for the membership of the European Union (EU) in Helsinki in December 1999. The conservative Islamic Justice and Development Party (AKP), which won elections in November 2002, has adopted a seven point "EU harmonization package" to meet the Copenhagen criteria requirements for accession to the EU. Despite massive resistance from conservatives, the AKP government has continued the process of constitutional reforms with considerable pain.

This article focuses on the effects the reforms have entailed so far for the situation of the Kurdish population in Turkey. The objective of the article is not meant to provide a comprehensive analysis of each reform article, but to ascertain their impact on Turkey's traditional Kurdish policy regarding possible improvements in the political and cultural rights of the Kurdish population.

Turkey's Policy on the Kurds: between dogmatism and liberalization

Constants of Turkey's Kurdish policy.
The basis of the Turkish concept of the state, i.e. the state ideology which is marked by a stringent nation-state concept and rigid

political and legal system, is a pivotal constant and thus a primary cause of the Turkish-Kurdish conflict. The rigid application of the prevalent concept of the nation has been cemented by a centralist unitary state whose make-up has no room for decentralization or a federal system of government. The strict nation-state concept defines the Turkish nation as a sum of subjects and negates in its legal definition the existence of ethnic minorities and thus the necessity for maintaining the status-quo. This concept of the nation in Turkey aims at creating a nationally and culturally homogenous unitary state on the territory of what is today the Republic of Turkey following the demise of the Ottoman Empire.

The Turkish nationalist state ideology has been devoid of any spiritual or demographic basis in the Kurdish region from the very outset. During the period when the new Republic of Turkey emerged, its founder, Kemal Attatürk, spoke of a partnership between Turks and Kurds in the new "Nation of Turkey," a joint parliament, and the possibility of self-government in areas where the Kurds formed the majority. These promises, however, were broken in favor of a centralist state based on a nationalist Turkish doctrine which met with massive resistance from traditional Kurdish rulers. The new state structure not only completely eliminated the tradition of the administration of the Kurdish principalities, de facto autonomies that existed during the Ottoman Empire, but it also ushered in a qualitatively new and systematic policy of assimilation vis-à-vis the Kurds.

As a consequence, a host of local Kurdish uprisings—led by traditional tribal leaders who also clearly had Kurdish nationalist ambitions—occurred during the 1920s and 1930s. Sources in the Turkish general staff indicate that there were as many as 30 Kurdish uprisings during that period. From then on the Kurds were officially declared "non-existent" and any expression of their Kurdish identity was consistently prosecuted politically and legally.

The military state of emergency and the use of force by the government in Kurdish areas in the southeast of Turkey lasted for decades. Forced expulsion from their homes and farms and resettlement in other localities, banning the expression of Kurdish identity, arbitrary arrest and persecution, and torture have become the everyday experience for the Kurds in Turkey.

In the new nation-state, the Kurds were left without any protection as a minority. The protection for minorities, as derived from the Lausanne peace treaty of 1923, applies only to non-Muslim minorities (Greeks, Armenians and Jews). Turkey has not accepted the term minority as it is applied in the international arena, i.e. chiefly ethnic and language minorities apart from religious ones. Any articulation of a cultural deviation was and has been perceived as a danger to the cultural and national unity and thus vehemently rejected. Based on the Kemalist definition of the Turkish nation and the postulate of the principle of equality derived from it, any expression of Kurdish identity has been banned and prosecuted.

The Kurds are enjoying equality as subjects of the Turkish nation. However, they are denied equality in terms of using and developing their own identity, culture and language. The state, nation and culture are considered a unity and placed under unchangeable protection by the constitution. Consequently, the existence of ethnic minorities is being ignored. Moreover, this concept of the nation-state is being translated into a systematic policy of assimilation and homogenization. This forced assimilation has been responsible for Kurdish resistance and the use of force against the state. It is this policy which has caused not only the outbreak of numerous Kurdish uprisings in the early years of the Republic, but also the emergence of the Kurdistan Workers Party (PKK) during the early 1980s.

A second component of the Kemalist concept of nation-state prevents the protection of minorities and the creation of any form of autonomy for the Kurds. The constitutional principle of an indivisible unity of territory and nation which upholds the rule of a centralized and unitary state and its ideology would be threatened should minorities be granted cultural autonomy or self-government. Fundamental rights and freedoms are being denied just to protect the unitary concept. This is reflected in a number of laws and decrees such as the penal code and Anti-Terror Act which seek to prevent "separatist propaganda." While a legal ban was imposed on the usage of the Kurdish language from 1983 to 1991, Turkish was considered to be the mother tongue of all

Turkish subjects. This was an attempt to assimilate the Kurds, above all, in terms of language and culture.

The amendments made in the constitution in June 1995—following strong European pressure in the run-up to the customs union between Turkey and the EU which started in 1995—have neither led to easing the centralized concept of the state ideology nor to an adaptation of the term minority to European standards. They rather provide for greater participation of associations, co-operatives and trade unions, academics, and students.

One must also stress the strong role of the military in the management of the state. As guardian of Kemalist principles, it has become an extraordinary factor in Turkish politics and an important decision-maker in the political system through its in-stitutionally ensured position in the constitutional body called the "National Security Council" (NSC). The NSC is a body which makes Turkey's Kurdish policy, and the military is its instrument to implement it.

Turkish politicians and the military regard the Kurdish con-flict as a national issue posing a threat to the indivisibility of Turkish territories and population, and consider Kurdish de-mands for self-development a priori as a "separatist danger." They reject any attempt for a solution based on autonomy, active protection of minorities, and/or a federal system of government. Regulations of any kind which seek to implement any of these options are seen as not in keeping with the strict state ideology (national and cultural homogeneity) and doctrine (centralism, unitarianism and the policy of homogenization).

Both an institutionalization of minority rights and autonomy regulations are considered early stages of secession and thus ve-hemently opposed. People who attempt to consider these or similar peaceful means are confronted with taboos and prose-cuted politically and legally for "separatist propaganda." Any cultural or political regulation requires approval by the military leaders in advance.

The foundation for the exclusive military option was laid down in the early years of the republic. It was then that the use of military force, and thus the campaign against any form of Kurdish self-determination, was declared a top priority. Not even the Social Democratic and Conservative coalition government—

which in its governmental protocol wanted to solve the Kurdish issue on the basis of the Paris Charter of the Organization for Security and Cooperation in Europe (OSCE) in order to recognize "the Kurdish reality" in December 1991—touched on this subject. Thus, the recognition of the "Kurdish reality" has remained just as ink on the paper since no further steps have been taken.

Finally, one must analyze the main part of the Turkish policy on the Kurds: a legal representation of Kurdish interests in politics and in parliament is to be prevented and isolated from the political system especially by means of intimidation, control, repression, prevention and ban on political activities. This policy vis-à-vis legal and legitimate rights of political entities is clearly visible when one inspects the treatment of pro-Kurdish parties such as the Peoples Labour Party (HEP), Democracy Party (DEP), and Peoples Democracy Party (HADEP), all of which were banned although they always won the majority of votes in local and general elections in the Kurdish region of Turkey after 1991. They were banned under the pretext of "separatism" and support for the PKK. Large numbers of politicians were imprisoned and sentenced to several prison terms.

Attempts at Liberalization under Turgut Özal

In the late 1980s, President Turgut Özal ushered in a slight change of approach to the policy on the Kurds for the first time in the history of the Republic of Turkey. Apart from military and state repression and control, this change would have led to more liberal cultural practices by allowing the usage of Kurdish in education, radio, TV and the press; aided the development of areas with a Kurdish majority; extended the competencies of local government through comprehensive administrative reforms, and integrated the PKK into the Turkish political system. The farthest reaching gesture towards the Kurds living in Turkey was the legalization of the Kurdish language by lifting the law banning it in 1991.

Özal gave priority to a political solution to the conflict. He was convinced that genuine peace can be achieved only through dialogue with the PKK and by taking concrete steps towards a cease-fire. He regarded the MPs of the pro-Kurdish HEP, followed by DEP (which were both banned), as partners in addressing the civil war with the PKK. Ironically, however, the talks between some HEP MPs and the PKK leader, Abdullah Öcalan, led to the lifting of immunity and sentencing their members. Özal did not believe that granting cultural autonomy and political liberalization would pose any subsequent danger to the unity of the state. Contrary to the coalition government and army generals, Özal regarded the one-sided truce announced by the PKK in March 1993, as a positive step in the right direction. He saw it as a chance to integrate the PKK politically with the help of such concrete steps as an amnesty, thus paving the way for a political solution. The sudden death of Özal in April 1993, however, put an abrupt end to this early fling at liberalism in the Turkish policy on the Kurds.

After Özal.
It was noticeable that all prime ministers who followed the late President Özal (Tansu Ciller, Mesut Yilmaz and Necmettin Erbakan) initially announced that they would champion improvements and reforms regarding the conflict. Concrete steps, however, never followed. Some political parties even officially drew up reports about the Southeast Anatolia problem. Basically, the conflict was thought to be a result of economic underdevelopment, so the ethnic and national dimensions of the problem were ignored. Most of the proposals were related to decentralization of the state, democratization, liberalization of state politics, and an economic recovery program for the region.

The political Islamic forces of the country have stressed a humanitarian approach to the Kurdish conflict with priority given to Islam. They considered Islam as a uniting political framework which would provide a unified identity to all Muslims in Turkey. By making Islam as something which all citizens have in common, they thought that they could solve the Kurdish conflict. This vague religious Islamic concept of society, however, is unable to provide solutions to ethnic and national conflicts because it does not recognize either the identity of Kurds or the identity of any other ethnic groups. Like any other political groupings, the Islamists fail to accept the Kurdish reality. What needs to be emphasized is that Özal's attempts at liberalization have ushered in an irreversible process of change. Since Ozal's administration, there has been a gradual process of rethinking of cultural and local administrative issues in some political quarters in Turkey. Unfortunately, these changes have so far been largely theoretical in nature.

Change in the PKK's Strategy Following Öcalan's Arrest in 1999

When the PKK was strategically defeated in 1999, the state had the opportunity to fundamentally liberalize its policy on the Kurds. The seizure and sentencing of Abdullah Öcalan, the PKK[1] renouncement of violence, and the scaled back substance of its political demands should have created another favorable condition for the reorientation of Turkey's Kurdish policy. Since these developments coincided with the beginning of the Helsinki process, they generated considerable internal and external pressure on Ankara to step up its democratization and liberalization policies.

For the most part, the military and civilian decision-makers were hesitant to exploit the situation to make significant changes in their traditionally repressive Kurdish policy. On the other hand, the termination of the war led to a general easing of the political climate and the return of a degree of normalcy to the everyday life in the Kurdish region. Although the state of emergency was being gradually lifted officially, the security forces were far from observing it. So far, the internally displaced Kurds have not yet been allowed to return to their villages. Hardly

---

[1] After Abdullah Öcalan was arrested in February 1999, the PKK changed its former violent strategy. These changes included the termination of armed struggle, the withdrawal of its militant activists to Northern Iraq, a new definition and reduction of their objectives (only cultural rights within state boundaries), and renaming itself "Kurdistan Congress for Freedom and Democracy" (KADEK). For more reference, see Gülistan Gürbey, "Im Blickpunkt: Umkehr bei der PKK, Wandel in der türkischen Kurdenpolitik?" *Südosteuropa-Mitteilungen.* Munich. 2000/No.2, pp. 104, 123. At the end of 2003, KADEK was renamed *KONGRA-GEL* (Kurdistan Peoples Congress).

anything has changed about the disastrous situation in the fields of social and medical services and education. Moreover, obstruction of the work of pro-Kurdish civil-society organizations, arrests of democratically elected politicians, and the ban on pro-Kurdish parties are still the order of the day in the Kurdish region.

The conservative Islamic AKP government is now trying to meet the reform and liberalization requirements required for Turkey to have its candidacy accepted by the EU. This has ushered in a limited easing of Turkey's repressive policy toward its Kurdish population, especially in the cultural field. By means of the "Society Rehabilitation Act,"[2] Turkey has also tried to make sure that a large number of former PKK fighters would surrender their weapons without being punished. In contrast to earlier "Repentance Acts," ordinary PKK militants—who had not been involved in fighting against Turkish troops and/or police forces— are guaranteed to get off scot-free once they have put down their arms. However, civilian organizations and the pro-Kurdish Democratic People's Party (DEHAP) had demanded in the run-up to passing the bill a general amnesty for all PKK members and granting the organization the right to work legally in Turkey.

---

[2] The law, also known as "Home Coming Act," was adopted by the Turkish parliament on 30 July 2003. Erdogan said the law had been agreed on at the NSC meeting on 5 February 2003 and had been endorsed by the general staff from the very beginning. In the framework of the present consultations between Turkey and the USA regarding the deployment of Turkish troops in Iraq and the withdrawal of the Turkish troops from Kurdish Northern Iraq, the Turkish decision-makers had demanded as a pivotal condition the ultimate removal of the PKK/KADEK from the region. According to press reports, such an agreement had been reached. The USA had been ready for military action against the PKK had the PKK militants not surrendered voluntarily. At the same time the USA was looking for political asylum for PKK leaders (about 100 persons) in Scandinavian countries, such as Norway. *Milliyet*, 30 July 2003; and *Hürriyet*, 30 July 2003.

Consequences of the Helsinki Process and the Present Situation

At the EU Summit in Helsinki on 10/11 December 1999, Turkey was accepted as a candidate for accession to the organization on condition that it implemented the Helsinki resolution[3] and the related partnership[4] document which laid down conditions for accession to the EU. Turkey pledged to meet the membership requirements within the time frame laid out by the organization. The pre-accession strategy and the follow up political dialogue between the EU and Turkey are destined to stimulate and support the pending reforms. Turkey, like all other EU candidates, must fulfill the Copenhagen criteria (institutional stability as a prerequisite to democracy, the rule of law, human rights, and the recognition and protection of minority rights) so that accession talks can be initiated. At its summit in Copenhagen on 12 and 13 December 2002, the EU decided to hold its first talks with Turkey in 2004.

The Helsinki resolution requires that the Copenhagen criteria, which became effective in 1993, also applies to Turkey with a view to meeting the political criteria before the accession process starts. The accession partnership document stipulates short-term and medium-term objectives and sets a time frame for monitoring the fulfilment of the Copenhagen criteria. Although no exact date has been set for the latter, the former had to be put into practice by March 2004. Included in the short-term priorities are, among other things, the lifting of all bans on broadcasting in native languages; improvement in economic, social, and cultural conditions for all citizens; the abolition of regional inequalities; the right to free speech; and a campaign against all kinds of torture. The medium-term priorities are the abolition of the death penalty, the lifting of the state of emergency, the reduction of the role of the NSC in civilian affairs similar to the practices of in-

---

[3] See <*http://ue.eu.int/de/info/eurocouncil/index.htm*>.

[4] "Council Decision of 8 March 2001 on the principles, priorities, intermediate objectives and conditions contained in the Accession Partnership with Turkey," *Official Journal of the European Communities* (OJ). L 85. 24 March 2001, pp. 13-23.

stitutions in EU countries, guaranteed cultural diversity and cultural rights for all citizens (no matter what their origin might be), and the suspension of all legal obstacles to these rights including education.[5]

By means of the "National Programme for Adopting the Acquis Communautaire," Turkey reacted to the EU demands on 20 March 2001. Twenty-two months after the Helsinki resolution, the reform process began in Turkey. Shortly before the EU Commission published its progress report, the Turkish parliament agreed to the first partial reform of the Turkish constitution of 1982 in October 2001. Thirty-four sections of the constitution were adapted to European standards. Harmonization laws followed in February, March, and August 2002; and January, June and July 2003.[6] These laws have aligned the legal situation in Turkey with those of the EU standards and with the Turkish constitution. Though the amendments made were incorporated in the Turkish constitution of 1982, considerable scepticism prevails about putting these amendments into practice,.

Now that Turkey is a candidate and has entered the accession partnership, the military and civilian decision-makers are obliged to act and meet the requirements set by the Copenhagen criteria and the EU demands, the fulfillment of which is a prerequisite for starting negotiations. Until then, an internal reform process

---

[5] For more details on the reform process and the Copenhagen criteria, see Heinz Kramer, *Die Türkei und die Kopenhagener Kriterien. Die Europäische Union vor der Entscheidung* (Berlin: Stiftung Wissenschaft und Politik. SWP-Studie, November 2002); Heinz Kramer, *Ein Wichtiger Schritt in Richtung EU. Das Türkische Parlament Verabschiedet "Historisches" Reformpaket* (Berlin: Stiftung Wissenschaft und Politik, August 2002).

[6] The following Harmonization Packages have been adopted: First package adopted on 6 Februay 2002, enforced on 19 February 2002; second package adopted on 26 March 2002, enforced on 9 April 2002; third package adopted on 3 August 2002, enforced on 9 August 2002; fourth package adopted on 2 January 2003, enforced on 11 January 2003; fifth package adopted on 23 January 2003, enforced on 4 February 2003; sixth package adopted on 19 June 2003, not yet in force at the time this article was written; seventh package adopted on 31 July 2003, not yet in force at the time this article was written.

will continue with a view to reconciling the views of the proponents and opponents of reforms step by step. At least two groups
of politicians are engaged in the debate concerning the passage
of the harmonization bills. The opponents of reforms insist on
the political status quo and fear that the Turkish national and
cultural unitary state will be compromised if the EU demands are
met. For the most part, the military leadership, the state security
apparatus, parts of the legal authorities, and the state bureaucracy
who constitute the nationalist forces belong to it.[7]

On the other hand, the military leadership looks at membership in the EU as part of the Kemalist aspirations of westerniza-
tion. Though this group is trying to advocate and champion the
ongoing reform process, it still has no desire to see the foundations of the Kemalist unitary state altered.[8] The adversaries of the

---

[7] Columnist Ertugrul Özkök points out that the critics of the Turkish
ambitions to join the EU are now about to discover the term
"Lausanne" (relates to the Lausanne Treaty) for themselves by calling
themselves "Lausannists" and defaming the proponents of the efforts to
join the EU as "Seyrists" (relates to the Treaty of Sevres which had,
inter alia, plans for founding a Kurdish state). Özkök warns against
instrumentalizing Lausanne as the basis for the Turkish Republic and
its ideological arguments. Columnist Mehmet Ali Birand also stresses
that the actual problem was the retired civilians who had worked in the
field of security before (military, police, prosecutors, judges). They
were trying to create an atmosphere as if Turkey was running the risk
of being partitioned any time due to Kurdish nationalism and Islamists,
and that only the military could prevent this. If the military role were
restricted now, this would only facilitate activities by the enemies of
state. Birand emphasizes that the changes to the functions of the NSC
General Secretariat were not based on a power struggle between the
AKP and the military. Something like that was unthinkable anyway;
that is why it was high time to part with the taboos in people's minds.
See Ertugrul Özkök, "Lozan´i türban haline getirmeyelim," *Hürriyet*,
29 July 2003; and Mehmet Ali Birand, "CHP, AB´den rahatsiz mi?"
Hürriyet, 18 July 2003.

[8] The Vice Chairman of the general staff, Yasar Büyükanit, said that
the general staff endorsed EU membership on principle, but was scepti-
cal about some reform steps. He stressed that the general staff was not
opposed to the EU because the EU was a geopolitical and geostrategic
necessity of the modernization target projected by Attatürk. Turkey was

reform process mistrust the AKP government; they believe that the AKP actually wants to convert Turkey into an Islamic state and that membership in the EU is being used as a pretext to weaken the role of the military as a guardian of the secular system of government in Turkey.[9]

The proponents of the reforms want to speed up the democratization process and espouse far-reaching changes. One finds liberal forces in this group, such as pro-Kurdish parties, Kurdish and non-Kurdish civil organizations, and business associations. The Turkish entrepreneurs association TÜSIAD issued a one-page ad in Turkish daily newspapers strongly advocating necessary reforms. On 15 April 2002, all major foundations in Turkey issued a joint appeal for implementing the reforms. Numerous other organizations supported the sixth harmonization package by means of advertisements in daily newspapers in early June 2003.[10] The sixth and seventh harmonization packages, which contradicted the standard practices but were adopted by the NSC without prior discussions, triggered fierce debates in both camps.[11]

The sixth harmonization package focuses on regulations for broadcasting in native languages and the elimination of "separatist propaganda" clauses from Article 8 of the Anti-Terror Act. The seventh package deals mainly with the competencies of the NSC. The amendment made in the constitution in October 2001

---

part of Europe and would become an EU member. The unitary, laicist nature of Turkey was fully in keeping with the fundamental principles of the EU. The Copenhagen criteria had been fulfilled to a large degree. See Fikret Bila, "Org. Büyükanit: AB tarih vermeli," *Milliyet*, 30 May 2003; *Hürriyet*, 30 May 2003; Mehmet Ali Birand, "Büyükanit, AB icin ince ayar yapti," *Hürriyet*, 30 May 2003; and Sedat Ergin, "Ordudan küresellesmeye elestirel bakis," *Hürriyet*, 30 May 2003.

[9] For example, Oktay Eksi, "Paket iyi ama...," *Hürriyet*, 18 June 2003.

[10] See *Milliyet*, 10 June 2003.

[11] Hasan Cemal underscored the importance of the seventh harmonization package as it chiefly restricted the competencies of the NSC General Secretariat and the military's influence in politics. Cemal criticised those opposed to reforms who mainly tried to rally support against this reform package. See Hasan Cemal, "Süngünün Ucunda," *Milliyet*, 23 July 2003; and Hasan Cemal, "Yine madde 8!" *Milliyet*, 15 July 2003.

has already provided for a larger number of civilian members by adding the Deputy Prime Minister and Minister of Justice to the NSC and by stressing its advisory role. This amendment to the constitution, however, has not been effective, since a simple majority of civilian members in the NSC did not automatically bring about fundamental changes in Law 2945 of 1983 which regulates the NSC's tasks and organizational procedures. The seventh harmonization package of July 2003, however, does just that by restricting the far-reaching competencies and tasks of the NSC General Secretariat,[12] which is an executive decision-making body. The military control of the NSC has now been shifted to the civilian authority.[13] For the first time in the history of the Turkish republic, a government has dared to make changes in the NSC and restrict the role of the military.

Previously, the NSC's competency was to "determine, implement, coordinate and supervise national security policy." Now its tasks have been confined to simply "determining" national security policy and to executing secretariat chores stipulated by the NSC and the law. The Deputy Prime Minister is now in charge of supervising the implementation of NSC decisions. The NSC Secretary General, who is to be appointed upon the recommendation of the Prime Minister, can now also be a civilian. Furthermore, public institutions are no longer obliged to turn over information and documents demanded by the General Secretariat; the NSC will be convened every other month; and the responsibility for overseeing the military defence expenditures are being placed under the authority of the parliament for the first time.[14]

---

[12] The law regarding the NSC General Secretariat was initiated by the military leadership in 1983 during the short period between general elections and handing power over to civilians led by Turgut Özal. The law aimed to obtain control over the civilian government.

[13] See *Milliyet*, 19 July 2003; and *Hürriyet*, 18 July 2003.

[14] For a positive assessment of the changes in the powers of the NSC General Secretariat in the seventh harmonization package, see Mehmet Ali Birand, "MGK Genel Sekreterligi askeri denetim organi," *Hürriyet*, 22 July 2003; Hasan Cemal, "Askerin sivile tabi olmasi!" *Milliyet*, 18 June 2003; and Hasan Cemal, "CHP?" *Milliyet*, 18 July 2003.

The military Chiefs of Staff rejected this latter restriction on their functions and competencies, arguing that conditions in Turkey do not permit this change and that comparable bodies exist in the European Union. Although army generals declared that they agree in principle to have a civilian as a Secretary General of the NSC, they reserved the right to recommend a military officer for the post.[15]

The role played by the NSC has often triggered controversies in the past.[16] The planned changes have for the first time infringed on the NSC General Secretariat's competencies by restricting the military's role in making decisions on national security issues. Shifting the executive competencies of the NSC General Secretariat to the government is an attempt to strengthen the civilian authority and curb the de-facto dominance of the military. The political role of the military is now confined, by and large, to the functions of the NSC. Despite this change, the role and power of the general staff—which is free from oversight—have remained untouched in the political arena. In the absence of

---

[15] Columnist Ismet Berkan regarded the resistance put up by the general staff as inappropriate. Berkan criticized the position of the NSC within the political system. The NSC acted as a second government parallel to the civilian government which was not in compliance with democracy. Berkan used an example to illustrate this situation. The NSC General Secretariat monitored external airport and port security. These control measures were the result of decisions made during the military rule in the 1980s. Even if the government wanted to lift the control measures these days it could not do so because it would need an order from the NSC General Secretariat. See Ismet Berkan, "MGK ve yedinci paket," *Milliyet*, 29 July 2003. Columnist Güneri Civaoglu points out the military's fear that state secrets would now be made public which would then make keeping them strictly secret impossible. Therefore, it was necessary in the course of adapting to EU standards to establish some compensation and not allow the NSC to become just some decorative body or shutting it out altogether. Güneri Civaoglu, "Nasil bir MGK," *Milliyet*, 19 July 2003.

[16] The Turkish Industrialists' and Businessmen's Association demanded in an essay provided by the late Prof. Bülent Tanör that the NSC be subordinated to the general staff of the Defense Ministry. See Turkish Industrialists' And Businessmen's Association (TÜSIAD), *Perspectives on Democratizations in Turkey*, Istanbul, January 1997.

checks and balances, the military authority continues to function as an independent decision-making body. If and to what extent these changes will impact the balance of power in making political decisions remain to be seen.

To sum up, one can conclude that the prospect for Turkey joining the EU has triggered a reform process and has thus far shown some positive signs. The accession partnership debate and regular progress reports[17] by the EU Commission have served as a pressure mechanism for a gradual implementation of the Copenhagen criteria. The purpose of the progress reports is to make sure whether the Copenhagen criteria have been met and when the accession negotiations should start. However, because of ambiguities in the definition of the Copenhagen criteria, it will be difficult to accurately measure the progress made by Turkey.

The political criteria of Copenhagen are general in nature; the wording has been left vague for a variety of reasons concerning the lack of uniformity in the regulations applied for the protection of numerous and diverse minority groups in the EU. The practice of minority protection varies from country to country within the EU and does not lend itself to a given objective standard. The lack of concrete binding rules for implementing these general principles leaves some room for interpretation. The definition of minimum standards and the decision whether or not they have been met, therefore, depent primarily on political considerations. At the end of the day, the candidates for accession can determine to a large extend what they understand by these political criteria and how to put them into practice. Therefore, the EU urgently needs to fill this gap to arrive at better implementation criteria. One possibility would be to lay down clearly and unambiguously how these criteria should be interpreted and by whom.

This should also apply to the accession partnership process with Turkey. Since the EU has not specified how these criteria

---

[17] See the Kommission der Europäischen Gemeinschaften's two reports, *Regelmäßiger Bericht 2002 über die Fortschritte der Türkei auf dem Weg zum Beitritt*, Brussels, 9 September 2002 (SEK. 2002.1412); and *Regelmäßiger Bericht 2001 über die Fortschritte der Türkei auf dem Weg zum Beitritt*, Brussels, 13 November 2001 (SEK.2001.1756).

should be interpreted and implemented, an objective assessment of their fulfillment by Turkish and the EU officials becomes problematic. Apart from a few clearly defined demands such as the abolition of the death penalty, the ratification of the two 1966 UN human rights covenants, or the lifting of the state of emergency, it remains unclear when Turkey can justifiably claim that it has fulfilled the requirements for accession talks. This leaves considerable room to Turkish decision-makers for the interpretation and implementation of the criteria. Therein lies the danger: the EU criteria can be interpreted and implemented as restrictively as possible to maintain the dogmatic concept of the Turkish state and nation.

Relevance and Importance of Reforms for the Kurds of Turkey

EU Accession Partnership and the Kurdish Conflict.
Upon closer inspection of the EU accession partnership documents, there is no direct reference to the Kurdish conflict. Neither the words "Kurdish/Kurd" nor minorities can be found in the documents exchanged between Turkey and the EU. By avoiding these terms and a direct reference to the Kurdish conflict, the EU has clearly observed Turkish interests vis-a-vis its Kurdish population. This approach is expected to perpetuate the Turkish practice of denial and signals a far-reaching agreement with Ankara's fundamental views of the Kurdish conflict.

The EU views the Kurdish conflict in the context of human rights and democratization. Consequently, it demands measures that do not include the granting of political rights to minority groups, but rather promotes the implementation of human rights and democratization. From the EU point of view this includes granting individual human and civil rights, cultural rights, and an improvement of the economic and social situation in the Southeast (Northern Kurdistan). Specifically, the accession partnership simply demands: (a) the "elaboration of a comprehensive concept for removing the regional differences and improving the economic, social and cultural situation in the Southeast for all citizens"; (b) "safeguarding cultural diversity and ensuring human rights for all citizens irrespective of their origin"; and (c) the removal of "all legislations obstructing citizens from enjoying these rights, including education." These words do not contain any further demands such as the granting of political rights or political autonomy to the Kurdish population. Though the Kurds are not explicitly mentioned in the accession partnership documents, emphasis is being laid on the fact that the aforementioned demands touch on the situation of the Kurdish population.

From the Turkish point of view, it was important to avoid making an explicit reference to the Kurds or to their cultural and political rights in the accession partnership document. Although Ankara avoided making such a linkage for fulfilling the political requirements of the Copenhagen accession criterion, "respect for and protection of minorities," nevertheless, boils down to the acid test for the Turkish decision-makers. This difficulty results from the dogmatic Turkish concept of state and nation as well as Turkey's definition of minorities. The existence of the Kurds is no longer being denied today; however, officially they are not being recognized as a minority worthy of state protection. From the Turkish perspective, the demand of "respecting and protecting minorities" is to be interpreted as restrictively as possible in the framework of the adaptation regulations in order neither to jeopardize the foundation of the concept of state and nation nor to recognize the cultural independence of the Kurds as a group. The reforms are to be laid out in such a fashion that they rule out any interpretation specifically made for Kurds. Therefore, the reforms will not lead to the cultural independence of the Kurds as a group and make it also very difficult to put individual rights into practice.

Kurdish Cultural and Political Rights in the Context of the Reform Packages

Right to Use of Kurdish Language in Media and Education.
In general, no Turkish law mentions Kurdish as a language or the right to use it in education or publications. Nevertheless, everyone is aware that the changes in the framework of the adaptation packages centered primarily on permission to use Kurdish. While the accession partnership includes lifting the bans on Kurdish broadcasting as a short-term measure, Turkey is ex-

pected to continue its current policy of Turkish being the only language to be used in education, broadcasting, and official communications. However, this does not prevent other languages and dialects from being spoken in everyday life. It simply means that the freedom to speak Kurdish must not be used for separatist purposes.

Still, Kurdish is not even mentioned explicitly. When the constitution was amended in October 2001, Sections 26 (freedom of expression) and 28 (freedom of the press) were changed. The phrases "when voicing one's opinion no forbidden language must be used" (Section 26, paragraph 3) and "publications must not be made in a forbidden language" (Section 28, paragraph 2) were cancelled. However, in Section 26, paragraph 2 the protection of national security and the fundamental principles of the indivisible unity of territory and nation were added so that the freedom of speech was restricted again in a way which was and is always used to curb the rights of the Kurds.[18]

These reforms, celebrated as "the lifting of the ban on the Kurdish language,"[19] have not led to any real change because, since the annulment of the law banning languages in 1991, there has been theoretically no forbidden language. Kurdish broadcasts and education in Kurdish, however, have not been allowed. In addition, Section 42 of the constitution stipulates that Turkish is the mother tongue and fundamental language in educational institutions, while Article 2c of Law No. 2932 on education in foreign languages of 1983 provides for the Council of Ministers to regulate tuition in foreign languages with the opinion of the NSC being taken into account. In reality, these regulations mean that

---

[18] For more details about the legal reforms, see Türkiye Insan Haklari Vakfi (Human Rights Foundation of Turkey), *Meaning and Value of the Changes Made in the Turkish Law System in Relation with the European Union*, Ankara 2002; and Heidi Wedel and Riza Dinc, *Rechtsreformen im Rahmen der türkischen EU Beitrittsbemühungen und die Kurdenfrage.*

[19] In the context of allowing Kurdish to be used in radio and TV programs, as well as in private teaching institutions, the Turkish entrepreneurial association TÜSIAD spoke of "breaking through a psychological barrier." See TÜSIAD, *Towards European Union Membership: Political Reforms in Turkey*, Istanbul, October 2002, pp. 24-28.

one cannot even think of teaching Kurdish as a foreign language.[20]

The third harmonization package of August 2002, focused mainly on changes to the law on foreign language tuition and the law on broadcasts in response to the mid-term priority of implementing cultural rights in the educational field. The "law on foreign language tuition and education and learning of various languages and dialects of Turkish citizens" decrees: "In the framework of Law No. 625 of 8 June 1965 on private teaching institutions, private courses can be opened to enable Turkish citizens to learn various languages and dialects they have traditionally been using in everyday life. These courses must not contravene the fundamental principles of the republic and the indivisible unity of territory and nation as laid down in the constitution. The principles and procedures applicable to opening and supervising these courses will be determined in a bylaw issued by the National Ministry of Education."

On 20 September 2002, the "Bylaw on learning various languages and dialects Turkish citizens use in everyday life" came into force. Without using the word Kurdish, provisions were meant to be made for private Kurdish courses. Complex and restrictive stipulations in laws and bylaws, however, have thwarted

---

[20] The fact that especially the Turkish General Staff did not want broadcasts and education in the Kurdish language was illustrated by a remark the Vice Chairman of the General Staff, General Yasar Büyükanit, made: "It was a shame that nobody managed to teach the population in that area Turkish in 500 years." Therefore, one should make efforts to teach them the proper mother tongue, i.e. Turkish in the framework of Article 8 of the Copenhagen criteria. *Milliyet*, 31 May 2003; and *Hürriyet*, 23 May 2003. In contrast, the report on 14 July 2003 of the Minority Rights and Cultural Rights Working Group of the High Council for Human Rights affiliated to the Prime Minister's office came to the conclusion that Turkey had not yet fully complied with the Lausanne Treaty and that, if Article 39/4 of the Lausanne Treaty were applied, the discussion about the right to publications in the Kurdish language would be superfluous. The Article mentioned grants all Turkish subjects the right, *inter alia*, to be published and use the language they choose. This working group is headed by university teacher and political scientist Prof. Dr. Baskin Oran. See *Milliyet*, 29 July 2003.

the opening of private Kurdish courses in reality. As a result, not a single Kurdish course has been opened. All attempts have failed to fulfill the conditions made by the National Ministry of Education.[21]

The first reaction on the part of the Kurds to these reforms was to launch a campaign for introducing Kurdish as an optional class at universities, while parents demanded Kurdish education at school. The state reacted by massive arrests; hundreds of students and parents were imprisoned on charges of "supporting an illegal organisation" (Article 169 penal code); and students were thrown out of universities. At the end of the day, these reactions on the part of the authorities reflected not only the unwillingness to give up the current repressive practices, but also that it takes a bit longer to understand and implement each individual step of the reform.

The reform package of August 2002, also responded to the short-term priority of allowing broadcasts in Kurdish: "Furthermore, broadcasts can be made in various languages and dialects Turkish citizens use in everyday life. These broadcasts must not contravene the principles of the republic and the indivisible unity of territory and nation as laid down in the constitution. The principles and procedures for the production and supervision of these broadcasts will be stipulated in a bylaw by the High Council." This paragraph was added to Article 4 of Law No. 3984 on the High Radio and Television Council (RTÜK).

---

[21] In Urfa, e.g., a retired teacher tried to open the private "Urfa teaching institute for the Kurdish language and dialects." He was denied approval by the authorities who argued that the name contained the words Kurdish language and institute which was tantamount to recognizing Kurdish as a language. See *Aksam*, 7 June 2003. The owner of the "English Fast" language schools, Nazif Ülgen, who also wanted to offer Kurdish classes at his schools, complained that the changes to laws so far came to no avail with regard to Kurdish language classes, as it was impossible to offer Kurdish classes due to the regulations and decrees issued by the National Ministry of Education. Ülgen justifiably demanded a change of this bylaw so that the way would be paved for holding such classes. See Haber Türk, "English Fast, Kurdish Fast," *Acmakta Kararli,* 6 August 2003.

In December 2002, the RTÜK bylaw entered into force and decreed that, although radio and TV broadcasts must be in Turkish, they also could be in languages and dialects Turkish citizens traditionally use in everyday life. Article 5 of the law stipulates that such broadcasts "must only be produced by the state-run radio and TV station TRT and may only cover the . . . news, music and culture for grown-ups and not serve the purpose of teaching other languages and dialects. They must not exceed 45 minutes a day and 4 hours a week on the radio and 30 minutes a day and 2 hours a week on television. On TV they must be fully subtitled in Turkish; on the radio the programmes must be translated into Turkish afterwards."

The discussion about broadcasts in Kurdish illustrates the collective fear of Turkish decision-makers of not having control over such programs. The military fears it has insufficient control over Kurdish broadcasts on private stations and only endorses their airing on TRT. The AKP government and the Republican People's Party (CHP) opposition in contrast prefer broadcasts on private stations, arguing that TRT was overtaxed broadcasting in all languages and dialects, and that there was a danger of a perception that there was another official language apart from Turkish.

The government feels supervision of programming is guaranteed by RTÜK.[22] Despite criticism from the military leadership, the sixth harmonization package even allowed private stations to broadcast in other languages.[23] So far, however, TRT has not only failed to produce a single program in Kurdish, but it has also filed a request with the Higher Administrative Court to annul the bylaw.[24] Moreover, RTÜK has fined several private radio

---

[22] Foreign Minister Abdullah Gül especially favors programs in Kurdish primarily on private stations and not on the state-run station TRT. See the interview with Abdullah Gül by Fikret Bila, "Abdullah Gül: Genelkurmay'la ayri degiliz...," *Milliyet*, 18 June 2003. See also Sedat Ergin, "Baykal'dan uyum paketine destek," *Hürriyet*, 10 June 2003.

[23] NSC Secretary General, General Tuncer Kilinc, spoke out against giving private stations the chance to broadcast in other languages, arguing that this would give rise to separatism. *Hürriyet*, 19 May 2003.

[24] *Milliyet*, 12 June 2003.

and TV stations for playing Kurdish music and threatened to start proceedings to close them down.[25]

The current practice does not foreshadow an easy implementation of these new laws. This applies not only to the arrangement for Kurdish courses, but also to giving children Kurdish names. Lawsuits about Kurdish names are still pending.[26] Which effects the changes to the laws will have in public life and whether the executive bodies will still adhere to their rigid definitions and punish every move as a violation to the rule, remain to be seen.

Political Rights, Freedom of Expression, State of Emergency, Death Penalty

Political Rights.
With reference to Sections 68 and 69, numerous parties founded and/or supported by Kurds have been banned because they endorsed an approach to the Kurdish issue that differed from the official line; their political activities were obstructed; and countless members and leaders arrested and imprisoned.[27] The constitutional reform of October 2001, was meant to make it more dif-

---

[25] RTÜK forbade, e.g., the local Cinar TV station in Van to broadcast for 30 days because it had aired statements by Abdülmelik Firat (Chairman of the Party for Rights and Freedoms, HAK-PAR). In July 2003, Radyo Dünya based in Adana was taken off the air for one month for broadcasting a program named "History of the Kurdish Language and Literature" and playing Kurdish music. *Özgür Gündem*, 1 July 2003; and *Evrensel*, 15 June 2003.

[26] The sixth harmonization package allows giving names in other languages.

[27] Since 1991, the following pro-Kurdish parties have been banned: HEP (*Halkin Emek Partisi*, Labour Party of the People) 1993; ÖZDEP (*Özgürlük ve Demokrasi Partisi*, Party for Freedom and Democracy) 1993; DEP (*Demokrasi Partisi*, Democracy Party) 1994; DDP (*Demokrasi ve Degisim Partisi*, Party for Democracy and Change) 1996; DKP (*Demokratik Kitle Partisi*, Democratic Party of the Masses) 1999; and HADEP (*Halkin Demokrasi Partisi*, Democracy Party of the People) 2003. Lawsuits are pending to ban HAK-PAR (*Hak ve Özgürlükler Partisi*, Party for Rights and Freedoms) and DEHAP (*Demokratik Halk Partisi*, Democratic People's Party).

ficult to outlaw parties by adding Sections 69/6 and 149. Section 149 decrees that at least a three-fifths majority must exist in favour of banning a party by means of a court order. Section 69/6 was complemented by adding that the court decision to ban a party that has violated Section 68/4 can only be made if the constitutional court has established "that the party has become a centre of such activities." The present version of Section 68/4 stipulates *inter alia*, that the statutes, programs and activities of Turkish parties must not contravene the inseparable unity of territory and nation. For the pro-Kurdish parties, therefore, these amendments did not produce any substantial improvement. One example of this is that the pro-Kurdish HADEP party was banned after this reform.

In June 2003, Turkey complied with one of the medium-term priorities: The Turkish parliament agreed to ratify the two International Covenants on Civil and Political Rights, and on Economic, Social and Cultural Rights. Because of the rights to self-determination and speaking one's mother tongue, Turkey had not ratified them earlier. However, Turkey has reservations, which means the Kurds are still denied the political and cultural rights provided for in these Covenants. For example, according to Turkey, minority rights guaranteed by the Covenants are only to be afforded to minorities recognised in the Treaty of Lausanne.

Freedom of expression.
The accession partnership includes the short-term priority to strengthen the right to free speech and improve the situation of non-violent political prisoners according to Article 10 of the European Human Rights Convention (EHRC). A comprehensive reform of the laws and their everyday application are still missing, however, although some progress has been made. For example, it was long overdue to abolish the notorious Article 8 ("separatist propaganda" provision[28]) of the Anti-Terror Act. This finally was done by the sixth harmonization package in June 2003,

---

[28] Article 8, which threatened severe penalties for "separatist propaganda," was mainly used as an all-purpose clause against Kurdish intellectuals, civil rights activists, and publicists. The European Court for Human Rights criticized this dispensation of justice several times.

even though President Ahmet Necdet Sezer and the military leadership spoke out against it. Sezer considered the abolition alarming with regard to the unity of territory and nation, and proposed a reduced version of Article 8 so that it would not contravene Article 10 of the EHRC.[29]

The government, however, decided that the abolition of Article 8 would not leave a gap, since people could still be sentenced for violation of Article 312 ("incitement of the people", and "disturbance of public order" provisions) and Article 169 of the penal code. Indeed, in the past few years, the trials for voicing an opinion on the Kurdish issue were mainly based on Articles 312 and 169, not on Article 8.[30] Furthermore, the RTÜK and Parties Acts ban any propaganda against the inseparable unity of territory and nation, as well as parties which include such propaganda in their programs.[31]

State of emergency.
The state of emergency was completely lifted in the last two provinces in which it was still operative (Diyarbakir and Sirnak) on 30 November 2002. The governor for the state of emergency was renamed coordination governor. However, the lifting of the state of emergency has not yet led to any results worth mentioning. According to reports from human rights organizations, human rights violations are still prevalent and previous practices are still applied.[32] Mention must also be made of the fact that the

---

[29] President Ahmet Necdet Sezer signed the reform package, which was filed again unchanged. The former chief judge of the Constitutional Court viewed the policy by the AKP government with suspicion because of its roots in political Islam. *Milliyet*, 19 July 2003.

[30] See *Milliyet*, 18 June 2003.

[31] See Sedat Ergin, "Demokrasinin 8: madde sinavi," *Hürriyet*, 13 June 2003.

[32] See the Turkish Human Rights Association (IHD) and Amnesty International (AI) reports. In October 2001 and September 2002, AI documented systematic and widespread torture in Turkey today. See Amnesty International "EUR 44/026/2002," and "EUR 44/0402002." The Turkish Human Rights Association (IHD) spoke of an increase in human rights violations in the Southeast in the first six months in 2003. IHD Report, 2003.

reforms in no way facilitate a return of the Kurdish displaced persons[33] to their home villages and towns. Although a vast majority of internal refugees want to return, even the AKP government has not yet paid attention to their request. On the contrary, reports by the refugee association Göc-Der[34] have it that state bodies on the spot prevent people from returning and drive away those refugees who have already returned.

Death Penalty.
In August 2002, the death penalty was abolished in times of peace (exceptions are war and the threat of war) and changed into life imprisonment. Those sentenced to death for terrorist crimes are not eligible for any amnesty. Turkey made this move to comply with Protocol 6 of the EHRC which it has not ratified yet. As a result of this reform, Abdullah Öcalan's death sentence was commuted to life imprisonment. At the end of 2003, the death penalty was also abolished for cases occurring during war or its threat to comply with the EU standards.

Conclusion

Despite nascent legal reforms associated with its EU candidacy, the Turkish policy on the Kurds is still marked by severe problems and contradictions. For example, even though the state of emergency was lifted, the pro-Kurdish HADEP, which had won a clear majority in the region, was banned and numerous politicians barred from political life for several years. As a consequence, there is still no party representing legitimate Kurdish interests. As a result, the vast majority of the Kurdish population in the region still remains without a voice in politics and parliament.

---

[33] Regarding the situation of Kurdish internal refugees, see Gülistan Gürbey, "Vom Schrecken des Krieges ins Elend der Gecekondus: Die Lebenssituation von kurdischen Inlands-flüchtlingen in der Türkei," *Südosteuropa-Mitteilungen.* Munich, 2001/No. 3, pp. 290-306.

[34] For the latest developments, see by Göc-Der, *Köy bosaltmalar gündemde,* 31 July 2003; and *Basina ve kamuoyuna. Son aylarda bölgede gelisen olaylar kaygi verici,* 4 August 2003.

The handling of the Kurdish language issue, for example, illustrates Ankara's efforts to prevent any recognition of the Kurdish language or Kurdish cultural rights. This has been accomplished by means of complicated regulations in laws and decrees. It illustrates how Turkish policy vis-à-vis the Kurds is still swinging between dogma and liberal tendencies. It also reflects the indecision and the lack of political will to usher in a consistent and substantial change of the traditional dogmatic policy on the Kurds.

All in all, the reform process marks an important first step on the road to Europe. However, a breakthrough has not yet been achieved. Especially due to the prevailing major problems in implementing the reforms, it is much too early to speak of them as historic. Overcoming these problems requires as a sine qua non a change in the attitudes and conduct among the political class and the executive state bodies. At the moment, however, we cannot speak of any such process. If and to what extent the restrictive interpretation of the amendments to the laws will change remains to be seen.

Finally, we must conclude that the reforms do not meet the needs of the Kurdish population appropriately because they neglect both the historically grown and rooted efforts for Kurdish autonomy, as well as the historical and psychological depth and dimension of the conflict. That is why the reforms are insufficient for obtaining cultural and political autonomy for the Kurds which would be based on an institutional recognition of the Kurdish identity, political representation and integration.

As long as this is the case, the EU will continue to be affected by the Kurdish conflict. The question arises for the EU, therefore, whether it regards the conflict as finally settled with reference to the present reforms and is content with the situation, or whether the EU will take more pains to achieve a better implementation by specifying the very general political accession criterion "respect for and protection of minorities." The Turkish decision-makers are still faced with a great challenge, i.e. to muster the political will and break with the dogmatic concept of state and nation in favour of a substantial and continuous democratization and liberalization of the country. What is needed is to find appropriate regulations not just for the conflict over the political and cultural rights of the Kurdish population, but also about determining the identity of the entire country in the 21st century.

CHAPTER 8

Turkey's Kurdish-Centered Iraqi Policy

M. Hakan Yavuz

To understand the Turkish reaction to the 2003 Iraqi war, one needs to focus on two dominant interpretations. The foremost interpretation utilizes the concept of neo-colonialism. Public opinion in Europe and Turkey see what occurred as a "neo-colonial" US war to control the oil resources of Iraq. The second more dominant mode of reading the war focuses on the "neo-conservative/Likudnik" attempt to restructure the Middle East with a view to protecting the state of Israel and maintaining US hegemony. To support this second claim, many people invoked the appointment of US General Jay Garner as the "governor of occupied Iraq." General Garner, according to these people, has close ties with the right-wing think thank, Jewish Institute for National Security Affairs (JINSA). Although most Turks agree with the first interpretation, the second interpretation is dominant among the Turkish Islamic media, such as *Yeni Safak*, *Milli Gazete*, and *Vakit*.

If their real intentions are to bring "democracy" and "human rights" to Iraq and the Middle East, the Bush administration has failed to prepare the world and especially the Islamic world for this war. Many people remain skeptical of these US claims, as they remind their audience of the rights of the Palestinians. Clearly, the war has been very unpopular, and its morality has been undermined. Is there a legal justification for the war? The

UN Security Council did not endorse it, and has already called it an "occupation." Thus, the Bush doctrine of preemptive war is more likely to lead to a new world disorder and create a number of new problems.

This paper seeks to explain the unwavering, yet failed policy of the Turkish state toward Iraq by problematizing Ankara's fear and security-based policy on the Kurds.[1] In short, Turkey's foreign policy is an extension of its domestic civilizational project of becoming a homogenous secular nation-state.[2] For instance, Turkey's own Kurdish problem shapes its policy toward the Iraqi Kurds. Thus, Turkey has no Iraq policy, but rather an "anti-Kurdish policy" that is guided by fear of being partitioned. This policy, in turn, is the major obstacle to Ankara's options in the region.

The state fascination to make everything Turkish and the hegemonic role of the military are the two major obstacles that address the Kurdish question in Turkey. Turkey's foreign policy is the extension of its domestic "imagined enemies" of the Kurds and Islamists. Since Turkey is currently in the midst of major reform, however, its economy, public sphere, and political rights have been expanding and transforming. These changes will create an expected environment of political debate to formulate a new social contract of peaceful co-existence and a new approach to the Kurdish issue.[3]

---

[1] Christopher Houston, *Islam, Kurds and the Turkish Nation State* (Oxford, U.K.: Berg, 2001); M. Hakan Yavuz, "A Preamble to the Kurdish Question: The Politics of Kurdish Identity," Introduction to special issue on the Kurds, *Journal of Muslim Minority Affairs* 18 (April 1998), pp. 9-18; and M. Hakan Yavuz, "Turkey's Fault Lines and the Crisis of Kemalism," *Current History* 99 (January 2000), pp. 33-38.

[2] Andrew Mango, "Atatürk and the Kurds," *Middle Eastern Studies*, 35 (October 1999), p. 8.

[3] For greater detail on the Kurdish issue and its relationship with the state, see David McDowall, *A Modern History of the Kurds* (London: I.B. Tauris, 1996); and Martin van Bruinessen, *Agha, Shaikh and State: The Social and Political Structures of Kurdistan* (London: Zed Books, 1992).

Turkey's Policy Towards Iraq

Overall, Turkey's policy towards Iraq is shaped by its perception of the Kurdish problem in Turkey.[4] One cannot understand Turkey's policy by ignoring the perceptions of the Kurds in the state ideology of Turkey, known also as the Kemalist ideology. The goal of Kemalism has been the creation of a homogenous (Turkish) nation-state and secular society. These two goals of homogenization and centralization were regularly challenged by peripheral Kurdish and Islamic groups. For instance, the Sunni Kurdish groups organized the first rebellion against Mustafa Kemal's reforms in 1925.[5] This rebellion was very crucial for the collective memory of the Turkish state and securitization of the Kurdish identity claims. The British played a direct role in the rebellion because of Turkish resistance to accepting the border drawn between British-mandate Iraq and Turkey. The Kurdish region had been divided and had become the borders of four states. Thus, the Kurds and Kurdish regions acquired the status of being a "national security" problem for these states. The entire region became vulnerable to interference by regional and international powers.

At that time, Turkey had asked for a plebiscite in the region, but this was rejected by the British. Britain agreed not to support Kurdish claims, and Turkey agreed on the current border with Iraq, which ended Turkish claims on Mosul and Kirkuk.

Although divisions among the Kurds and aggressive Turkish state policies helped to suppress the Kurdish rebellion and led to

---

[4] For more on the Turkish Kurds, see M. Hakan Yavuz, "Five Stages of the Construction of Kurdish Nationalism in Turkey," *Nationalism and Ethnic Politics*, 7 (Autumn 2001), pp. 1-24; Michael Gunter, *The Kurds and the Future of Turkey* (New York: St. Martin's Press, 1997); Michael Gunter, *The Changing Kurdish Problem in Turkey* (London: Research Institute for the Study of Conflict & Terrorism, 1994); and Robert Olson, ed., *The Kurdish Nationalist Movement in the 1990s: Its Impact on Turkey and the Middle East* (Lexington, KY: University Press of Kentucky, 1996).

[5] Robert Olson, *The Sheikh Said Rebellion and the Emergence of Kurdish Nationalism, 1880 1925* (Austin: University of Texas Press, 1989).

the hanging of its leadership, the Kurdish-dominated provinces became hotbeds of spontaneous anti-reformist and anti-state rebellions. These rebellions shaped the collective memory of the Turkish state bureaucracy about the Kurds, in general, and the Kurdish question, in particular. Thus, these rebellions helped to create two fundamental parameters of the Turkish state: territorial integrity and political unity of the state (which means no federalism), and the secular and national character of the nation.[6] Any attempt to challenge these two principles was either criminalized or excluded from the body politic by force. Thus, this collective memory of the state elite is crucial in understanding the current policies towards Iraq.

Turkey always remained aloof from Iraqi domestic affairs, and the Kurdish issue remained a source of fear both in the domestic and foreign policy of Turkey. In the 1980s and 1990s, Turkey's policy toward Iraq was guided by three principles.[7] First was the border security against the Kurdistan Workers Party (PKK) and the prevention of transregional Kurdish politicization. Although Turkey actively engaged in the design and implementation of the "safe haven" concept for the protection of the Iraqi Kurds after the Persian Gulf War in 1991, it remained opposed to Kurdish statehood.

In the war against the separatist PKK, Turkey closely worked with the Kurdistan Democratic Party (KDP) of Massoud Barzani and the Patriotic Union of Kurdistan (PUK) of Jalal Talabani. The Turkish-Iraqi border was controlled by the forces of the KDP which provided much better security for Turkey than the Iraqi state under Saddam Hussein could. However, to obtain the support of the KDP, Turkey had to become involved in intra-Kurdish politics in Iraq and eventually even send troops to help stop the conflict between the KDP and PUK after 1994. Thus, Turkey's own Kurdish issue has forced Ankara to become involved in Iraqi Kurdistan for security reasons.

---

[6] Henri Barkey, "Hemmed in by Circumstances: Turkey and Iraq Since the Gulf War," *Middle East Policy*, 7:4 (2000), pp. 110-126.

[7] Michael Gunter, *The Kurdish Predicament in Iraq: A Political Dilemma* (New York: St. Martin's Press, 1999).

This is a security-based policy which totally ignores the Kurdish identity and political claims in Iraq. For Ankara, good Kurds are those who fight against the PKK, and bad Kurds are those who refuse to follow suit.[8] Due to Turkey's security concerns, the US supported the Turkish presence in Iraq until the 2003 Iraqi war.

The second issue was the distribution and usage of the waters of the Tigris River.[9] Turkey controls the water resources of the region and has built a series of dams for irrigation purposes and generation of electricity. The water remained the major source of tension between Turkey and the governments of Iraq and Syria. Both Syria and Iraq did not hesitate to use their "Kurdish card" against Turkey by providing shelter to the PKK.

Third, the chemical weapons of Iraq were a major concern for Turkey as well. When the Iraqi leader used these weapons against the Kurds, Turkey condemned the Iraqi leader and worried about the proliferation of these weapons. The US, however, did not react to the Iraqi use of chemical weapons against the Kurds and Iranian soldiers.

The 2003 Iraqi War and Turkey's Policy

The 2003 Iraqi War has altered the balance of power in the region. The current Turkish policy is still being made, and is guided by three key principles: (1) Turkish security concerns. This stems from the Iraqi Kurdish aspirations of secession or creation of a transregional Kurdish irredentism (pan-Kurdism). Turkey has a clear policy against an independent Kurdish state and uses every opportunity to support the territorial integrity and

---

[8] Michael Gunter, "Kurdish Infighting: The PKK-KDP Conflict," in *The Kurdish Nationalist Movement in the 1990s: Its Impact on Turkey and the Middle East*, ed. by Robert Olson (Lexington, KY: University Press of Kentucky, 1996), pp. 50-62.

[9] Michael B. Bishku, "Turkey's Water Usage in the Tigris-Euphrates Basin and its Impact on its Downstream Neighbors," *Journal of Development Alternatives and Area Studies*, 20 (September-December 2001), pp. 29-42; and Servet Mutlu, "The Southeastern Anatolia Project (GAP) of Turkey: Its Context, Objectives and Prospects," *Orient*, 37 (March 1996), pp. 59-86.

political unity of Iraq. In addition, Turkey supports non-ethnic administrative federalism for Iraq in which the oil is controlled by the central government. Turkey also vehemently opposes Kurdish moves to control Musul and Kirkuk, where a large Turkish minority lives. Thus, Ankara, just like many other regional governments, regards the Kurdish political aspirations of autonomy or independence in Iraq as a source of instability.

(2) Due to its involvement in the mid-1980s in intra-Iraqi conflicts, Turkey rediscovered the "Turkman" issue and created the necessary conditions for the politicization of the Turkman identity.[10] The Turkmans became the most important strategic card against unruly Kurdish groups. The assimilationist policies of the KDP against the Turkman community enhanced the Turkman sense of identity. Moreover, a powerful Turkman lobby has been forming in Ankara. This lobby is built around Bilkent University and the Dogramaci family. There are large numbers of Turkman students in Bilkent University and other institutions in Turkey. Today, there is a pro-Turkman public opinion in Turkey which is very sensitive to the treatment and rights of the Turkman community. Any attack or genocide against the Turkman population could easily be translated into anti-Americanism, as well as opposition against Barzani who has recently become very unpopular in Turkey.

(3) To counter the prospects of Kurdish independence and protect the Turkman community, Ankara supports the territorial integrity of Iraq within which the Shiite community is expected to play a determinant role. Thus, Ankara does not support any ethnic group (such as the Kurds) having the right to shape the constitution of Iraq.

---

[10] Tarik Oguz, "The Turkmans as a Factor in Turkey's Foreign Policy," *Turkish Studies* 3:2 (2002), pp. 139-148. The 1957 census—the last in which the Turkmans were permitted to register—counted 567,000 Turkmans (9 percent of the population) among Iraqi's population of 6,300.000. The Kurds were 13 percent.

US Misreading of Turkey

The US had a very positive standing in Turkey due to the Cold War and its support for the Muslim communities in the Balkans. This pro-American public opinion, however, has been diminishing as a result of US policies in Iraq. The US failed to understand Turkey's sensitivity on the Kurdish question. Some powerful lobbies, especially the neoconservatives, wanted to create an independent Kurdish state. The US began making competing commitments to the Kurds and Turks at the same time.

For instance, shortly before the 2003 Iraqi War, Zalmay Khalilzad—the special US envoy to the Iraqi opposition—held a meeting in Saladdin with the Iraqi opposition which excluded the Turkman minority. When Khalilzad was in Iraq, there also was a number of anti-Turkish demonstrations, and the houses of the Turkman minority groups were attacked in Sulaymaniya and Arbil. In addition, Khalilzad's speeches to please the Kurds angered the Turks. Moreover, many Turks believed that Barzani's intransigence and anti-Turkish statements were fed by the United States to "control" Turkey. This was also known as the US Kurdish card against Turkey. People referred to statements of Khalilzad and US Ambassador Peter Galbraith who declared at a meeting in Odense, Denmark in November 2002 that "the main threat to Kurdish self-determination is Turkey, not Saddam." The US debate over Kurdish statehood has undermined Turkish confidence in the American policy to keep Iraq as a unified entity.

These US actions helped to influence the Turkish parliament on March 1, 2003 to vote against the US demand to station over 50,000 American troops in Turkey to open the second front in Iraq. This vote in the Turkish parliament reflected the over 70 percent anti-war public mood in Turkey. The Turkish public interpreted the US actions as the "ordering of the Turks to allow troops," "heavy-handed diplomacy," and a reflection of "evolving deep suspicion on the Kurdish issue."

In addition, the US treatment of the Turkish parliament and sending of military hardware to the Turkish bases without even waiting for the decision of the parliament did not help the situation. In retrospect, U.S. officials admit they made unrealistic demands on the new government of Turkey (which was installed only in November 2002) by insisting on a vote on whether it would accept as many as 90,000 U.S. troops, even as President Bush was still publicly claiming he had made no decision to attack Iraq. US officials repeatedly set deadlines for action, but then took no action when the deadlines passed, costing the administration credibility and inflating Turkey's sense of importance. A day before the voting, a number of articles were published by *Milliyet* which claimed there was close cooperation between the US and the PKK groups in Iraq. This was later denied by the US Embassy.

Turkey also made a number of mistakes before the 2003 parliament vote. The Turkish military and foreign ministry believed that the US could not fight nor win the war without opening a second, northern front in Turkey. The Turks overplayed their strategic importance and misread the US resolve and capabilities to win the war without the Turkish front. The Justice and Development Party (AKP) government of Prime Minister Abdullah Gül did not work hard enough to get its own motion to pass. This blunder was very much an outcome of a deliberate game of deception played by the Gül government, and also a strategic blunder deriving from miscalculations by the Turkish military.

The result was a political catastrophe for US-Turkish relations. The AKP either did not have resolute leadership and cohesion, or this is the outcome its leadership wanted. The prime minister and his advisors were led by their Islamic convictions more than the national interest of Turkey.

In the parliament, the vote turned into a battle over the leadership and orientation of the party. The conservative Islamic group won the motion by voting "no." Not national interests, but rather Islamic conviction determined the color of their vote. The government deliberately sent mixed signals to the US. The lack of governmental coordination played a key role. The AKP tried to use public opinion to negotiate, but eventually became hostage to public opinion, preferring instead to follow it. This public opinion was utilized by Gül and his Islamist advisors who were influenced by Samuel Huntington's writings and very much in the business of reverse orientalism. Clearly, the AKP did not want the motion to pass and did not impose enough party discipline.

The Turkish government was new and inexperienced in foreign policy issues. In secular Turkey, the religious-minded AKP (which evolved from the ruins of the Islamic parties banned by the army-influenced Constitutional Court) still regarded many state institutions as suspicious political forces. The AKP wanted to orient its foreign policy around membership in the European Union (EU). Since many European countries were against the war, the AKP did not want to be seen as a "US puppet."

The AKP leadership realized that the political space in Turkey could only be expanded with human rights, democracy, and the joining of the EU. These new ideas allowed the AKP leadership to expand their social base and create new coalitions with liberal-secular forces in Turkey. The West has become an ally to protect the social spaces against the excesses of the Kemalist state. Turkey has indeed become a model with its liberal and pluralist Islam, and this opportunity could be destroyed if the US does not support Turkey.

The AKP is not Islamist, but has deep roots in the Islamic movement in Turkey. The government and the military do not have a fully shared security map. The military is very uneasy with some of the key appointments of the AKP government. The military was upset when the White House opened its doors for the AKP's leader, Recep Tayyip Erdogan. When the AKP was elected to office in November 2002, the military allowed it to take over the government and also make the key decisions such as the US deployment. The US administration preferred to work with the civilian government and relied on a few journalists who misled the US. There was too much reliance on informal networks. Washington preferred to work with individuals, rather than institutions. Ahmet Necdet Sezer, the president of Turkey, has always been very critical of the US.

Post-War Situation

During the war, the Iraqi Kurdish militia fought on the side of the US and entered Kirkuk and Mosul without much of a fight. Turkey was totally excluded from the war, while the administration of Kirkuk became dominated by the Kurds. Afterwards, when the US wanted over 10,000 Turkish troops to be stationed in the Iraqi Sunni areas, Turkey responded positively. In October 2003, the Turkish parliament under Erdogan's leadership passed a motion to send Turkish peacekeeping troops to help the Americans in Iraq. However, the Iraqi Kurdish resistance to the Turkish troops obliged Washington to ignore the Turkish offer.[11] Thus, Ankara lost its strategic "utility" to the US policy towards Iraq, and the Iraqi Kurds emerged as dominant actors in shaping not only US policy in Iraq, but also US policy towards Turkey.

To get rid of all Turkish military presence in Iraq, in July 2003, the US forces detained 11 Turkish soldiers in Sulaymaniya who were originally deployed there as peacekeepers between the KDP and PUK. The Turkish troops were arrested on the basis of the PUK information that the Turkish troops were preparing an attack against the Kurdish governor of Kirkuk. The US regarded the Kurdish statelet in northern Iraq as a keystone to the stability of the Middle East, while Ankara perceived this evolving Kurdish statelet as a threat to its national security.

Turkey must realize that the return to a pre-1991 unified Iraq is out of the question. As a result of the "safe haven" zone, there is now a well-developed Kurdish state in northern Iraq. The institutions created in the two autonomous territories controlled by the two Kurdish factions (KDP and PUK) have served to deepen and consolidate Kurdish ethno-national consciousness and develop a sense of collective memory of being free in their own land. The Iraqi Kurds will not give up their hard-earned freedom.[12]

Turkey has to recognize Iraqi Kurdish autonomy as a fact of political reality, and develop a framework of relationship with these two Kurdish autonomous regions. Ankara must realize that the only option for the future of Iraq is federalism, and that there are more opportunities in Iraq today than a decade ago. If Turkey solves its Kurdish question by offering full cultural and political

---

[11] For background, see Michael Gunter, "United States Foreign Policy toward the Kurds," in *The Kurdish Question in U.S. Foreign Policy: A Documentary Sourcement*, ed. by Lokman I. Meho (Westport, CT and London: Praeger, 2004), pp. 3-12.

[12] M.Hakan Yavuz and Michael M. Gunter, "The Kurdish Nation," *Current History* 100 (January 2001), pp. 33-39.

rights within the framework of the EU, northern Iraq would not become a center of attraction for the Turkish Kurds.

In order to develop productive relations with the Iraqi Kurds, Ankara must regard the Kurds as a "friend," not a "foe," and stop seeing them as a source of instability for Turkey and the Middle East. Turkey needs a new social contract to overcome its domestic fault lines and a framework of foreign policy to consolidate this social contract. This first step is to see the Kurds as a natural ally and friend of Turkey.

CHAPTER 9

The Impact of the Iraq War on the Future of the Kurds in Iran

Nader Entessar

Introduction

The purpose of this article is to analyze the implications of the war against Iraq for the condition of the Kurds in Iran. The ouster of the Baathist government in Baghdad has created developments that will have some predictable and some unforeseen consequences for Iraq's neighbors and the broader Middle East. As for Iran, Saddam Hussein's demise should allow for greater regional cooperation between the two neighbors. As Anoushiravan Ehteshami has aptly noted, the notion that Iran and Iraq are destined for perpetual rivalry and hostility towards each other is false.[1] Hostile relations between Iran and Iraq in the past 40 years had more to do with *realpolitik* and regional developments than their purported historical rivalry dating back to the Ottoman-Persian competition over Mesopotamia. The Kurds certainly played a significant part in Iran-Iraq competition. It is beyond the scope of this chapter to analyze how each side tried to use its Kurdish card in recent conflicts with each other. However, we need to place the contemporary developments in the context of changing Kurdish fortunes in Iran since

---

[1] Anoushiravan Ehteshami, "Iran-Iraq Relations after Saddam," *The Washington Quarterly* 26 (Autumn 2003), pp. 115-16.

the overthrow of the Pahlavi monarchy and the establishment of the Islamic Republic in Iran.

The Kurds enthusiastically supported Iran's anti-monarchical revolution of 1978-79, and a broad spectrum of the Kurdish population participated in the revolutionary process from the outset. However, the initial Kurdish euphoria over the demise of the Pahlavi monarchy soon gave way to the bitter realization that the Kurdish autonomy demands would go unheeded by the new Islamic government. After the establishment of the Islamic Republic of Iran, it became quite evident that Ayatollah Khomeini's objective of establishing a strong and centralized Islamic state would clash with the goals of autonomy-seeking Kurds. Notwithstanding Khomeini's rejection of the concept of ethnic distinctiveness and attachments among Muslim nationalities in Iran, the Constitution of the Islamic Republic does recognize the existence of linguistic diversity among the Iranian people. Article 15 of the Iranian Constitution recognizes Persian as the official language of the country. All official communications as well as instructional and educational materials must be in Persian. However, the use of local languages in the media and in the classroom are permitted so long as they are used in conjunction with Persian.[2] The only specific recognition given to the minorities in Iran's Islamic Constitution is to the country's non-Islamic minorities (Christians, Jews and Zoroastrians), not to the Islamic groups, such as the Kurds. The latter category is viewed as an integral part of the Islamic *umma*, or community, and hence is not to be treated differently from other Muslim groups in the country.

The Kurds, however, saw an unrivalled window of opportunity created by the downfall of the Shah to push for autonomy and recognition of their cultural rights in post-monarchical Iran. Dr. Abdul Rahman Ghassemlou, who had become the Secretary General of the Kurdistan Democratic Party of Iran (KDPI) in 1973, returned to Iran after several years of exile in Europe on

---

[2] *Matn-e Kamel-e Qanoon-e Assassi-e Jomhoori-e Eslami-e Iran* [The Complete Text of the Constitution of the Islamic Republic of Iran] (Tehran: Hamid Publications, 1983), p. 28.

the eve of the Iranian revolution. He then sought to transform what was then a dormant KDPI into the principal Kurdish political organization in the country. On March 30-31, 1979, the Iranian government conducted a referendum asking Iranians to vote on a single proposal—to maintain the monarchical system or replace it with an Islamic republic. The KDPI, as well as many other secular groups in the country, boycotted the referendum because it only offered two choices to the voters. Given the general antipathy toward the Shah's regime at that time and mesmerized by revolutionary euphoria, it was evident that the majority of voters would opt for the choice of the Islamic republic. Ayatollah Khomeini's exhortations for a massive turnout resulted in an overwhelming victory for the new regime as 98.2 percent voted to replace the monarchy with an Islamic republic.[3] The Kurds had lost their first political battle with the revolutionary regime in Tehran.

The Kurds then shifted the focus of their political struggle to affect the draft of Iran's new constitution. The proposed constitution was unveiled by the provisional revolutionary government of Prime Minister Mehdi Bazargan in June 1979. Although the draft of the constitution contained democratic provisions to safeguard the rights of all Iranians, the Kurds felt that it did not address their autonomy demands adequately.[4] The KDPI joined many other nationalist and secularist groups and demanded that a constituent assembly, consisting of no more than 500 representatives, be elected to debate and revise the draft constitution.

Khomeini feared the dilution of the Islamic elements of the draft constitution if a constituent assembly, representing several constituencies and interests, were to review the document. Consequently, he ordered the establishment of a 73-member Assem-

---

[3] Shaul Bakhash, *The Reign of the Ayatollahs: Iran and the Islamic Revolution* (New York: Basic Books, 1984), p. 73.

[4] For a critical analysis of Iran's constitution from a Kurdish vantage point, see Farhad Akbari, "Jaygah-e Qanooni-e Khalq-e Kurd dar Qavaneen-e Asasai-e Iran" [The Legal Status of the Kurdish People in Iran's Constitutional Law] *Kurdistan* (Organ of the Central Committee of the Democratic Party of Iranian Kurdistan), no. 355, December 21, 2002, pp. 6-7.

bly of Experts to review the proposed constitution. Kurdish nationalists were not included in this body. Nevertheless, the Kurds continued to articulate their views on the shape of the new constitution in formal and informal gatherings. For example, Sheikh Ezzedin Hosseini, the spiritual leader of the Sunni Kurds in Mahabad, argued that since Iran was a multinational state, its constitution must legally recognize the cultural, economic, and sociopolitical rights of all ethnic and religious groups in the country.

Furthermore, many Sunni religious leaders opposed the inclusion of Shiism as the official religion of the state in the new constitution. According to Ayatollah Montazeri, the head of the Assembly of Experts at the time of the drafting of the Islamic Republic's constitution, conflicting opinions were expressed by the members of the Assembly on this issue. The Sunni clerics, as well as some Shiite members of the Assembly, preferred Islam, rather than Shiite Islam, to be listed in the new constitution as the official religion of the country.[5] Ahmad Moftizadeh, a Sunni Kurdish cleric sympathetic to the Islamic Republic, was also asked to express his views on this topic to the members of the Assembly of Experts. In the final analysis, those favoring the inclusion of Shiite Islam as the official state religion prevailed. They argued that the overwhelming majority of Iranians are Shiite Muslims, and that even the monarchical constitution had recognized Shiite Islam as the official state religion. It would be unthinkable for the Islamic Republic to do less than what the Shah had done in this respect. Moreover, they reasoned that the Sunnis would still be able to follow their religious practices and the rulings of their own judges in religious courts.[6] However, some Sunni minorities in today's Iran have expressed dismay at the de facto discrimination against them. A number of Sunni mosques have been closed down or destroyed since 1980, in-

---

[5] Ayatollah Hossein Ali Montazeri, *Matn-e Kamel-e Khaterat-e Ayatollah Hossein Ali Montazeri* [The Complete Text of the Memoirs of Ayatollah Hossein Ali Montazeri] (Essen, Germany: Union of Iranian Editors in Europe, 2001), p. 252.

[6] *Ibid.*, pp. 252-53.

cluding some in the Kurdish cities of Sanandaj and Saqqez.[7] Furthermore, Tehran is still without a single Sunni mosque despite its expanding multi-religious population.

Acrimonious debates about the draft constitution and Kurdish autonomy demands conjured up memories of the Mahabad Republic. Furthermore, Ayatollah Khomeini and his supporters within the clergy feared that the foundation of their preferred system of government would be weakened if ethnic demands, especially secular ones, were accommodated in the revised constitution. To make matters worse, tensions between the Islamic authorities and the Kurds manifested themselves in a series of armed clashes between the forces of the KDPI and the newly-created *pasdaran-e enghelab* (Revolutionary Guards). In order to stem the tide of armed conflict in Kurdistan, Sheikh Mohammad Sadegh Sadeghi Guivi (better known as Sadegh Khalkhali) was dispatched to the region to try and punish those who had taken up arms against the new regime in Tehran.

As the first judge of the revolutionary courts who condemned scores of high level officials of the Pahlavi regime to death, Khalkhali's arrival in Kurdistan bode ill for a peaceful resolution of the conflict. In a series of trials that lacked even the most basic elements of fairness, Khalkhali sentenced scores of Kurdish nationalists to death. He blamed Prime Minister Bazargan, who had tried unsuccessfully in the past to reign in Khalkhali's free-wheeling dispensation of justice, for the deterioration of conditions in Kurdistan. In particular, Khalkhali accused Bazargan of currying favor with Ghassemlou and other high officials of the KDPI. As Khalkhali put it, by placing "known communists" in key positions in Kurdistan, Bazargan was responsible for the martyrdom of Revolutionary Guards in the region, and by undermining the authority of the revolutionary courts, Bazargan "weakened their steadfastness."[8]

---

[7] A. William Samii, "The Nation and Its Minorities: Ethnicity, Unity and State Policy in Iran," *Comparative Studies of South Asia, Africa and the Middle East* 20:1&2 (2000), p.130.

[8] Ayatollah Haj Sheikh Sadegh Khalkhali, *Khaterat-e Ayatollah Khalkhali, Avalin Hakim-e Shar'-e Dadgahaye Enghelab* [Memoirs of Ayatollah Khalkhali, the First Religious Judge of the Revolutionary Courts] (Tehran: Sayeh Publications, 2001), pp. 293-94.

Continuing armed clashes between the Kurds and the Iranian military and Revolutionary Guards led to, *inter alia*, the banning of the KDPI at the end of autumn 1979 followed by Ayatollah Khomeini's labeling of Ghassemlou as *mofsid-e fil azr* (corrupter of the earth). However, shortly before the complete breakdown of negotiations between the Kurds and the representatives of the Iranian government, Khomeini issued a conciliatory message addressed to the people of Kurdistan. In his message, Khomeini, for the first time, publicly acknowledged the legitimate grievances of the Kurds. He promised to continue negotiations with Kurdish religious and nationalist leaders until peace and calm were restored in the area. Khomeini's message further stated that a lot of people in Iran had suffered under both the monarchy and the revolutionary government, and he asked for their patience and forbearance. In the last paragraph of the letter, Khomeini beseeched the Kurds to join him in the name of God and Islam to "save our country and to direct our energies against the real enemies of the country led by the United States."[9] The content and tone of Khomeini's last message to the Kurds was profoundly different from his previous message issued three months earlier in which he had issued an ultimatum to the Kurds to lay down their arms. It was apparent that Khomeini had feared that continuing armed clashes in Kurdistan would redound to the detriment of the Islamic Republic and could have broadened the conflict with unforeseen consequences for the integrity of the country.

Khatami's Administration and the Kurdish Challenge

The election of Mohammad Khatami as Iran's president in May 1997 and the defeat of the conservative forces in the February 2000 parliamentary elections generated a great deal of expectation for political change in Iran. Khatami, a mid-level Shiite cleric, received some 70 percent of the popular vote with a man-

---

[9] For the complete text of Ayatollah Khomeini's November 16, 1979 letter to the Kurds, see *Ettalaat*, November 17, 1979.

date to reform Iran's political system and allow the emergence of a genuinely pluralistic political structure in the country. As Khatami had stated, "we cannot expect any positive transformation anywhere [in Iran] unless the yearning for freedom is fulfilled."[10] Furthermore, Khatami, from the beginning of his first presidential term, has continued to emphasize the notion of inclusiveness—*Iran baray-e hamy-e Iranian* (Iran for all Iranians)—and the importance of the rule of law in nurturing and enhancing the foundation of Iran's political system.[11] The Kurds, as well as several other ethnic groups in the country, welcomed Khatami's election.

The reform movement (the Second of Khordad Movement) that guided Khatami's electoral victories in both of his terms, however, proved to be a weak and fractious coalition unable to withstand the onslaught of the hardliners in and out of the government. In addition to legal limits imposed on the authority of the president by the Iranian constitution, Khatami and his supporters have continuously been challenged in all arenas by their conservative opponents. When challenged, Khatami has always conceded. Closing down of the reformist newspapers and organizations as well as jailing of journalists, lawyers, students, writers, and other supporters of political reform have gone largely unchallenged by Khatami, save occasional speeches he delivers denouncing violations of the rule of law.

The arrest of officials in Kurdistan, some of whom had identified with Khatami's programs, has intensified since 1999. City council elections have been nullified by anti-reform forces, and the credentials of either pro-reform or independent Kurdish politicians and candidates are rejected when they seek to run for various offices in the province. In a crackdown on Kurdish officials, then Governor General of Kurdistan Abdullah Ramazan-

---

[10] Mohammad Khatami, *Islam, Liberty and Development* (Binghamton, NY: Institute of Global Cultural Studies, Binghamton University, 1998), p. 4.

[11] For a selection of President Khatami's speeches on this and similar topics, see Seyyed Mohammad Khatami, *Tose'-e Siyasi, Tose'-e Eghtesadi va Amniyat* [Political Development, Economic Development and Security] (Tehran: Tarh-e No, 2000), especially pp. 55-97.

zadeh was summoned before the Special Court for Public Officials in April 2001 and was charged with the "dissemination of lies." Although Ramazanzadeh was later released, his arrest highlighted the precarious nature of the Second of Khordad coalition in the country. Ramazanzadeh's "crimes" were his objections to the nullification of the votes of two constituencies in the Kurdish cities of Baneh and Saqqez; thus he was accused of libelous statements against the powerful watchdog body, the Council of Guardians, that had ordered the nullification of the aforementioned constituency votes.[12]

Another significant political obstacle between Khatami and the Kurds is the presence of several individuals in the reform movement who had earlier participated in the suppression of Kurdish uprisings. Many Kurds believe that today's reformists are yesterday's oppressors, and thus they cannot be trusted. The case of Hamid Reza Jalaipour is illustrative of this point. Jalaipour, who became a significant architect of the Second of Khordad reform movement and an editor of *Asr-e Azadegan*, the now banned reformist Tehran daily, spent 10 years in the province of Kurdistan fighting Kurdish autonomy demands.

As a commander of a Revolutionary Guards unit, and later the Governor of Naqdeh and Mahabad, and Deputy Governor General for Political Affairs in Kurdistan; Jalaipour was directly and indirectly responsible for some of the worst revolutionary excesses in that region. When asked if he had any remorse about ordering the execution of 59 Kurdish nationalists, Jalaipour refused to offer any apology for his past actions by claiming that he could not be held responsible for actions undertaken when he was a revolutionary in his 20s or for undertaking actions that were necessary during wartime and in the interest of saving the nascent Islamic Republic.[13] However, when Jalaipour was invited to participate in the Berlin conference organized by the Heinrich Boll Foundation in Germany to initiate a dialogue between the representatives of the reform movement in Iran and the outside world, Jalaipour claimed that he had been misquoted by

---

[12] Islamic Republic News Agency (IRNA), April 9, 2001.
[13] *Asr-e Azadegan*, March 6, 2000.

the correspondent of *Asr-e Azadegan*, who was a Kurd himself.[14] These exchanges also demonstrate the existing gap between the reform movement and the Kurds.

The lingering suspicion that the Kurdish demand for autonomy is, in fact, a disguised attempt at secession has hindered meaningful dialogue between Iranian reformists and the Kurds. From the outset, the Kurds have denied that their aim is to establish a sovereign nation-state of Kurdistan inside Iran. As Ghassemlou stated emphatically: "Let me make one thing clear: no political force in Iranian Kurdistan wants to secede from Iran. Our demands are framed within the context of [the] Iranian state."[15] He also helped coin the slogan "democracy for Iran, autonomy for Kurdistan" as the motto of the KDPI. Abdullah Hassanzadeh, the KDPI's current Secretary General, has reiterated this point on numerous occasions. In an interview with *Al-Zaman*, Hassanzadeh further stated that the KDPI believes that the time for establishing small, nonviable countries has long passed. That is, the legitimate rights of the Kurds can be best guaranteed within a democratic Iran. Besides, Hassanzadeh continued, regional geopolitical realities in the region will not allow the creation and/or survival of an independent Kurdish state.[16]

In response, the Iranian authorities have insisted that the KDPI must prove its loyalty to Iran and the principles of the Islamic Revolution. In the words of Mostafa Chamran, the first Defense Minister of the Islamic Republic who oversaw some of the most intense battles in the Kurdish regions during the early

---

[14] Mohammad Ali Zakariaee, ed., *Konferanc-e Berlin: Khedmat ya Khiyanat* [The Berlin Conference: Service or Treason] (Tehran: Tarh-e No, 2002), p. 211.

[15] See Abdul Rahman Ghassemlou's interview in the *MERIP Report*, no. 98, July-August 1981, p. 17. Also, see "Barnameh va Assassnameh-e Hezb-e Demokrat-e Kurdistan-e Iran" [The Platform and Constitution of the Kurdish Democratc Partry of Iran], Third Congress of the KDPI, 1973, and "Asnad-e Kongereh-e Dahom-e Hezb-e Demokrat-e Kurdistan-e Iran" [The Documents of the Tenth Congress of the Kurdistan Democratic Party of Iran], April 1995.

[16] See *Kurdistan* (Organ of the Central Committee of the Kurdistan Democratic Party of Iran), no. 278, December 1999, p. 4.

months of the post-revolutionary period, if the KDPI and other Kurds really believe in the Islamic revolution, "we would give them autonomy not just in Kurdistan but also would ask them to show us how to give autonomy and freedom to every ethnic group in the country. However, if they simply use fancy and misleading slogans to hide their intention to harm Islam and our revolution and to serve foreign powers whose interests are diametrically opposed to those of the Iranian people, including the Kurds, we will fight them to the end."[17]

Hamid Reza Jalaipour has criticized the very notion of autonomy (*khodmokhtari*) as proposed by the KDPI. What does autonomy entail for Iran? What guarantees will Iran have that outside powers would not take advantage of the situation and harm our territorial integrity, inquired Jalaipour? He further declared that the recipe for Kurdish autonomy is anathema to Iran's national identity and is a foreign concept to most Iranian Kurds. Jalaipour also stated that because Kurdish history in Iran is so vastly different from the Kurdish experience in Iraq or Turkey, models of autonomy imported from outside Iran are not applicable to Iranian Kurdistan.[18]

Finally, Kurdish autonomy demands may run counter to similar demands by other ethnic groups in Iran. There are several areas of Iran where the Kurds, Azeris and other ethnic groups live side-by-side. For example, the provinces of West Azerbaijan, Ilam and Kermanshah are inhabited by numerous groups, including the Sunni Kurds, Shiite Kurds, Lurs as well as the Armenians and Assyrians. The exclusive ethnic claims of each group may generate inter-ethnic conflict in these provinces. This problem first came up during the negotiations between the KDPI and the provisional revolutionary government of Iran in 1979, and it is still a sensitive issue under Khatami. In fact, when a group of Azeri intellectuals, journalists, students and

---

[17] Mostafa Chamran, *Kurdistan* (Tehran: Foundation of Martyr Chamran, 1985), p. 153.

[18] Hamid Reza Jalaipour, *Kurdistan: Elal-e Tadavom-e Bohran-e An Pas Az Enghelab-e Eslami* [Kurdistan: Reasons for the Continuation of its Crisis after the Islamic Revolution] (Tehran: Institute for Political and International Studies, 1993), pp. 164-65.

parliamentary representatives wrote an open letter to President Khatami asking for greater cultural autonomy for the Azeris, they also referred to a "specific ethnic group" that seeks to create another "Karabagh enclave" in Azerbaijan. It was clear that the Kurds were the target of this letter. Consequently, the KDPI criticized both the Azeris and Khatami for ignoring Kurdish claims in the province of West Azerbaijan.[19] Notwithstanding political and logistical problems, it is clear that the long-term stability of Iran requires the recognition of the rights of all of its inhabitants.

Constitutional and Legal Engineering:
A Preliminary Proposal

As the experience of post-Saddam Hussein Iraq has shown, the fear of "Balkanization" of the country had been highly exaggerated. In fact, a fully functioning federal democracy in Iraq will have a major spill-over effect in Iran. If the Iraqi experiment in establishing a viable federal state through constitutional engineering and other legal remedies leads to the accommodation of ethnic and minority rights in that country, it can be used as a model for similar experiments in Iran. For example, constitutional and legal reforms can be implemented with the specific intention of promulgating statutes to protect the status of various ethnic groups through constitutionally-mandated changes. Such laws could also extend to specific institutional arrangements to ensure equal treatment for the Kurds not only by the state apparatus, but also by private institutions.[20] Nondiscrimination statutes that have been enacted in the United States since the 1960s and similar ones that are being considered in a new federal Iraq's

---

[19] For details, see *Kurdistan* (Organ of the Central Committee of the Kurdistan Democratic Party of Iran), no. 294, October 6, 2000, pp. 1 and 4-5; *Kurdistan*, no. 297, November 20, 2000, pp. 1-3; and *Kurdistan*, no. 304, March 5, 2001, pp. 1 and 5.

[20] For details, see Claire Palley, "The Role of Law in Relation to Minority Groups," in Anthony E. Alcock, Brian K. Taylor, and John M. Welton, eds., *The Future of Cultural Minorities* (London: Macmillan, 1979), pp. 121-26.

constitution are examples of such devices. Provisions already exist for the implementation of indigenously-designed equal rights legislation in Iran. Electoral laws, systems of proportional representation, and the like are useful beginnings for the utilization of legal/constitutional remedies to seriously deal with the Kurdish predicament in Iran.

A carefully crafted scheme leading to the establishment of a genuine pluralistic polity in Iraq will have a significant repercussion for the Kurds in Iran. Pluralism in post-Saddam Iraq with the aim of creating a condition of diversity within unity in which different ethnic groups coexist in a single territorial state in a relationship of interdependence, will become a model for not only the Kurds but other groups to follow. In many ways, the multiethnic empires of the Middle East, such as the Persian and Ottoman systems, were characterized by the existence of ethnic pluralism. It was only after the creation of the European-style nation-state system that ethnic chauvinism replaced old loyalties and cross-cutting alliances that had developed over the centuries among various ethnicities in Iran and elsewhere in the Middle East. Furthermore, as Patrick Thornberry has observed, for pluralism to succeed as a viable option for a multi-ethnic state like Iran, there must be a "large measure of freedom within the state for minorities in the interest of real rather than formal equality."[21] Various autonomy agreements signed between the Iraqi governments and the Kurds in the 1960s and 1970s failed because of the absence of such freedom for the Kurds. However, if the post-Baathist Iraq succeeds in implementing genuine rights for the Kurds, then the federal structure of the new Iraq can become a viable model for Iran to consider.

All in all, two techniques, both of which require constitutional restructuring, can be mentioned as desirable ways to reduce conflict between the Kurds and the central authorities in Iran. The establishment of a genuine federal structure and a move away from the strong centralism that has characterized Iran for almost a century may presage the onset of a democratic, participatory political system. This process must be gradually

---

[21] Patrick Thorberry, *Minorities and Human Rights Law* (London: Minority Rights Group, 1987), p. 4.

implemented in stages and not imposed in a short time frame. Imposed federalism will likely fail in the long run, as it did in the former Yugoslavia in 1991. Iran will have to develop its federal structure within its own unique political milieu and with respect to its own unique Kurdish problem. Again, a successful Iraqi model of federalism may lead to the acceleration of a similar process in Iran, but the two countries will have to pursue their goals within the specific framework of their own political requirements.

A second technique, which can be implemented without the federal system, will require changes in the electoral laws to implement a system of proportional representation.[22] Although this system of representation may lead to the proliferation of political parties and unstable coalition governments, it seems to provide an equitable channel for ethnic groups to develop a stake in the viability of the larger state within which they live. In other words, if ethnic groups are not underrepresented in the decision-making institutions of the national government, as is the case with the Kurds today, they will likely develop greater loyalty to the broader interests of the state. This, in turn, may lead to the development of political alignments that are based on national interests rather than on parochial interests of various ethnic entities. Ethnic identification and demands for the recognition of ethnic rights would most likely persist even with the successful constitutional/legal restructuring discussed above. However, such demands will not always lead to violent conflict when avenues of genuine political participation are open to all segments of society.

Prospects for the Future

As Iraq develops into a functioning society with the Kurds playing a much more significant role in the political life of the country than they have played since the establishment of an independent Iraq in the early twentieth century, collaboration between Iran and the Iraqi Kurds will inevitably mature. This, in

---

[22] See Donald L. Horowitz, *Ethnic Groups in Conflict* (Berkeley, CA: University of California Press, 1985), pp. 628-33.

turn, will have an impact on the Iranian government's policies towards the country's Kurdish population. At the theoretical level, even high-level government officials already pay more heed to the needs of the Kurds, as reflected in the number of speeches given by Iranian officials on this issue. Today, there are more Kurdish publications and cultural enterprises than at any time since the establishment of the Islamic Republic in 1979. The Tehran Kurdish Association, or *Kory Kurdani Taran* (KKT), which is a recognized Non-governmental Organization (NGO), has had a renaissance of some sort in recent times. According to the KKT, there are 1,800,000 Kurds in greater Tehran.[23] This would make greater Tehran a city with one of the largest Kurdish communities in the world. Notwithstanding barriers that continue to hamper the publication of Kurdish magazines and newspapers, there is a growing body of such publications, the latest of which is the bi-weekly *Kil-e Shin* published in Ushnovieh.[24]

The Iraqi Kurds and Iran were in regular contact in the months preceeding the ouster of Saddam Hussein. Both Massoud Barzani, the head of Iraq's Kurdistan Democratic Party (KDP) and Jalal Talabani of the Patriotic Union of Kurdistan (PUK), as well as Ahmad Chalabi of the Iraqi National Congress (INC) conducted several discussions with Iranian leaders regarding issues of common interest. These Iraqi Kurdish organizations also maintained offices in Iran.[25] Emerging security issues have also allowed for a modicum of cooperation on common threats, both in the pre- and post-Saddam era. For example, Iran has provided some support in the fight against Ansar al-Islam, the militant Islamic group with reputed links to al-Qaeda. Notwithstanding charges made by L. Paul Bremer, the U.S. administrator of Iraq, against Iran's laxity in guarding its Kurdish borders, thus allowing the Ansar forces to move freely between Iranian and Iraqi Kurdistan, Iran has for sometime been engaged

---

[23] See H.S. Soran, "An Introduction to the Tehran Kurds' Association," *Kurdish Media*, June 13, 2003 [http://www.kurdishmedia.com/reports.]
[24] For a report on this, see *Kurdistan* (Organ of the Central Committee of the Democratic Party of Iranian Kurdistan), no. 369, July 22, 2003, p. 8.
[25] See, for example, *Iran Times*, December 13, 2002, and December 27, 2002.

in low-level confrontations with both al-Qaeda and Ansar al-Islam forces. The Iranian government had conveyed its desire to help the Kurdish forces in Iraq to oust the militants from northern Iraq.[26] Although the Ansar forces in the PUK-controlled areas of Iraqi Kurdistan were heavily bombed by the U.S. forces, the regrouped Ansar may have returned to Iraq in a new attempt to carve out a place for themselves.[27]

Iran's stance vis-à-vis Ansar was severely criticized by Mulla Krekar, the groups's purported leader, in an interview published in the independent Iraqi Kurdish newspaper *Hawalati*. Recalling his treatment in Iran, Krekar stated:

> From the outset, it was like a snake, which hates garlic; we came and planted ourselves on its pit. We are a group of Salafis; and we know how much Iran hates the Salafis. We came and emerged just close to it [Iran] in the [border] region of Tora Bora [nickname for Biyarah area in northern Iraq...], as the PUK would call it. At the same time we have a religious and national empathy with Iranian Kurds. It is certain that Iran was not happy with the establishment of our group... Yes, they [Iranians] took me to the airport in a savage and Stalinist manner [and deported me to the Netherlands]....[28]

Despite changes in Iraq and regional geostrategic developments that may create a framework for closer Iranian-Kurdish cooperation in Iraq, there remain serious shortcomings with re-

---

[26] Daniel J. Wakin, "Iran Has Reportedly Pledged Help in Ousting Al-Qaeda From Northern Iraq," *New York Times*, November 6, 2002, p. A14; James C. Helicke, "Iraqi Kurdish Leader: Iran Is Helping to Fight Islamic Militant Group," The Associated Press, November 13, 2002; and Karl Vick, "Iran Denies Care to Militants, Kurdish Official Says," *Washington Post*, March 24, accessed over the Internet.

[27] Jeffrey Fleishman, "Routed During the War, Ansar Returns to Join in Iraq Attacks," *Los Angeles Times*, September 3, 2003, accessed over the Internet.

[28] *Hawlati* (Sulaymaniya), January 27, 2003, as quoted by the BBC Monitoring, January 31, 2003.

spect to Iran's posture towards its own Kurdish population. The Iranian government continues to consider the KDPI as an obstacle to peace and tranquility in Iranian Kurdistan. General Yahya Rahim Safavi, the commander of the Revolutionary Guards, has referred to the KDPI as a "spent force." In a speech given in Sanandaj, Safavi stated that insofar as Iran was concerned, the KDPI was politically "dead." He also accused the KDPI of facilitating the deployment of the Ansar al-Islam in Iran's border regions so as to pave the way for the stationing of American forces in Iraqi Kurdistan.[29]

Similarly, the KDPI has adopted a more assertive stance towards the Islamic Republic since the overthrow of Saddam Hussein's regime. For example, it has accused Iran of colluding with Turkey to strangle Kurdish aspirations in the region.[30] More recently, the KDPI criticized the detention of many members of the *Mojahedin-e Khalq* (MKE), including the arrest of Maryam Rajavi, the wife of the organization's leader Massoud Rajavi, and the confiscation of the assets of the MKE on terrorism-related charges.[31] The MKE's close cooperation with the Baathist regime has been censured by both the Kurds and the Iranians, and the absolute cultish devotion to its leaders that it demands from its members has made it into a despised force among Iranians of all political stripes. The KDPI's ill-timed position on the MKE may diminish its standing among the Iranian opposition groups as well as the Kurds.

Still another problem arising after the fall of Saddam Hussein's government is the status of Iranian Kurdish refugees who have been stranded in Iraq. It is estimated that some 13,000 Iranian Kurds have left Iran for Iraq since the establishment of the Islamic Republic. During Saddam Hussein's reign, many of

---

[29] *Kurdistan* (Organ of the Central Committee of the Democratic Party of Iranian Kurdistan), no. 348, September 6, 2002, p. 1.

[30] Abdullah Bahrami, "Turkiya va Iran, Negarani va Totehay-e Moshtarek" [Turkey and Iran, Common Apprehension and Plots], *Kurdistan* (Organ of the Central Committee of the Democratic Party of Iranian Kurdistan), no. 363, April 20, 2003.

[31] See the KDPI's announcement in *Kurdistan* (Organ of the Central Committee of the Democratic Party of Iranian Kurdistan), no. 367, June 21, 2003, p. 2.

these refugees were housed at the Al Tash camp outside Baghdad. With the fall of Iraq to the American forces, they were left stranded without water, electricity and food.[32]   Some of the Al Tash refugees fled to Jordan and Turkey.   However, most of them were returned to Iraq and a few are still languishing in Turkey.   It would behoove the Iranian government to allow the repatriation of these refugees to their homeland on humanitarian grounds.   Such a move would certainly contribute to the much needed confidence-building measures between the Iranian government and its Kurdish citizens.

Finally, the most assertive challenge to Iran's security has emerged in the aftermath of the Bush administration's new Middle East policy with its emphasis on "regime change" and "axis of evil."   The neoconservative hawks, both inside and outside the U.S. government, have drafted grandiose plans to redraw the geostrategic map of the Middle East.   Neoconservative strategists have long viewed the war against Saddam Hussein's Iraq as a prelude to a more significant intervention in Iran.   Given the difficulty faced by U.S. forces in governing Iraq and the complex nature of Iranian society itself, an assault on Iran will not necessarily involve a direct U.S. military intervention.   When asked what the KDPI's position on a possible U.S. attack on Iran would be, the KDPI's Abdullah Hassanzadeh opined thus: "It is not easy to conjecture about something hypothetical like this. My party and I, however, prefer peaceful solution of conflicts and consider war as a last resort.   We do not like our country to be attacked militarily.   But we would be happy to see the United States, Europe and the rest of the international community to adopt policies in support of the liberation movements of the Iranian nationalities."[33]

---

[32]   For details, see K. Nagasaka, "Iranian Kurdish Refugees in the Al Tash Camp in Iraq," United Nations High Commission for Refugees (UNHCR), reported in the WorldNews Network, July 8, 2003 [http://cgi.wn.com/?action=display&article=21926947&template=worldnews/index.txt@index=recent]. Also, see the KDPI's announcement on this issue, April 30, 2003.

[33] *Kurdistan* (Organ of the Central Committee of the Democratic Party of Iranian Kurdistan), no. 365, May 21, 2003, p. 2.

Such sentiments heighten the fear among the ruling elites in Iran that the Iranian Kurds may be willing to cooperate with the United States in a possible future attack on or encirclement of Iran if the United States provides them with the necessary tools to achieve their political goals. This, coupled with the Pentagon's plans to establish new forward bases in Iraq, including at Bashur in northern Iraq,[34] have created genuine concerns that Kurdistan may turn into a staging ground for an attack on Iran or for destabilizing the country. These and similar fears may be misplaced, but they nevertheless highlight some of the unintended consequences of the war in Iraq for the future of Kurdish-Iranian relations.

---

[34] Thomas Shanker and Eric Schmitt, "Pentagon Expects Long-Term Access to Four Key Bases in Iraq," *New York Times*, April 20, 2003 [http://www.nytimes.com/2003/04/20/international/worldspecial/20BASE.Html].

CHAPTER 10

Obstacles Hindering the Kurdish Question in Iran

Farideh Koohi-Kamali

Introduction

This paper will try to analyze the present situation of the Kurds in Iran, the nature of their relationship with the Iranian government and people, and the obstacles and future for the Kurds in the light of the reform movement in Iran. Though the situation on the ground is still too fluid, one can still identify the following two major obstacles that face the Kurds in Iran: (1) Iranian official nationalism, whether wrapped in a royalist or Islamic flag, and (2) the lack of social justice and democracy in Iran.

Official Nationalism

Let us first see what official nationalism is. From the early nineteenth century, popular national movements, with great emphasis on the national language, played a central role in the formation of the modern nation-state. Nationalism for certain language communities meant that communities with separate languages perceived themselves as separate national groups. The response to this popular, linguistic nationalism was a special kind of nationalism implemented by the ruling elite of empires in the middle of the nineteenth century. Hugh Seton-Watson called it "official nationalism."[1]

Official nationalism was the nationalism of the state and the ruling aristocracy. Characteristics of official nationalism were: state controlled education, state organized propaganda, rewriting of history, a strong army and militarism. The leaders of the powerful states saw it almost as their obligation to impose their nationality on the multi-religious, multi-linguistic and multi-cultural communities they ruled. They did so as an attempt to safeguard the "higher" standard of existence and the unity of the community which, as the result of popular, linguistic nationalism, was breaking apart.

However, the implementation and pursuit of the policies of official nationalism in itself, at a later stage, created new waves of nationalism by the communities seeking independence from the authority of that official nationalism, and reinforced those movements already in existence. Now, let us see how this current in world history translated itself into Iranian history and politics.

In the case of Iran, the doctrine of official nationalism was adopted by Reza Shah and his son, Mohammad Reza Shah, in pursuit of a modern nation-state. The formation of a strong army and establishment of a secular state were the hallmarks of this system. Civil laws were adapted from the European civil codes; the state was in control of education, propaganda, political parties, and the writing of history.[2] The national rights of those who thought of themselves differently from the dominant nationality group were denied.

In most of the Middle East, limited attention given to the right of minorities to self-determination was only recognized by the British and French in mandate and protectorate territories. In

---

[1] Hugh Seton-Watson, *Nations and States: An Enquiry into the Origins of Nations and the Politics of Nationalism* (London: Methuen 1982), pp. 147-48.

[2] The Belgian constitution was the model for the Iranian constitution, with two major adaptations to suit the country's conditions: numerous references to religion and the importance of religious leaders. The constitution also made a point of recognizing the existence of the provincial councils.   Ervand Abrahamian, *Iran Between Two Revolutions* (Princeton, NJ: Princeton University Press, 1982), p. 90.

these territories, the western powers had certain obligations to respect the right of minorities to self-determination and to prepare the territories for the establishment of future independent states based on a constitution, the rule of law, and ideas of democracy. In Iran, however, the state of affairs was very different. Despite the indirect control of the imperialist powers over the country, there existed no international mandate to pressure the government to treat its ethnic minorities with some degree of respect for their rights. Minority rights to self-determination in Iran were not even a matter for consideration.

In many documents and in the minds of many Iranians, Reza Shah is referred to as the founder of modern Iran. He probably deserves such a title, because he did, to some extent, modernize and centralize the country. This was done, however, at the expense of its democratic development and minorities, such as the Kurds.

A very important feature of Reza Khan/Reza Shah's government was its militarism. Reza Shah, even prior to proclaiming himself Shah, aimed at creating a modern army to control the many regions of the country, such as Kurdistan, which were practically autonomous. The new army proved to be effective in establishing the government's authority in the outskirts of the country, defeating many tribal uprisings.

Reza Shah prohibited the appointment of numerous local personalities to official positions in their own locality. The minority communities were also adversely affected culturally and politically because priority was given to the Persians and Persian culture. Economically, the modernization process ignored the fringes of the country. While roads and a communication system were built and factories began to operate in the central and northern provinces, Baluchistan, Kurdistan, and Luristan remained as backward as ever.

After the sedentarization of the nomadic tribes and the formation of a relatively cohesive and strong central government by Reza Shah, the political/military power of the tribes was greatly reduced. Before this, for centuries, the tribes had been instrumental in assisting groups and individuals to achieve power, and once in power, they had tended to depend on the continued support of tribal forces. Obviously, such political influence caused great apprehension for the states, which wished to control the tribes. Kurdish tribes were no exception to this general role. Reza Shah's rise to power meant that Kurdish tribes no longer were able to seriously and systematically threaten the state, because now it was the state which controlled them.

Reza Shah's regime had all the characteristics of "official nationalism," which later was passed on to his son, Muhammad Reza Shah. Kurdish nationalism developed as a reaction to the Pahlavis' "official nationalism."

Kurdish Nationalism

How Kurdish nationalism in Iran developed to the stage that is today is a subject for another paper. However, in order for the national consciousness of a community to materialize into a fully developed national movement, that community has to pass through several political and social phases. Kurds in Iran had to go through a transformation from a nationally conscious community to a fully developed national movement. Reza Shah's rule is the start of the developing process of Kurdish nationalism in Iran, where Kurds began to see themselves as an ethnic/national community separate from the other groups. Kurds not only felt a sense of community because of their distinct language, common culture, history and ancestry, but also because of the treatment they received from the central governments. This was particularly true during Reza Shah's reign, when Persian official nationalism, in centralizing the country, chose repressive measures towards the practically self-ruled rebellious regions of the country such as Kurdistan.

The Islamic Republic and the Kurds in Iran

The Islamic revolution provided a golden opportunity for Kurdish nationalism, which by 1979 had become a well-organized movement. Kurdistan stood in the front line of opposition to the Shah's regime. The Iranian revolution, which was welcomed as the harbinger of democracy in Iran by the opposition to the Shah, failed to live up to people's expectations. Despite promises, the Kurds received very harsh treatment. Later, the war between Iran and Iraq was thought to provide a golden opportunity for the Kurds of both countries. However, this also proved to be another period of repression for the Kurds. A report by the Minority Rights Group on the Kurds stated that: "by early 1984 a Kurdish-controlled region of Iran had been virtually eliminated. At least 27,500 Kurds were reckoned to have died by this stage, of which only 2500 were fighters."[3]

Why did the situation for the Kurds not change with the Islamic Republic? The simple answer is that the Islamic Republic could not have responded favorably to the Kurdish demands because it is a non-democratic regime, a situation very similar to its predecessors. If there was any misunderstanding at the beginning of the revolution in Iran about the intentions of the regime, it did not take long to change. The idea of an autonomous Kurdistan, or any autonomous region in Iran, does not accord with the idea of the universality and expansion of Islam, as it was understood by Khomeini and his followers. Khomeini's attitude to the nationalism of minorities was that "there is no difference between Muslims who speak different languages.... It is very probable that such problems have been created by those who do not wish the Muslim countries to be united.... They create the issues of nationalism, of pan-Iranism, pan-Turkisim, and such isms, which are contrary to Islamic doctrines."[4] As Khomeini expressed repeatedly, in Islam and Islamic countries there is no room for such divisive ideas, which aim at weakening the unity of the Islamic community.

Despite all the claims about the universalism of Islam, we have seen too often in the last few decades in Iran that when Islam is the state ideology, it is bound to act within the limits of national boundaries. Since it is also non-democratic, it would have its own version of official nationalism with such characteristics as state-controlled education, propaganda, political participation, and, since the state is an Islamic one, control over many

---

[3] David McDowall, *The Kurds*. no. 23 (London: Minority Rights Group, 1989).

[4] Charles G. MacDonald, "The Kurdish Question in the 1980s," in Milton J. Esman, and Itamar Rabinovich, ed., *Ethnicity, Pluralism, and State in the Middle East* (Ithaca, NY: Cornell University Press, 1988), p. 245.

aspects of what has often been thought of as the private sphere. For Kurds, this meant the same treatment as before, with additional limitations that the rest of the country was also experiencing.

Social Justice and Democracy

The question could be asked whether Kurds could achieve their political and cultural demands within a non-democratic state in Iran. Past experience would suggest a simple NO answer. A non-democratic Iran, regardless of its ruling regimes, is unable to recognize the rights of ethnic groups, as this would immediately lead to competing centers of power. It is important to note that, throughout the history of the Kurdish movement in Iran, Kurds always have seen themselves as part of Iranian society and politics. This is true even at two significant moments in their history, when it seemed as if the Kurds had the upper hand in their relationship with the Iranian government: (1) during the Mahabad Republic, when at all times peaceful negotiations were sought, and (2) during the Iranian Revolution, when Kurds were the most recognized and well-organized opposition group.

One slogan has always been the focus of the political demands of the Kurds in Iran, regardless of their situation: "Democracy for Iran, autonomy for Kurdistan." It is critical to remind ourselves that the Kurdish movement in Iran is the only one among the main Kurdish movements in the three countries containing the bulk of the worldwide Kurdish population, which has never demanded a separate state. This is an understanding that the Kurdish movements in Turkey and Iraq arrived at much later. The reason for this relates to the relationships between the Kurds and the rest of Iran. Thus, it is necessary to briefly examine some of the factors which have contributed to the Iranian Kurdish interest in pushing for autonomy, rather than independence.

Why Do the Kurds in Iran See Their Future in Iran?

The Kurds in Iran have more in common with other members of the Iranian opposition than with the other Kurds in the region. It might not be a politically correct statement regarding the national aspirations for a united country of Kurds, but it is the reality. Let us look at a few of the factors which contribute to this reality.

(1) Demography. The Kurds in Iran are a smaller proportion of the total national population of Iran, than are the Kurds in Turkey or Iraq. It is estimated that only 10 per cent of the Iranian population is Kurdish, as opposed to 19 per cent in Turkey and 23 per cent in Iraq.[5]

(2) Culture. The Iranians and Kurds share a common history and culture. Their common celebration of *Newruz* is a good example. Furthermore, the Persian language is similar to Kurdish. One, therefore, would expect a degree of mutual comprehension not easily duplicated between Kurds and Arabic or Turkish speakers.

(3) Inter-ethnic Conflict. There have not been significant instances of inter-ethnic hostility between Kurdish and Iranian people. This is to be contrasted with what has happened in Iraq and Turkey.

(4) Economy. The perception is that a connection with the larger Iranian economy would be beneficial for the Kurds in Iran. Kurdistan has some possible avenues of development, both in agriculture and in mining, from which the country as a whole can benefit. However, its infrastructure is poorly developed. As well as having fewer roads, hospitals, and schools compared with the rest of the country, it has far fewer doctors, nurses, and teachers per capita. Economic development would be further hindered without the support of a central government.

It might be argued that the relatively underdeveloped state of the Kurdish economy is a powerful argument for independence and separation from Iran. However, in the absence of a larger Kurdish nation, or a Kurdish Diaspora with significant capital resources, the road to further economic development of Iranian Kurdistan runs through Tehran.

The same economic characteristic led, for a time, to a very different political demand from the Turkish Kurds, but this is, at

---

[5] David McDowall, *The Kurds: A Nation Denied* (London: Minority Rights Publications, 1992), p. 12.

least in part, due to the lack of any recognition of their identity by past Turkish governments, which is not precisely the case in Iran.

(5) Religion. The Kurds are predominantly Sunni, but there is a considerable number of Shiite Kurds concentrated in southern Iranian Kurdistan. The statistics show that about 20 percent of the Kurds are Shiites.[6]

(6) The Iranian Government. The Iranian government's attitude towards its Kurdish population, is, to some extent, the result of a combination of cultural concession and political repression that has historically characterized previous regimes' dealings with the Kurds. Unlike Iraq and Turkey, Iranian governments have not, at least in recent history, pursued either a policy of "ethnic cleansing," or one of systematic forced assimilation, with their Kurdish population.

It is true that Kurdish areas are among the less developed regions of Iran, but Kurdistan is not the only one which is underdeveloped. It is also true that Kurds have been tortured and executed all through the modern history of Iran, but it is also important to bear in mind that they were persecuted not as Kurds but as part of a larger opposition movement. It is fair to say that, generally speaking, it is not the cultural identity of the Kurds that bothers the governments in Iran, but their political aspirations that challenge the central government's authority.

(7) Iranian Kurds. Kurdish nationalism has not explicitly been transnational in nature, a result of Kurds in different countries having been subjected to the different conditions and political environments in those countries. This ensures that the overall unity of the Kurds will be a rather difficult goal to achieve, and one which has not been explicitly formulated in the past. Furthermore, it has so far not been an evident part of the Iraqi or Turkish Kurdish programs to include appeals to Iranian Kurds or refer to Iranian Kurdistan.

---

[6] Martin van Bruinessen, "Kurdish Society, Ethnicity, Nationalism and Refugee Problems," in Philip G. Kreyenbroek and Stefan Sperl, ed., *The Kurds: A Contemporary Overview* (London and New York: Routledge, 1992), p. 36.

This makes the formation of a united state of Kurdistan highly unlikely, not so much because Kurds are divided by their dialects or their political expressions, but simply because of the political realities in the region. Strong Iranian and Turkish governments and lack of international support are the main aspects of such reality.

Iran's mainstream Kurdish movement, the Kurdistan Democratic Party of Iran (KDPI), while not forswearing violence, has shown interest in negotiation. As mentioned above, its declared aim since 1946 includes autonomy, not independence. The Kurdish movement in Iran has not been a separatist movement.

Such an attitude still exists amongst most of the Kurdish leaders in Iran. The late Abdul Rahman Ghassemlou was convinced of the need to pursue a peaceful settlement for autonomy with the Iranian government. In 1979, in a letter presented to Ayatollah Khomeini, Ghassemlou formulated his views on Kurdish aspirations:

Our people have fought for two major goals: the overthrow of the dictatorship and its replacement by a humane regime which would respect political freedoms and rights throughout Iran, and the realization of national rights for all nations in the form of autonomy or a federation in free Iran. As there are several oppressed groups in Iran, the most suitable formula would be a federal system.... Autonomy, or a federal structure, is in no way a contradiction with the unity and internal integrity of Iran.[7]

Iranian Kurds not only realize that militarily they cannot win a war—after 1980, when the Iranian army entered Kurdistan, armed struggle was practically abandoned—but furthermore, they probably also realize that war against the government would likely be hopeless. The military alternative is becoming more and more useless because engagement in modern warfare is dangerous when one is not properly equipped. The respective states in the region have far more advanced weaponry, destructive forces and means of control than the Kurds can match.

Therefore, the Kurds in Iran seek a peaceful solution, grounds for compromise, and guarantees which safeguard their cultural heritage and identity, and allow for economic development and a

---

[7] MacDonald, "The Kurdish Question in the 1980s," p. 242.

large measure of self-rule. The Kurds do this within the frame-work of the struggle for democracy in Iran.

Participation of the Kurds in the Iranian Reform Movement

To understand the future of the Kurds in Iran, we need to understand the present situation in connection with the reformist movement in Iran, and how the future of the Kurds is an integral part of the future of Iran as a whole. This is how it is understood and being articulated by the Kurds themselves. Respect for ethnic and women's rights, social justice, and political freedom and democracy are part of an indivisible package. It is within a democratic Iran that Kurdish rights would be respected. The reality of Kurdish politics is that its fate is tied to the fate of Iranian politics as a whole. Despite the political suppression, imprisonment, executions, and social and economic deprivation, the Kurds, similar to the other ethnic groups in Iran, have attempted to work within the system. The example of the participation of the Kurds in the recent Iranian parliamentary and local elections demonstrated the great extent to which the Kurds are part of the general opposition politics in Iran.

The 1997 presidential election, which resulted in a landslide victory for Mohammad Khatami, also gave hope to the Kurds. Khatami promised greater political and social freedom for the people and a better economic situation. The Kurds, just like others, though skeptical, participated in the election to protest against the policies of the hardliners and to encourage the ideas of the reformists. They overwhelmingly voted for the reformist platform, demanding more local representation in parliament and a larger allocation of local positions for Kurdish officials.

Abdullah Ramazanzadeh, a Shiite Kurd, became the first Governor General of Kurdistan. He appointed several Sunni Muslims to important positions, including key roles in economic and financial affairs. Ramazanzadeh not only enjoyed immense popularity among the local people, but also received endorsement from President Khatami for his reformist ideas. His ascent to power and the degree of support he received from his constituencies should all be seen as part of the attempt by the Kurds to achieve their demands through peaceful and participatory representative methods. These developments coincided with an important political change in Kurdistan, the end of military control of the region and the start of law enforcement control.

The lifting of nearly two decades of military control in Kurdistan was perceived as a great victory for the reformist government of Khatami and the Kurdish delegates. However, the Kurdish representatives, like the others who demanded change, realized the obstacles in achieving their goals. The most dramatic manifestation of their demands for equal treatment came in the form of a mass resignation of Kurdish representatives.

In October 2001, a legislator and five deputies of the Majlis from the province of Kurdistan collectively resigned in protest, accusing Khatami's government of double standards in discriminating against the Kurds. In the letter they presented to the interior minister, they asked for equality and social justice. One of their main concerns was their unhappiness with the appointment of a non-Kurd as the new governor general after the popular Ramazanzadeh had been summoned to Teheran to become a member of President Khatami's Cabinet. The mass resignations were a political embarrassment for Khatami's government, which also has had to deal with many other political problems.

In a report by the United Nations on human rights issues, including the treatment of minorities in Iran, the Special Representative of the Commission on Human Rights, Maurice Danby Copithorne, summarized the major concerns of the Kurds.

* Violent deaths of individual Kurds, apparently the result of reckless or intentional acts of the law enforcement forces.

* The recent kidnapping and death of a popular local cultural figure.

*Death sentences imposed and in most cases carried out against Kurdish activists.

* The continuing refusal of the authorities to allow Kurdish to be taught at any level in schools in Kurdistan.

* The limited use of Kurdish in the print and electronic media and, even then, usually only as a translation of Persian; the air time for Kurdish programming is "drastically shorter" than it was before 1979.

* Various forms of economic discrimination, including access to jobs in general; in the case of the Piranshehr Sugar Company, the

discharge in May 2001 of 80 percent of the Kurdish employees by a non-Kurdish president, and their replacement by workers of other ethnicities "and those who collaborate with the Pasdaran."

* The use of Kurdish territory, particularly Kermanshah province, as a "resting place" for drug addicts, criminals and other difficult groups from around the country.

* The disallowance of the election to the Majlis of two Kurds representing Orumieh and Naghade districts.

* The gross under-representation of Kurdish districts in the Majlis, as also perhaps other districts dominated by other ethnic groups, as seen for example in the failure to add any new seats for Kurdish districts in the latest (fifth) Majlis redistribution.[8]

Many analysts believe that the Kurds, as did other Iranians, cast their votes in the most recent presidential elections not to endorse Khatami, but to reject the hardliners. There is an element of "rejection voting," but many Kurds genuinely hoped that the reformist government would act on the promises of "Iran for all Iranians" and a greater recognition of their minority rights. Their disappointment with the reformist government is the same as that of the rest of the country, which had put its trust in the Khatami government for change. As mentioned above, Kurdish politics is, and has been, an integral part of the bigger political picture in Iran.

Another recent example of solidarity between the Kurds and other opposition groups was seen with the recent students' uprising in Iran. Reports from the sit-down protest at Sanandaj University indicated that the students had the same demands as the students in Tehran University. The International Relations Bureau of the KDPI reported that the students at the Teachers' College of the University of Sanandaj organized a demonstration on 10 June 2003 to use the lack of coolers in dormitories to protest in support of the dissident movement of the universities all over Iran. The university officials requested assistance from the security forces and anti-riot troops to contain the crowd. The arrival of these forces on campus angered the students to the extent that they threw rocks and bottles at the forces from inside the buildings. The regime's forces succeeded in dispersing the

---

[8] International Relations Bureau of KDPI on 24 June 2003.

students using brutal beatings and firing in the air. Several students were detained and charged with "disorder and riots. . . . Their whereabouts are not known so far."[9]

Another report declared that the students of Kurdistan University (Sanandaj), in support of the dissident movement of the students in Iran, attempted to gather at the university campus on 21 June 2003, and along with chanting slogans against the regime, demanded the release of the detained students. The special units and the security forces followed their arrival, and gave warnings to disperse to the students; however, the students continued their protests on campus. The security forces, attempting to prevent the students from joining the general public, surrounded the university. Following two days of protests, the anti-riot special units attacked the students, which resulted in the death of one student and the detainment of 150. The university fell under the occupation of the regime hard-liners. Further protests occurred in the "Mordabiyan" parts of Sanandaj.[10]

In addition, it was reported on 22 June 2003, that a considerable number of people from the city of Mahabad, in support of the dissident movement of the students, gathered in the center of the city to shout slogans against the regime and in support of the Kurdish movement. These people also attempted to distribute a portrait of Ghassemlou among the people. "The security forces, aided by the special anti-riot units, encircled the demonstrators; however, they avoided confrontation with the protesters, so the crowd dispersed. As a result of these events, the security forces in all the Kurdish regions are on high alert, and most of the recruits have been ordered to work two shifts."[11]

In an interview in May 2003, Abdullah Hassanzadeh, the general secretary of the KDPI, told the *Financial Times* that his party was willing to open negotiations with Tehran, provided the Islamic Republic "declared its willingness publicly." He emphasized that he wanted "Kurdish rights," but he played down his past commitment to replace the Islamic Republic with a democratic, secular state. Interestingly enough, the secretary general

---

[9] *Ibid.*
[10] *Ibid.*
[11] *Ibid.*

of the party welcomed the overthrow of Saddam Hussein, and hinted that the strong US position in a new Iraq would put pressure on Tehran. However, he also added that "we do not want outside interference in Iran, but we would like the international community to support the Iranian opposition."[12] After explaining the difficulties for the KDPI to continue armed struggle after 1980 when the Iranian army and pasdarans took control of the Kurdish regions, he then went on to say: "We continue [unarmed] activities inside Iran . . . because we no longer have a military presence, [and] the regime has stopped shelling Kurdish areas."[13]

Iranian Kurds voted overwhelmingly in 1997 for Mohammad Khatami, the reformist president, despite a call by the KDPI to abstain, and there are at least 30 Kurdish deputies in the 290-strong Iranian parliament. The number of Kurdish publications has increased, although the language is not allowed in schools and the Kurdish region is one of Iran's poorest.

Conclusion

The Kurdish issue in Iran should be seen as part of the Iranian peoples' demands for political freedom and democracy, as well as recognition and respect for ethnic and women's rights. An Iran that respects its women would also respect its different ethnic groups. Therefore, what happens to Iranian Kurds depends very much on what happens to the rest of Iran. The main obstacle preventing the Kurds in Iran from achieving their goals has always been, and still is, the lack of democracy and social justice in Iran.

---

[12] Gareth Smyth, "Kurdish Party Sets Out Terms for Talks with Tehran," PDKI-Canada/Daily News and Reports in English (FT.com site), 2 May 2003.

[13] *Ibid.*

CHAPTER 11

Durable Solution for the Internally Displaced Iraqi Kurds: Legal and Practical Considerations

David Fisher

The people of Iraq have suffered numerous and well-recorded horrors over the last few decades. While many disfavored ethnic and religious groups, including the Marsh Arabs, Turkmans, Assyrians and certain Shiite factions, have found themselves targets of the Baathist regime, the Kurds have been the hardest hit. The Iraqi government's deliberate and, at times, genocidal campaign to force the Kurds from the fertile and oil-rich lands that they have occupied for centuries in the northern governorates has generated forced displacement on an epic scale. Whereas significant numbers of Kurds and other Iraqis driven from their homes have gone on to flee the country, hundreds of thousands have remained within national borders, becoming what is known in humanitarian parlance as "internally displaced persons" or "IDPs." Once ignored by the West, Kurdish and other Iraqi IDPs have become the engines of some extraordinary shifts in the global security order and in international law, in particular with regard to an emerging doctrine of humanitarian intervention.

Now that "regime change" has been partially completed with the removal of the Saddam Hussein government from power, but with the question of what is to permanently succeed it as yet undecided, the internally displaced Kurds of Iraq are again set to test the limits of legal and institutional frameworks for humanitarian response, in particular with respect to the issue of their return. Moreover, as noted in a recent study by John Fawcett and Victor Tanner,[1] the approach taken by the various players—including the American and allied forces, the nascent Iraqi government, the Kurdish authorities and the United Nations—to the question of the resolution of the displacement issue in northern Iraq will serve as a litmus test for the future direction of the country. Unfortunately, the decisions they take on these questions in the coming months will be greatly complicated by ongoing ambiguity over the roles and responsibilities of the various players, and their room for maneuver is limited in the still-dangerous environment that prevails in Iraq, as evidenced by the recent bombing of the UN compound in Baghdad which killed, among others, the UN's top official in the country, Mr. Sergio Vieira de Mello.[2]

This paper will attempt to illustrate some of the legal and practical questions that face the various authorities with regard to issues of the return and resettlement of internally displaced Kurds in northern Iraq, with a focus on the rights of the displaced. After reviewing the history and situation of the internally displaced Kurds, it will discuss the relevant international normative framework and how it applies to the particular issues of IDPs and the responsibilities of the various authorities. It will conclude with recommendations on several issues on which this framework offers concrete guidance.

Background to the Kurdish Displacement in Iraq

The Kurds have long suffered from discrimination at the hands of the distant powers that have ruled over their territory in what is now northern Iraq. Various rulers, starting with the Ottomans

---

[1] John Fawcett and Victor Tanner, *The Internally Displaced People of Iraq* (Washington DC: Brookings Institution-SAIS Project on Internal Displacement, 2002), p. 2, available at http://www. brookings. edu/ fp/projects/IDP/articles/iraqreport.htm.

[2] "Top UN Envoy Killed in Baghdad Blast," BBC News August 20, 2003, available at http://www.bbc.co.uk.

and continuing through the British and Iraqi monarchy, have encouraged non-Kurds to move into Kurdish areas, for example by
building additional housing for them and employing them in key
civil service posts, in hopes of quelling Kurdish aspirations—and
periodic military attempts—to gain independence.[3]   Kurdish
culture has been regularly suppressed over the years and the
Kurdish language banned in schools and in the press.[4] The discovery of vast oil reserves—considered the largest and highest
quality in Iraq—in the region of Kirkuk in the 1920s, and the
increasing importance of the water resources of the Greater Zab,
Lesser Zab and Diyala Rivers, rendered subsequent Iraqi administrations all the more determined to strengthen their control over
the Kurdish north.[5]   This eventually expressed itself not only
through intentional displacement of Kurds by government forces,
but a genocidal campaign designed to destroy the Kurdish presence almost entirely.

Arabization

By the 1930s, the Iraqi regime had begun not only moving non-
Kurds into the north, but also sometimes moving the Kurds
themselves off of their lands.[6] However, it was not until after the

---

[3] Nouri Talabany, "The Displacement of Kurds and Others in the
Kirkuk Region," Statement to the Conference on Refugees and Displaced   Persons,   Paris,   July   4,   2002,   available   at
http://kurdweb.humanrights.de; Middle East Watch; and *Genocide in
Iraq: The Anfal Campaign Against the Kurds* (New York: Human
Rights Watch, 1993), hereinafter, *HRW Anfal Report*, available at
http://www.hrw.org.

[4] Talabany, "The Dispalcement of Kurds and Others in the Kirkuk Region"; and David McDowall, *A Modern History of the Kurds* (New
York: I.B. Taurus, 1996), p. 75.

[5] Fawcett & Tanner, *The Internally Displaced People of Iraq*, p. 3;
McDowall, *A Modern History of the Kurds*, p. 7; and Human Rights
Watch, "Iraq: Forcible Expulsion of Ethnic Minorities," hereinafter
"HRW, Forcible Expulsion Report 8,"(March 2003.

[6] "HRW, Forcible Expulsion Report 8"; Brenda Oppermann, "The
Many Causes of Internal Displacement in Central and Northern Iraq:
Consequences and Recommendations," Refugees International, 2003,
available at http://refugeesinternational.org.

second accession to power of the Baath party in 1968 that truly systematic efforts to "ethnically cleanse" the Kurds and other minorities, including the Turkmans and Assyrians, began to emerge.[7]

It was the Kurds themselves who facilitated the first Baathist takeover in 1963, having weakened the government of coup leader Brigadier Abdul Karim Qasim through three years of revolt. Kurdish leaders agreed with the Baathists to withhold attack while the latter engaged government forces in exchange for promises of autonomy.[8] However, upon the success of the putsch, relations broke down over Kurdish demands for autonomy and a proportionate share of oil revenue for the Kurdish region, in particular from the area of Kirkuk.[9] In support of its rejection of Kurdish claims, the government pointed to a 1947 census indicating that Kurds made up only 25 percent of the population of Kirkuk town, and 53 percent of the surrounding province.[10] This attention to the ethnic proportions of the population around the oilfields has been an enduring theme in the Iraqi-Kurdish conflict.

The government responded to the stalemated negotiations in 1963 by rounding up and massacring 80 men in Sulaymaniya, a portent of atrocities later to come.[11] This led to more fighting between the Kurds and the government and the forcible eviction by government forces of dozens of Kurdish villages that were then repopulated with Arabs.[12]

Intermittent periods of Kurdish revolt against Iraqi rule continued between 1963 and 1975. By 1970, this conflict had resulted in 60,000 Kurdish casualties, 3,000 Kurdish villages (representing 75 percent of the total) seriously damaged, and hundreds of thousands of Kurds displaced.[13] Around this time, too, Iraq began expelling from the country tens of thousands of per-

---

[7]   "HRW, Forcible Expulsion Report 8"; McDowall, *A Modern History of the Kurds*, pp. 390-420

[8]   McDowall, *A Modern History of the Kurds*, p. 313.

[9]   "HRW, Forcible Expulsion Report 8."

[10]   *Ibid.*

[11]   McDowal, *A Modern History of the Kurds*, p. 314.

[12]   *Ibid.*

[13]   *Ibid.*, pp. 319, 326.

sons of one sub-group of Kurds—the Faili—who had lived in Iraq since the time of Ottoman rule, on the grounds that they lacked Iraqi citizenship and should be considered Iranians.[14]

After the withdrawal of Iranian support to the Kurdish separatists incident to the 1975 Algiers Agreement between Iran and Iraq and the collapse of the latest revolt, the Iraqi government embarked on a sustained campaign of "Arabization" to change the ethnic equation in the north.[15] Over the next three years, the government razed an estimated 1,400 Kurdish villages, deporting at least 600,000 Kurds to *mujamaat* "collective" resettlement camps, and others to the south of the country.[16] The government also moved up to a million Kurds away from disputed areas within the Kurdish lands, replacing them with Egyptian and Arab Iraqi settlers.[17] The authorities also resorted to restricting Kurds' ability to alienate and purchase property, providing financial rewards to Arabs taking Kurdish wives, transferring Kurdish civil servants and soldiers away from disputed areas and Arabizing place names.[18] The 1977 census clearly reflected the results, with significant drops in Kurdish and Turkman populations in Kirkuk compared to earlier tallies.[19]

The Arabization campaign continued through the 1980s, with an estimated 4,500 villages destroyed between 1976 and 1986.[20] Before the 1987 census, respondents from cleared areas were required to live in settlement camps or risk losing their citizenship, being "legally" considered as military deserters, and punished accordingly.[21]

Anfal.
In 1987, the campaign against the Kurds escalated yet further. That year, Ali Hasan al-Majid, cousin of Saddam Hussein, was appointed as Secretary General of the Northern Bureau of the

---

[14] *Ibid.*, p. 330.
[15] "HRW, Forcible Expulsion Report 9."
[16] McDowall, *A Modern History of the Kurds*, p. 339.
[17] *Ibid.*, p. 340.
[18] *Ibid.*
[19] "HRW, Forcible Expulsion Report 10."
[20] *Ibid.*
[21] *Ibid.*

Baath Party Organization, with extraordinary powers to issue mandatory orders to all military, civilian and security agencies.[22] His appointment grew out the regime's fury over signs of collusion between the Kurdish parties and its Iranian enemy, and al-Majid's response to that challenge was equally furious.[23]

The Anfal, (or "spoils of war"), was an organized campaign of mass murder and destruction designed to wipe out the Kurdish presence in the targeted areas. Iraqi military units, accompanied by pro-government Kurdish militia (the *josh*), surrounded villages, killed the inhabitants and bulldozed them into the earth.[24] Between 150,000 and 200,000 civilians were killed.[25] Thousands more "disappeared" and over a million were reportedly driven from their homes.[26] Over the course of one year, more than 2,000 villages were destroyed. Moreover, al-Majid ordered the use of chemical weapons on the Kurdish civilians, most infamously against the town of Halabja where 5,000 civilians died.[27] It was later estimated that 250 towns and villages were subjected to chemical bombardment in the 1987-88 period.[28] Western reaction was largely mute.[29]

The Persian Gulf War and 1991 Uprising

The memory of the Anfal was very fresh when, at the public invitation of the first President George Bush in the aftermath of the first Iraq war, the Kurds in the north and Shiite Arabs in the south rose in revolt against the Hussein regime.[30] Both the Arabs and the Kurds were quickly routed, and approximately 2,000,000 Kurdish civilians fled what they feared would be another massacre, as the Americans and British (the "Coalition")

---

[22] *HRW Anfal Report.*
[23] *Ibid.*
[24] Fawcett & Tanner, *The Internally Displaced People of Iraq*, p. 10.
[25] McDowall, *A Modern History of the Kurds*, p. 359.
[26] *Ibid.*, p. 357; *HRW Anfal Report.*
[27] McDowall, *A Modern History of the Kurds*, p. 358.
[28] Fawcett & Tanner, *The Internally Displaced People of Iraq*, p. 10.
[29] McDowall, *A Modern History of the Kurds*, p. 362.
[30] Fawcett & Tanner, *The Internally Displaced People of Iraq*, p. 11; McDowall, *A Modern History of the Kurds*, p. 372.

stood by. Iran accepted 1,500,000 Kurdish refugees, but an additional 500,000 were blocked at the Turkish border.[31] Fearful that its victory would be tainted, the Coalition called for the Security Council to act.[32] On April 5, 1991, the Security Council passed Resolution 688, the first such resolution ever to authorize international intervention for the express purpose of protecting civilians from their own government.[33] Resolution 688 did not expressly refer to *military* intervention or to "Chapter VII" of the UN Charter, which is the operative section concerning military intervention. Nevertheless, the Coalition subsequently declared the northwestern portion of Iraq north of the 36th parallel a "safe haven" and "no fly zone," which they were prepared to enforce militarily pursuant to Resolution 688.[34]

Kurdish In-Fighting.

The imposition of the "safe haven" allowed the displaced Kurds to return from the border and govern themselves with near complete autonomy for over a decade. However, by 1994, the competition between the two main political factions, the Kurdistan Democratic Party (KDP) and the Patriotic Union of Kurdistan (PUK) descended into armed conflict, which continued intermittently for the next three years.[35] During the conflict, adherents of rival parties were expelled or fled from both KDP and PUK areas.[36] Some of these were able to return after a cease-fire was agreed in 1997 and the parties moved to create a single governing structure.[37] Additional displacements were caused by fighting between the members of the main Kurdish parties and the Turkey-based Kurdistan Workers Party (PKK) and the *Jund al-Islam*.[38] As of 2000, it was estimated that over 92,000 Kurds remained displaced as a result of these internecine conflicts.[39]

---

[31] *Ibid.*
[32] *Ibid.*
[33] *Ibid.*
[34] *Ibid.*
[35] McDowall, *A Modern History of the Kurds*, p. 386.
[36] Fawcett & Tanner, *The Internally Displaced People of Iraq*, p. 13.
[37] *Ibid.*
[38] *Ibid.*
[39] *Ibid.*, p. 16.

Post Persian Gulf War Arabization.

The "safe haven" declared by the Coalition did not include the cities of Kirkuk and Mosul, and the Iraqi regime continued and even accelerated its Arabization campaign in these areas through the 1990s, albeit with methods not as extreme as the Anfal.[40] The government again targeted Kurds, Assyrians and Turkmans, using a range of tactics. Non-Arabs were pressured to sign forms "correcting" their ethnic identity to "Arab," join the Baath Party and/or volunteer for paramilitary forces.[41] Those who refused were arrested and ordered expelled, after "voluntarily" signing documents stating that they had freely chosen to depart.[42] Departing families were forced to leave most of their belongings behind. The government also acted more nakedly at times, simply seizing farms from non-Arabs without prior notice and reallocating them to new Arab owners as part of a purported land reform campaign.[43] Arab settlers were offered additional incentives, including cash grants and monopolies in oil-for-food related businesses, to encourage them to move north.[44] As a result, ethnicity-based displacement in these areas continued up to the eve of the 2003 Iraq war.

The 2003 Iraq War and its Aftermath

In the months leading up to the start of the 2003 war in Iraq on March 20, the United Nations humanitarian community grew convinced that the impending conflict could cause massive new internal displacement. The capacity of Iraqi civilians to withstand the ravages of conflict and remain in their homes was thought to be at its lowest ebb after decades of war, ten years of sanctions, and an equally long dependency by an astonishing 80 percent of the population on the central food rationing system.[45] Several neighboring countries had made public statements about

---

[40] "HRW, Forcible Expulsion Report 6."
[41] *Ibid.*, p. 13.
[42] *Ibid.*, pp. 13-14.
[43] *Ibid.*, p. 24.
[44] Fawcett & Tanner, *The Internally Displaced People of Iraq*, p. 12.
[45] United Nations, "Flash Appeal for the Humanitarian Requirements of the Iraq Crisis," March 28, 2003, p. 9.

their intentions to block would-be refugees at their borders, and several of them began turning away those seeking to flee before the start of war.[46] It was further feared that Turkish forces would invade in the north to quell any Kurdish attempts to use the situation to consolidate their autonomous position. A confidential UN planning document that was leaked to the press in January 2003 predicted that up to 2,000,000 additional Iraqis might be internally displaced in the event of new war, and between 600,000 and 1,450,000 might become refugees.[47]

In the event, there were early reports of several hundred thousands of persons newly displaced in northern Iraq, mainly in anticipation of fighting rather than as a direct result of it, including a number of Kurds leaving Kirkuk for fear of Iraqi retaliation against them.[48] However, the overwhelming majority of these

---

[46] Kim Gattas, "Syria Blocks Iraqi Exodus," BBC World News, March, 19 2003, on file with author; Refugees International, "Kuwait Will Not Admit Iraqi Refugees," available at http://www.refugeesinternational.org; "Iran Ready to Help Iraqi Refugees Despite Lack of Support," Deutsche Presse Agentur, March 13, 2003, on file with author noting that Iran had announced plans to assist Iraqi refugees but only on Iraqi soil at the border; "Oxfam Sets up Iraqi Camps," BBC News March 21, 2003, available at http://news.bbc.co.uk, noting that Turkey had given indications of unwillingness to accept Iraqi refugees.

[47] "Integrated Humanitarian Preparedness and Response Plan for Iraq and Neighboring Countries," January 16, 2003, p. 9, available at http://www.casi.org.uk/info/undocs/internal.html. The report was posted on the Internet by a British NGO, the Center for Economic and Social Rights, which reportedly obtained it from "several UN personnel who believe that the potential humanitarian impact of war is a matter of global public concern that should be discussed fully and openly." See CESR website, cited above.

[48] E.g., Sebastian Alison, "Rising Flow of Fearful Iraqi Kurds Leaves Kirkuk," Reuters, March 13, 2003, on file with author; International Committee of the Red Cross, "Operational Update on Iraq 20-25 March 2003," Mach 27, 2003 hereinafter "March ICRC Update," available at http://www.icrc.org; United States Committee For Refugees, "Updates on Developments Concerning Iraqi Refugees and Displaced Persons," March 25, 2003, available at http://www.refugees.org.

persons were said to have quickly returned to their homes.[49] With the lack of UN presence in the center and south, reporting on population movements in these areas during the war was minimal, but reports from the International Committee of the Red Cross and other observers indicated that very few fled their homes.[50]

As it became clear that the conflict would not provoke a massive outflow, and with the end of "major combat" declared by President George Bush on May 2, 2003,[51] humanitarian planners concerned with displacement turned to the issues of the "old caseload" of IDPs and refugees and, in particular, to planning for their return and reintegration.[52]

Even before the end of the war, however, a wave of new displacements began to occur in the north as returning Kurds turned out the Arab occupants of properties they claimed as their own, with the reported encouragement of local authorities of the Patriotic Union of Kurdistan (PUK).[53] At least some of these expulsions were accomplished at gunpoint, and there were reports of some killings.[54] However, many others occurred spontaneously, as Arabs fled properties to avoid facing returning Kurds.

The initial reaction of Coalition forces to these expulsions was confused. In some areas, Coalition troops reportedly did nothing, and in others they forcibly removed Kurds and reversed their ad hoc expulsions.[55] However, after several weeks, a policy

---

[49] Norwegian Refugee Council Global IDP Project, *Global IDP Database: Iraq*, hereinafter, *Global IDP Database*, available at http://www.idpproject.org.

[50] International Committee of the Red Cross, "Operational Update on Iraq 20-25 March 2003."

[51] "Bush Calls End of Major Combat," CNN, May 2, 2003, available at http://www.cnn.com.

[52] "Humanitarian Appeal for Iraq: Revised Inter-Agency Appeal," June 2003, pp. 15, 39-41, on file with author.

[53] Human Rights Watch, "Iraq: Killings, Expulsions on the Rise in Kirkuk," April 15, 2003, available at http://www.hrw.org.

[54] *Ibid*; see also Brenda Oppermann, "The Many Causes of Internal Displacement in Central and Northern Iraq: Consequences and Recommendations."

[55] Interview by author with UNOCHI source, June 2003.

was decided upon to prevent expulsions pending the creation of a process to deal with property claims in an orderly fashion. Enforced by the American military, the policy was agreed to by Kurdish leaders, despite initial hesitation.[56] Nevertheless, an UNOPS mission to the Khanaquin and Kifri areas of Diyala found ongoing expulsions of Arabs by Kurdish groups as of August 2003.[57] Many of the Arabs thus displaced are reportedly squatting in public buildings or living in other makeshift accommodations.[58]

The Current State of Kurdish Displacement in Iraq.
Many Kurds and persons from other ethnic groups remain displaced within and from the north as a result of all of the foregoing events, whereas others have returned or permanently resettled. Just before the 2003 war, it was estimated that there were over 1,000,000 internally displaced persons in all of Iraq, with between 600,000 and 800,000 in the north and 300,000 in the center and south of the country.[59] The overwhelming majority of those displaced in the north were Kurds, but the figures also in-

---

[56]   *Ibid*; Hiwa Osman, "Ethnic Tension Divides Kirkuk," BBC News, May 24, 2003, available at http://www.bbc.co.uk, quoting Kurdish Prime Minister Barham Salih to say "The US cannot become the guardian of the evil of ethnic cleansing . . . liberation means that ethnic cleansing should be reversed."; Andrea Nusse, "The Arabs Should Leave Kurdistan Again," interview with Massoud Barzani, *Frankfurter Rundschau*, Sept. 16, 2003, available at www.kurdishmedia.com, quoting KDP chairman Massoud Barzani to say "These Arabs should leave, because they were brought here to 'Arabize' Kurdistan. It is impossible for the Kurds to say that the Arabs can remain. But we will be patient until a legal solution can be found." Reaction from the Kurdish population has sometimes been less patient. See, e.g., Rashid Karadaghi, "An Orderly Return," Kurdisatan Observer, Aug. 18, 2003, available at www.kurdistanobserver.com, expressing outrage at statements by the Kurdish governor of Kirkuk about the need for an "orderly return" of Kurds to their homes.
[57]   UN Office of the Humanitarian Coordinator for Iraq, "Iraq: Weekly Update 4 Jul–10 Aug 2003," August 10, 2003, available at http://www.reliefweb.int.
[58]   *Ibid.*
[59]   Fawcett & Tanner, *The Internally Displaced People of Iraq*, p. 3.

cluded Turkmans, Assyrians and Arabs.[60]   In the center and
south of the country, the majority of the displaced were thought
to be Marsh Arabs and Shiites considered to be opponents of the
Saddam Hussein regime.[61]   However, there was also some unknown number of Kurds who had been forced out by the Arabization and Anfal campaigns, as well as some 45,000 so-called
josh Kurds, who fought with or supported the Iraqi government
in the 1980s and who later fled from the north.[62]   It was further
estimated that there were between 1,000,000 and 2,000,000 Iraqi
refugees living outside Iraq as of 2002, although only 400,000
had formal recognition.[63]   These included the Faili and other
Kurds, in unknown total numbers.

Preliminary figures from the International Organization for
Migration (IOM) indicate that there remain some 40,000 "new
caseload" IDPs (i.e., those displaced by the 2003 war) in the
south and center of the country as of this writing.[64]   On the other
hand, the United Nations Office for Project Services (UNOPS)
has reported that virtually all of those displaced during the war in
the north have returned.[65]   No official figures are yet available
for the number of newly displaced Arabs as a result of Kurds
returning to Kirkuk and surrounding areas, but some media reports indicate that they number in the thousands of families.[66]

According to a survey carried out in 2001 by the UN
HABITAT, the conditions of life of the internally displaced in
the northern governorates were very poor, and worse than those
of the general population. Roughly half still lived in the collective resettlement centers to which they were forced by the government, many of which were in an advanced state of decay.[67]

---

[60]   *Ibid.*, pp. 6-17.
[61]   *Ibid.*, pp. 32-33.
[62]   *Ibid.*
[63]   United States Committee for Refugees, *World Refugee Survey 2003*, p. 162.
[64]   *Global IDP Database*, entry for Iraq.
[65]   *Ibid.*
[66]   E.g., Nadra Saouli, "Iraqi Kurds Returning Home, Drive Out Shiites Relocated by Saddam," Agence France Presse, July 9, 2003, on file with author.
[67]   Fawcett & Tanner, *The Internally Displaced People of Iraq*, p. 19.

Over 50,000 were living in barracks or other buildings not designed for family accommodations and of these, over 6,000 were
living in tents.[68] The HABITAT study also reported that "about
40 percent of internally displaced persons lived in settlements
with standards of water, electricity supplies, sanitation, drainage
and road access that are below average for the area."[69] A smaller
study conducted the previous year by the Ahmed Foundation for
Kurdish Studies concluded that the purchasing power of IDPs in
the north had collapsed after their displacement, that many of
them had been forced to leave many or even all of their personal
effects behind, and that a substantial number suffered from dis-
abling emotional problems.[70] Equally disturbing, the great majority of displaced children were not attending school.[71]

Internally Displaced Kurds and International Law

Based on the foregoing, it should be plain to any lay observer
that Iraq's Kurds, and in particular those who have been displaced, have suffered monumental injustice. Likewise, it requires no particular expertise in the issue of internal displacement to realize that, in a country with a population of approximately 24,600,000, of whom approximately one-fifth are
Kurds,[72] no long-term stability can be expected so long as durable and just solutions have not been found for the over 1,000,000
displaced persons, the majority of whom are Kurds.
    However, the questions of what precisely are the rights of the
internally displaced when it comes to these solutions and what
kind of assistance they can and should expect from the occupying powers, the new national government, the local authorities
and the international community are complex. Kurdish IDPs,

---

[68] *Ibid.*

[69] *Ibid.*, p. 22.

[70] Mohammed Ahmed,"The Chronic Problem of Kurdish Refugees
and Internally Displaced Kurds in Southern Kurdistan – Iraq, " in
Mohammed Ahmed and Michael Gunter, ed., *Kurdish Exodus: From
Internal Displacement to Diaspora* (Sharon, MA: Ahmed Foundation
for Kurdish Studies, 2002), pp. 33-34.

[71] *Ibid.*

[72] *CIA World Factbook 2003: Iraq*; see http://www.cia.gov.

like the estimated 25,000,000 persons who share their plight around the world,[73] stand at the crossroads of the differing regimes of international humanitarian, human rights and refugee law that do not always gel smoothly together.

Nevertheless, consensus is emerging internationally around a normative framework focused on IDPs and designed to rationalize the various strands of applicable law. This framework is expressed in the Guiding Principles on Internal Displacement, which, while not a binding legal instrument in itself, provides a useful basis for examining the rights and responsibilities of the various parties in situations of internal displacement. Accordingly, this author will structure his analysis around the Guiding Principles and examine the "hard law" issues through its lens. He begins with a description of the origins and scope of the Guiding Principles.

Background to the Guiding Principles.
Although internal displacement is nothing new in world history, the international community did not start to organize around the issue until the early 1990s.[74] In large part, this was because it had previously been considered that displacement within the borders of a state concerned its national authorities alone and national sovereignty precluded international interference.

Attitudes on this question began to change after the end of the cold war with an easing in relations between the two superpowers and an end to proxy wars in different countries, heightening international willingness and ability to consider intervention for humanitarian purposes.[75] At the same time, "[t]he political advantage that motivated many states to accept refugees during the cold war gave way . . . to a desire to limit their entry" and an interest in finding ways to persuade potential asylum seekers to stay home.[76] The end of the cold war also led to new, especially violent, internal wars as the system of rival geo-strategic patron-

---

[73] "Global Overview," in *Global IDP Database.*

[74] Roberta Cohen and Francis Deng, *Masses in Flight* (Washington: Brookings Institution, 1998), p. 3.

[75] *Ibid.*, p. 3.

[76] *Ibid.*, p. 4.

age collapsed.[77] These internal conflicts particularly contributed to a precipitous rise in the number of internally displaced persons. In 1982, when IDPs were first tallied, the global number was estimated to be 1,200,000 persons. By 1992, that figure had grown to 24,000,000.[78]

World opinion on this issue was also galvanized by a series of highly publicized humanitarian crises beginning in the 1980s, including in Ethiopia and the Sudan, and continuing into the 1990s with the war in the Balkans.[79] However, as mentioned in the introduction to this paper, it was the situation of the Iraqi Kurds themselves that arguably contributed the most to this momentum. Security Council Resolution 688 of 1991 and the American and British decisions to intervene militarily to protect the displaced Kurds trapped on the Turkish border have been identified as turning points in the international debate on whether internal displacement is an issue of international concern.[80]

Thus, in 1992, the Commission on Human Rights, "the Commission," called on the Secretary-General to appoint a Representative on Internally Displaced Persons, hereinafter, "the Representative."[81] The Secretary-General designated Dr. Francis Deng, a former Sudanese diplomat and a human rights scholar, to this post.[82] The first task entrusted to him was to analyze the international normative framework applicable to internally dis-

---

[77]   *Ibid.*

[78]   "Report of the Representative of the Secretary-General on Internally Displaced Persons," Francis M. Deng, submitted pursuant to Commission on Human Rights Resolution 2002/56, UN. Doc. E/CN.4/2003/86, ¶4, hereinafter, "2003 CHR Report."

[79]   *Ibid*; see also United Nations Office for the Coordination of Humanitarian Affairs–Internal Displacement Unit, "No Refuge: The Challenge of Internal Displacement," hereinafter "OCHA IDP Unit, No Refuge", New York: 2003, p. 3.

[80]   "OCHA IDP Unit, No Refuge," pp. 16-17.

[81]   U.N. Doc. E/CN.4/1992/73 ¶2 (1992). The international community also reacted with institutional changes in the United Nations approach to internal displacement, as briefly described below.

[82]   Simon Bagshaw, "Developing the Guiding Principles on Internal Displacement: The Role of a Global Public Policy Network," p. 11, available at www.globalpublicpolicy.net.

placed persons in light of their needs.[83] Working with a team of legal experts, Dr. Deng undertook a comprehensive study of existing international law, resulting in the "Compilation and Analysis of Existing Norms," presented to the Commission in two parts, the first analyzing the range of protections for persons already displaced, presented in 1996,[84] and the second focusing on protections from displacement in the first instance, presented in 1998.[85]

This study illustrated the basic dilemma of internal displacement in the international system. Although the situations and needs of IDPs strongly resembled those of refugees, the fact that they had not crossed a border put them outside the scope of the refugee law regime and its particular protections. Nevertheless, the study concluded that existing human rights and humanitarian law (also known as "the laws of war"), applicable to the internally displaced as to other human beings and non-combatants, respectively, covered many of the IDPs' needs. However, in light of certain gaps and grey areas in the coverage identified, and the diffusion of the various rights in various instruments, the study recommended that some sort of new instrument be created.

Accordingly, and with the approval of the Commission and the General Assembly,[86] the Representative and his legal team turned to developing a new framework. They decided early in their deliberations not to attempt to draft and promote a new treaty addressing the internally displaced, fearful that such an endeavor would take decades to complete and might result in reopening the question of rights already guaranteed in existing law.[87] Instead, they developed the Guiding Principles, a non-

---

[83] U.N. Doc. E/CN.4/1992/73 ¶2 (1992).

[84] U.N. Doc. E/CN.4/1996/52/Add.2.

[85] U.N. Doc. E/CN.4/1998/53/Add.1.

[86] E.g. Commission on Human Rights Resolution E/CN.4/RES/1996/52 ¶9, 19 April 1996, "call[ing] upon the representative of the Secretary-General to continue on the basis of his compilation and analysis of legal norms, to develop an appropriate framework in this regard for the protection of internally displaced persons..."

[87] Walter Kälin, "How Hard is Soft Law? The Guiding Principles on Internal Displacement and the Need for a Normative Framework," Statement Presented at Ralph Bunche Institute for International Studies

binding instrument comprised of 30 articles restating, interpreting and applying existing humanitarian and human rights law and, where appropriate, relying on refugee law by analogy.

The Guiding Principles prohibit arbitrary displacement,[88] set forth a broad range of rights addressing the protection and assistance needs of persons if and when they are displaced, including the right to access to basic humanitarian assistance (e.g., food, medicine, shelter), the right to be protected from physical violence, the right to education, freedom of movement and residence, political rights such as the right to participate in public affairs and the right to participate in economic activities.[89] They also provide for rights relevant to the end of displacement, notably the rights to return and or resettle elsewhere voluntarily in safety and in dignity and to receive restitution or compensation for lost property.[90] As a general matter, the Guiding Principles call for particular attention to the needs of particularly vulnerable groups, including children, female heads of household, persons with disabilities and the elderly, as well as persons uniquely attached to their lands, such as indigenous peoples, peasants, minorities, and pastoralists.[91]

Since the Guiding Principles were first presented in 1998, various UN organs, including the Commission on Human Rights, the Economic and Social Council and the General Assembly, have taken note of them and expressed their appreciation for their increasing use by governments, intergovernmental bodies and non-governmental organizations. [92] The Security Council has likewise noted their rising application.[93] The heads of the major international humanitarian agencies, acting through the Inter-Agency Standing Committee, have welcomed and endorsed the Guiding Principles, and encouraged their members to share

---

Roundtable, New York, December 19, 2001, available at http://www.brookings.edu.

[88]   Guiding Principle 6.
[89]   Guiding Principles 10-27.
[90]   Guiding Principles 28-29.
[91]   Guiding Principles 4, 9.
[92]   "2003 CHR Report," ¶15-20.
[93]   *Ibid.*, ¶19.

them with their staff and apply them in the field.[94] Regional and sub-regional organizations around the world, including the Organization of African States, the Economic Community of West African States, the Inter-Governmental Authority on Development, the Organization for Security and Cooperation in Europe, and the Council of Europe have expressed their appreciation for the Guiding Principles and incorporated them into aspects of their work.[95]

The Guiding Principles have also formed the basis for national law in a number of states, including Angola, Burundi and Colombia,[96] and of legislation currently pending approval in Uganda and Peru. They have even been taken up by a few non-state actors, including the de facto Abkhaz authorities in Georgia and the Sudan People's Liberation Movement and Army.[97] Furthermore, non-governmental organizations and civil society around the world have begun using the Guiding Principles as a means of evaluating existing national policies and laws and suggesting means to strengthen them.[98]

It is therefore no exaggeration to say that, although they are not a binding instrument and some of their provisions go beyond what is expressly provided in existing international instruments, the Guiding Principles represent an important convergence of opinion in the international community on the appropriate international norms applicable to the internally displaced.

International Law Related to Return and Resettlement through the Lens of the Guiding Principles.
There are several elements of the Guiding Principles that are worth examining in greater depth as a means of illustrating the underlying "hard law" issues involved for the return of the

---

[94] *Ibid.*
[95] *Ibid.*, ¶30-37; see also the "Khartoum Declaration: Ministerial Conference on Internally Displaced Persons in the IGAD Sub-Region," September 2, 2003, available at:
http://www.brookings.edu/dybdocroot/fp/projects/idp/conferences/Dec Khartoum.pdf.
[96] *Ibid.*, ¶23.
[97] *Ibid.*, ¶28.
[98] *Ibid.*, ¶29.

Kurds. It is noted that both Iraq and the United States are sig-
natories to the four Geneva Conventions of 1949[99] and to a number of the major international human rights instruments.[100]

1. Application to State and Non-State Actors.
First, by their terms, the Guiding Principles are not exclusively
directed to state governments. Principle 2 provides that "[t]hese
Principles shall be observed by all authorities, groups and persons irrespective of their legal status" making clear that this call
"shall not affect the legal status of any authorities, groups or persons involved." Elsewhere in the Guiding Principles, it is further
clarified that they are designed to guide not only these "authorities"—defined essentially by their power to affect the lives of the
displaced rather than by their legal legitimacy—but also inter-
governmental and non-governmental organizations that interact
with and assist the displaced.[101]

These provisions are reflective in some measure of existing
international law. In situations of armed conflict, humanitarian
law, on which a number of the Guiding Principles are based, applies both to state actors and insurgent groups, and certain provisions apply also to humanitarian organizations. Apart from these
areas, however, it has traditionally been considered that human
rights and other international norms apply exclusively to states,

---

[99] International Committee of the Red Cross, "States Party to the Geneva Conventions and their Additional Protocols," available at
http://www.icrc.org noting that Iraq acceded to the Geneva Conventions of 1949 on February 14, 1956, but has not yet signed the two additional protocols.

[100] Office of the High Commissioner for Human Rights, "Status of
Ratifications of the Principal International Human Rights Treaties as of
07 July 2003," available at http://www.ohchr.org, noting that Iraq is a
party to the Convention on Economic, Social and Cultural Rights
(CESCR), the Convention on Civil and Political Rights (CCPR), the
Convention on the Elimination of All Forms of Racial Discrimination
(CERD), the Convention on the Elimination of All Forms of Discrimination Against Women (CEDAW) and the Convention on the Rights of
the Child (CRC), but not the Convention Against Torture (CAT). The
same report further noted that the United States is a party to the CCPR,
CERD, and CAT.

[101] *Ibid.*, Introduction, ¶3.

as the primary subjects of the international legal regime.[102] In asserting a wider scope, the Guiding Principles are part of a growing challenge to this traditional notion. This trend is evident in the field of international criminal law, which has seen the creation of ad hoc international criminal tribunals in Yugoslavia and Rwanda in the early 1990s, and of the International Criminal Court in 2002, and the extension of "universal jurisdiction" over war crimes and crimes against humanity by a number of states, notably Belgium and Spain, to prosecute individuals for violations of human rights. Likewise, increasing civil litigation, such as that under the Alien Tort Claims Act in the United States, is beginning to hold both individuals and corporate entities responsible for such violations.

As between international and national actors, Principle 3 makes clear that "[n]ational authorities have the primary duty and responsibility to provide protection and humanitarian assistance to internally displaced persons within their jurisdiction." This is an expression of the notion that state sovereignty entails a positive responsibility for state authorities to care for and protect persons within their borders.[103] Where state governments are too weak or lack control over a particular area within their purported jurisdiction, Principle 5 alludes to the duties in international law of "all authorities and international actors."[104]

As a result of these provisions, the Guiding Principles purport to speak to all of the major sources of power and authority over the internally displaced in northern Iraq, including the Kurdistan Regional Government (KRG), the new national government, the occupying powers and the UN and other humanitarian organizations.

2. Definition of Internally Displaced Persons.

Of equal importance, the Guiding Principles provide the most widely accepted definition of what is meant by the term "inter-

---

[102] Peter Malanczuk, *Akehurst's Modern Introduction to International Law* (7th ed. ; New York: Routledge, 1997), p. 91.

[103] "2003 CHR Report," ¶67-68.

[104] Walter Kälin, *Annotations on the Guiding Principles on Internal Displacement* (Washington: American Society of International Law, 2000), pp. 2-3.

nally displaced persons": "persons or groups of persons who have been forced or obliged to flee or to leave their homes or places of habitual residence, in particular as a result of or in order to avoid the effects of armed conflict, situations of generalized violence, violations of human rights or natural or human-made disasters, and who have not crossed an internally recognized State Border."[105] This definition is not a legal classification, unlike the status of "refugee" accorded by the 1951 Refugee Convention.[106] Rather, it was designed to be inclusive of a large group of persons with shared types of needs, including those fleeing armed conflicts, natural disasters, and other reasons for displacement.[107] The primary elements of the definition are forced, i.e. involuntary, displacement, and the fact that those displaced stay within national borders.

Although not expressly stated, the wording of this definition extends to persons displaced for legitimate as well as illegitimate reasons. Thus, a person required to leave his home for a legitimate public project, such as the building of a road or a dam, is considered an "IDP" just as someone forced to flee persecution and conflict.[108] Likewise a person living in the home of a returning displaced person, e.g., an Arab living in a Kurdish home, should also be considered an IDP if he is obliged to leave in favor of the original owner. Although the circumstances in these two examples have important legal and moral differences, it is nonetheless useful to make clear, by extending the definition of IDP to both, that the needs of the persons so displaced are similar.

3. The Prohibition of Arbitrary Displacement and Procedures for Non-Arbitrary Displacement.

Guiding Principle 6 provides that "every human being shall have the right to be protected against being arbitrarily displaced from

---

[105] Guiding Principle 2.

[106] Kälin, *Annotations on the Guiding Principles on Internal Displacement*, pp. 2-3.

[107] *Ibid.*

[108] Guiding Principles 6 and 7 clarify what might be considered legitimate and illegitimate purposes and means of displacement, as discussed below.

his or her home or place of habitual residence."[109]   It also provides a non-exhaustive list of what might be considered "arbitrary," including ethnic cleansing, evacuation in the absence of danger to the civilians involved or imperative military reasons, and displacement as a collective punishment.[110]

There is no language in existing human rights or humanitarian instruments exactly matching the injunction against "arbitrary displacement" of Guiding Principle 6. However, the principle can reasonably be inferred from rights included in many of the major international and regional human rights instruments to free movement, privacy in the home and the right to housing.[111] Moreover, article 49 of the fourth Geneva Convention, applicable during inter-state conflicts, provides that "individual or mass forcible transfers, as well as deportations of protected persons from occupied territory to the territory of the Occupying Power or to that of any other country, occupied or not, are prohibited, regardless of their motive." Exceptions to this rule include, as in Guiding Principle 6, the safety of the civilians and imperative military reasons. Violation of article 49 is considered a "grave breach" of the Geneva Conventions, and therefore a war crime.[112] Additionally, depending on the circumstances, the wilful displacement of civilians can be considered a crime against humanity, even outside the context of armed conflict.[113]

---

[109] Guiding Principle 6(1).

[110] Guiding Principle 6(2).

[111] See Kälin, *Annotations on the Guiding Principles on Internal Displacement*, p. 14. Likewise, article 16 of "International Labor Organization (ILO) Convention No. 169 concerning Indigenous and Tribal Peoples" provides that such groups "shall not be removed from the lands which they occupy." However, neither the United States nor Iraq is party to this convention. See website of the International Labor Organization, http://www.ilo.org.

[112] "Geneva Convention Relating to the Protection of Civilian Persons in Times of War (IV)," Aug. 12, 1949, art. 147, 6 U.S.T. 3114, 75 U.N.T.S. 31, entered into force, Oct. 21, 1950; see also "Rome Statute of the International Criminal Court," hereinafter, the "Rome Statute," U.N. Doc. A/CONF. 183/9 July 17, 1998, art. 8.

[113] "Rome Statute," art. 7(1)(d) ; "Statute of the International Criminal Tribunal for the Prosecution of Persons Responsible for Genocide and Other Serious Violations of International Humanitarian Law Commit-

Guiding Principle 7 sets out steps authorities should take before undertaking population displacement, even if justified by
the particular circumstances of the case, in order for it to be considered non-arbitrary. Among these are exhausting all feasible
alternatives and acting to minimize the negative effects.[114] It
also provides, *inter alia*, that, where displacement occurs in non-
emergency situations, authorities should ensure that it is carried
out only on the order of an authority empowered by law to do so
and that the right to an effective remedy, including judicial review be guaranteed.[115] These steps "reflect the requirement of
Article 12(3) of the International Covenant on Civil and Political
Rights and similar human rights guarantees that restrictions on
the rights to freedom of movement and residence must be necessary and proportional" and are also reflected in the World Bank's
operational guidelines for involuntary resettlement.[116]

These provisions are clearly relevant to Kurds displaced by
the Iraqi government as part of its campaign of ethnic cleansing,
as well as those displaced by rival Kurdish factions because of
their political opinions. They are also applicable to the actions
of some displaced Kurds themselves, to the extent that they are
using threats, force or other extra-legal means to evict Arabs
from lands they claim as their own. If authorities encourage or

---

ted in the Territory of Rwanda and Rwandan Citizens Responsible for
Genocide and Other Such Violations Committed in the Territory of
Neighboring States Between January 1, 1994 and December 31, 1994,"
S.C. Res. 955, U.N. SCOR, 49th Sess., Annex, 3453d mtg, pp. 15, 16,
art. 3, U.N. Doc. S/RES/955 (1994); "Statute of the International
Criminal Tribunal for the Prosecution of Persons Responsible for Seri-
ous Violations of International Humanitarian Law Committed in the
Territory of the Former Yugoslavia since 1991," S.C. Res. 827, U.N.
SCOR, 48th Sess., 3217th mtg., U.N. Doc. S/RES/827 (1993), Implementing Report of the Secretary-General Pursuant to Paragraph 2 of the
Security Council Resolution 808 (1993), U.N. GAOR, Annex, art. 5.
See generally, Marco Simons, "The Emergence of a Norm Against Arbitrary Forced Relocation," *Columbia Human Rights Law Review,* vol.
34(2002), pp. 95-156.
[114] Guiding Principle 7(1) and (2).
[115] Guiding Principle 7(3).
[116] Kälin, *Annotations on the Guiding Principles on Internal Displacement,* p. 20.

are complicit in such actions without providing for any law-based framework to reverse ethnic cleansing or remedies in case of false claims, they could be said to be contravening the procedural requirements detailed in Principle 7.

4. Non-Discrimination.

Guiding Principle 4 prohibits discrimination in the application of the Guiding Principles on the bases, *inter alia*, of race, language, and national or ethnic origin. Express language prohibiting discrimination in the application of humanitarian and human rights principles can be found, *inter alia*, in the fourth Geneva Convention, and the Covenant on Civil and Political Rights and the Convention on the Elimination of All Forms of Racial Discrimination.[117] Thus, it is incumbent on the various authorities to ensure that any programs of return or resettlement for the displaced do not discriminate between the various ethnic groups involved. For example, incentives should not be offered to Kurdish IDPs to return or resettle in a particular area that are not offered to Assyrian or Turkmans IDPs in similar circumstances.

5. The Right to Return or Resettle in Safety and Dignity.

Of obvious relevance to the issue of return and resettlement for the Kurds, Guiding Principle 28 provides that "competent authorities," in other words those with jurisdiction and power over the relevant areas and populations, have the "primary duty and responsibility to establish the conditions, as well as provide the means, which allow internally displaced persons to return voluntarily, in safety and with dignity" or, at their option to resettle in another part of the country. It also calls upon the authorities to assist in the reintegration of these persons. A crucial component of this Principle is the right of free choice of the displaced to choose between options of return, integration where they have fled, or resettlement elsewhere.

The drafters of the Guiding Principles inferred this rule primarily from the right of free movement provided, *inter alia*, in

---

[117] *Ibid.*, p. 11, citing, *inter alia*, CCPR article 2(2), CESCR art. 2(2), and GCIV art. 27(3).

the Covenant on Civil and Political Rights (CCPR) article 12. [118] Article 49 of the Fourth Geneva Convention also provides that persons evacuated by occupying powers must be speedily assisted to return.[119] There is a long tradition in the realm of refugee protection of UNHCR assistance to and encouragement of the voluntary repatriation of refugees to their places of origin. [120] Nevertheless, and despite the fact that the CCPR and other human rights instruments posit a specific right to return to one's own country (i.e. CCPR art. 12(4)), there remains debate in legal circles whether the drafters of these instruments meant to include persons expelled in situations of mass displacement (whether internal or external) within the ambit of the right of return.[121] Regardless of the outcome of this debate, however, the trend is clearly to recognize a right of return both for refugees and IDPs. This was, famously, a crucial component of the Dayton Peace Agreement of 1995 concerning Bosnia, and has been recognized on several occasions in resolutions of the Security Council and other organs of the United Nations.[122]

6. The Right to Restitution of Property or Compensation.

Also plainly pertinent to the situation of returning Kurds in Iraqi Kurdistan, Guiding Principle 29(2) posits that the "competent authorities" should assist returned or resettled IDPS "to recover, to the extent possible, their property and possession which they left behind or were disposed of upon their displacement." If this is not possible, the authorities should provide or assist these persons in obtaining compensation or reparation.

The key drafter and annotator of the Guiding Principles has acknowledged that explicit provisions for restitution and compensation are not included in human rights instruments, and that humanitarian law provisions are limited to compensation for the

---

[118] *Ibid.*, pp. 69-70.

[119] *Ibid.*, p. 20.

[120] *Ibid.*

[121] John Quigley, "Mass Displacement and the Individual Right of Return," *British Yearbook of International Law* 75 (1998), p. 68.

[122] *Ibid.*; Kälin, *Annotations on the Guiding Principles on Internal Displacement*, p. 70.

grave breaches of parties to the conflict. [123] However, he identified a trend to apply remedies for violations of human rights in the jurisprudence of regional tribunals in the European and Inter-American systems, and in the international criminal tribunals for Yugoslavia and Rwanda. [124] Such a right was also strongly asserted by annex 7 to the Dayton Agreement. [125] Accordingly, this may be deemed at least an emerging area of international law and should be considered by the parties in situations of return and resettlement.

Responsibilities and Roles of the Various Authorities with Regard to the Return and/or Resettlement of Internally Displaced Kurds

In order to understand which "authorities" might be called upon to carry out the responsibilities and ensure the rights discussed above, this section will briefly discuss the mandates of the four main centers of authority of particular importance with regard to the return of displaced Kurds.

Coalition Forces and the Coalition Provisional Authority.
The American and British presence in Iraq is divided between their military forces, some additional troops contributed by allied states such as Spain and Poland, and the Coalition Provisional Authority (CPA) led by Ambassador Paul Bremer. Under the Geneva Conventions, all of these elements together are considered the "occupying power," with particular rights and responsibilities.

In addition to the considerations discussed in the previous section, these responsibilities include the duty to restore public order and safety (GC IV art. 64) and public health and sanitation (GC IV art. 56), and the availability of food and medical supplies (GC IV art. 55)—including by granting access by humanitarian assistance organizations (GC IV art. 59). In general, humanitar-

---

[123] Kälin, *Annotations on the Guiding Principles on Internal Displacement*, p. 72.
[124] *Ibid.*
[125] *Ibid.*

ian law "is strong in protecting the *status quo ante*, while weak in responding to new needs of the population of the occupied territory." [126] Thus the Authority's responsibility, in addition to providing for basic humanitarian needs, is to "rehabilitate and maintain infrastructure essential to the survival of the civilian population (e.g., water supply, sewage) as it existed prior to the conflict, and not to significantly alter the state structure and planning." In general, however, humanitarian law would not authorize occupying powers to undertake long-term reconstruction projects unless critical for the survival of the civilian population. [127]

On May 22, 2003, the Security Council adopted resolution 1483, which recognized "the specific authorities, responsibilities, and obligations under applicable international law of [the United States and the United Kingdom] as occupying powers under unified command" to be known as "the Authority" and calling upon them "to promote the welfare of the Iraqi people through the effective administration of the territory." [128] The resolution also provided the Authority with powers well beyond those automatically accorded to occupying powers under humanitarian law. It sanctioned the Authority's management of a "Development Fund for Iraq" to be "used in a transparent manner to meet the humanitarian needs of the Iraqi people, for the economic reconstruction and repair of Iraq's infrastructure, for the continued disarmament of Iraq, and for the costs of Iraqi civilian administration, and for other purposes benefiting the people of Iraq." [129] The United Nations Secretary-General was directed to terminate UN administration of the Oil for Food Program as of November 2003 and to transfer authority for the program to the Authority, placing oil proceeds in the Development Fund. [130]

---

[126] International Humanitarian Law Research Initiative, "Military Occupation of Iraq: I. Application of IHL and Maintenance of Law and Order," p. 3, April 14, 2003; http://www.ihlresearch.org/iraq.

[127] International Humanitarian Law Research Initiative, "Military Occupation of Iraq: II. International Assistance in Occupied Territory," p. 3, April 22, 2003; http://www.ihlresearch.org/iraq.

[128] U.N. Doc. No. SC/556/1483 (2003).

[129] *Ibid.*, para. 14.

[130] *Ibid.*, para. 16.

Given its extensive mandate for administration of the country, its oil wealth, and its reconstruction, the Authority should arguably be expected to play an important role in facilitating the return and resettlement of displaced Kurds. In theory, the CPA, as the branch in charge of all non-military affairs, should have the greatest part to play in this. However, the numbers and seniority of CPA personnel devoted to such issues is reportedly low, particularly outside of Baghdad, and it is therefore the military that has had the most day-to-day contact with the issue of IDP returns.[131]

Nevertheless, the CPA has taken a few steps of significance. In September 2003, the CPA adopted "Guidelines on Relocating Displaced Populations" aimed at IDPs and urban poor "'squatting' in various municipal or government buildings around Baghdad."[132] The Guidelines contemplate eviction of these persons to be "brought about by negotiation and persuasion, not by force" after 2-4 week notice to the "squatters." They commit the CPA to provide assistance for anyone so relocated and to work with UN agencies and NGOs to identify relocation sites. It is contemplated that these Guidelines might be extended to the rest of the country.

Of potentially greater importance, in June 2003, the CPA issued a regulation establishing an "Iraqi Property Reconciliation Facility" (hereinafter, "IPRF, or "facility").[133] The regulation notes that "large numbers of people from different ethnic and religious backgrounds in Iraq have been uprooted and forced to move from their properties to serve political objectives of the Ba'athist regime," that "many individuals have conflicting claims to the same real property, resulting in instability and occasional violence" and that "pending the establishing of a means of finally resolving property-related claims by a future Iraqi government, certain of these claims may be amenable to a voluntary reconciliation immediately, thereby avoiding instability and

---

[131] Interview by author with UNOCHI Representative, July 2003.

[132] On file with author.

[133] "Coalition Provisional Authority Regulation Number 4, Establishment of the Iraqi Property Reconciliation Facility," CPA/REG/25, June 2003/05.

violence."[134]   The regulation creates a "facility" designed to "collect real property claims and promptly resolv[e] such claims on a voluntary basis and in a fair and judicious manner." It also contemplates the possibility of the creation of an "IPRF Fund" to be used "in connection with the operations of the IPRF."

The CPA has contracted with IOM to perform the functions of the IPRF, and IOM has begun gathering property claims and offering its services to mediate property disputes.[135] It is not yet clear what is planned to be done with the property claims gathered but not submitted to the voluntary resolution mechanism.

The Governing Council and Cabinet of Ministers.

By an order of July 13, 2003, Ambassador Bremer recognized a "Governing Council" of Iraq consisting of 25 members chosen by the Authority to represent Iraq's various ethnic and religious groups, with limited powers of governance, including the power to appoint a cabinet of ministers, which has recently taken place.[136]   The leaders of the KDP and PUK are both members of the council.[137]   On August 14, the Security Council welcomed the creation of the Council "as an important step towards the formation by the people of Iraq of an internally recognized, representative government[.]"

As the recognized interim national government, the Council and the Ministers theoretically carry the primary responsibility for guaranteeing the rights of the displaced, per Guiding Principle 3. However, the current reality appears to be that the Council and its Cabinet are still very much creatures of the Coalition and not yet exercising effective control over national institutional apparati. Moreover, this interim government is unlikely to exercise any significant control over KRG-controlled areas in the absence of long-term agreements with the Kurdish leadership about the future governance of the region.

---

[134] *Ibid.*

[135] Interview with IOM representative by the author, August 2003.

[136] "CPA Regulation 6," July 13, 2003, available at http://www.cpa-iraq.org.

[137] "Iraq Governing Council Members," BBC News, July 14, 2003, available at http://www.bbc.co.uk.

The Kurdish Regional Government.

As discussed above, Kurdish authorities have been controlling and administering the territory in the "safe haven" since 1991. In the early 1990s, the KDP and PUK together formed the Kurdish Regional Government (KRG) to govern the area, consisting of a cabinet, a parliament, and various ministries, including the Ministry of Reconstruction and Development, which has responsibility, *inter alia*, for assisting IDPs and rebuilding destroyed villages.[138] As the main authority on the ground with capacity to respond to the needs of returning displaced persons in the north of Iraq, the KRG will have particular responsibility to ensure that the rights of IDPs of all ethnicities are met.

The United Nations, Other Intergovernmental and International Organizations and International NGOs.

Prior to and during the war, the United Nations and collaborating NGOs organized and planned their response to the humanitarian situation in Iraq under the leadership of the Humanitarian Coordinator for Iraq, Romero Lopez da Silva. In resolution 1483, the Security Council called upon the Secretary-General to appoint a Special Representative on Iraq with supervisory authority, *inter alia*, over humanitarian assistance.[139] The Special Representative was specifically tasked with "promoting the safe, orderly, and voluntary return of refugees and displaced persons" in coordination with the Authority.[140] The post of special representative was filled by Sergio Vieira de Mello (the sitting High Commissioner for Human Rights) until his death on August 19, 2003 in the bombing of UN headquarters in Baghdad. On August 14, 2003, the Security Council approved the creation of a full UN mission to Iraq, which will include the offices of the Special Representative, the Humanitarian Coordinator and other elements of the current UN humanitarian structure in Iraq.[141]

---

[138] "Ministry for Reconstruction and Development Mission Statement," available at http://www.krg.org.
[139] U.N. Doc. No. SC/556/1483, para. 8.
[140] *Ibid.*
[141] U.N. Doc. No. SC/7843/1500 (2003).

Prior to the war, the Humanitarian Coordinator assigned two UN agencies to serve as focal points on issues involving IDPs.[142] In the north, this agency was UNOPS, inasmuch as it had already been on the ground assisting the internally displaced through its administration of the Oil for Food program in the Kurdish "safe haven." IOM, a non-UN intergovernmental organization with a wide-ranging mandate for responding to issues of population movement, was invited to take responsibility for assisting IDPs in the center and south of the country. UN HABITAT was given responsibility for looking to the housing and shelter needs of the internally displaced.

This arrangement sparked criticism from some outside observers, who asserted that these agencies lacked experience with dealing with issues of protection, a crucial question in situations of displacement.[143] They would have preferred to see authority extended instead to the United Nations High Commissioner for Refugees (UNHCR) and/or the International Committee of the Red Cross (ICRC). However, neither of these agencies had shown real interest prior to the war in being designated as "lead" on IDPs, concerned that their other responsibilities would be prohibitive.

A new arrangement was struck after it became clear that the war would not cause huge new outflows of refugees and IDPs. UNHCR indicated its willingness to deal with IDPs, and in particular with issues of return. Accordingly, as described in the UN's Revised Humanitarian Appeal for Iraq issued in June 2003, responsibility for IDPs within the humanitarian system was divided among three separately identified IDP "caseloads": (1) IDPs in the three northern governorates as well as the governorates of Ninewah and At Taheem, (2) the Marsh Arabs in the south, and (3) the "new IDP caseload" in various urban centers

---

[142] Unless otherwise indicated, the following few paragraphs are based on information gained by the author as a participant in IASC planning meetings in Geneva through the spring and summer of 2003.

[143] E.g., Arthur Helton and Gil Loescher, "Internally Displaced Persons in Iraq: A   Potential   Crisis?"   April   10,   2003,   available   at www.opendemocracy.org.

displaced as a result of the war and its aftermath. [144]   UNHCR
was assigned to be the coordinating agency for returns and protection for the first caseload, and to collaborate with other agencies in the care and maintenance of IDP relocation villages for
the second caseload. [145]   The third caseload would be addressed
"within the inter-agency assistance framework" without a particular "coordinating" agency. [146]   With regard to the "first"—
essentially Kurdistan—"caseload", UNHCR would coordinate
with UNOPS and HABITAT as well as other agencies to, *inter
alia*, "negotiate a plan for the gradual and voluntary return of
IDPs to their homes or settlements, including solutions for those
who have to vacate occupied property," "monitor the treatment
of IDPs," "advocate for necessary legislation and property restitution and/or compensation procedures to be established by the
Authority," and "assisting in the ongoing relief and rehabilitation
initiatives to those not seeking to return and assistance to their
host communities[.]"[147]

Recommendations

In light of this normative framework and the areas of de jure and
de facto responsibility described above, the author concludes
with a few recommendations concerning the return and resettlement of the displaced Kurds of Iraq.   The practical problems involved in bringing about such solutions are legion and he cannot
hope to address them all here, in particular given the sketchy
information now available about the needs and current status of
the displaced.   Instead, he will highlight a few issues for which
the assistance of the Guiding Principles is particularly relevant.

Ensuring Voluntariness.
The first element of a successful program of return for the internally displaced emphasized by Guiding Principle 28 is the free

---

[144] United Nations, "Humanitarian Appeal for Iraq: Revised Inter-
Agency Appeal," p. 42.
[145] *Ibid.*
[146] *Ibid.*
[147] *Ibid.*

choice of the displaced persons themselves. Too often, authorities in post-conflict situations have manipulated the return and resettlement process in order to gain political advantages or to minimize expense. The Guiding Principles require, on the contrary, that returning displaced persons be viewed as human beings with individual rights, not as political pawns.

That there is a tendency nevertheless to do so can be made clear by several examples. After the dissolution of the Soviet Union in 1991, Georgia was granted independence and international recognition as a new state.[148] Abkhaz ethnics living in the Georgian province of Abkhazia harbored ambitions for their own state, and armed conflict soon broke out between them and ethnic Georgians over unmet demands for political and cultural autonomy, eventually leading to their unilateral declaration of independence.[149] In the first five years of conflict, 300,000 persons were displaced outside of Abhkazia, overwhelmingly ethnic Georgians.[150] Outside observers concluded that this was the result of ethnic cleansing meant to consolidate the Abkhaz position in their new "state" (which has not, as of this date, been recognized by the international community). Additional, plainly ethnicity-based, displacements occurred in 1995 and 1998. A ceasefire declared in 1994 has frozen the conflict, but a political solution has yet to be found. A parallel conflict with South Ossetia, led to displacement of approximately 60,000 individuals in 1991 and 1992.[151]

When the Representative visited Georgia in 2000, he found that the Georgian Government had vigorously pursued the goal of return of persons displaced from Abkhazia and Ossetia, to the exclusion of other potential long-term solutions such as assistance for local integration and resettlement.[152] Indeed, although

---

[148] "Report of the Representative of the Secretary-General on Internally Displaced Persons, Submitted Pursuant to Commission on Human Rights Resolution 2000/53, Profiles in Displacement: Georgia," U.N. Doc. No. E/CN.4/2001/5/Add. 4, p.14 (2001), hereinafter, "RSG Georgia Report."

[149] *Ibid.*

[150] *Ibid.*, ¶15.

[151] *Ibid.*, ¶20.

[152] *Ibid.*, ¶¶75, 105.

the Government offered emergency assistance to the displaced, it actively resisted attempts to enable the internally displaced to become self-reliant and socially and economically integrated in their places of refuge, for fear of losing momentum for its political objective of returning them to Abkhazia and Ossetia in hopes of reversing the gains of the insurgencies.[153] Many ethnic Georgians also strongly harboured the desire to return to Abkhazia, but the de facto authorities in that area did not facilitate return, despite verbal and formal agreements to do so.[154] On the contrary, Abkhaz authorities limited discussion of the return of ethnic Georgians to a single district, and had done little to address the potential for violence in that district that had caused renewed displacement of returnees in the past.[155] A similar dynamic of central authorities favoring return and authorities in local areas resisting it has been seen in the Kosovo region of Serbia-Montenegro; Serbian authorities insist upon return of displaced Serbs whereas local Albanians and their leaders have resisted it.[156] In Afghanistan and Russia, observers charge that central authorities are pressing return of the internally displaced in a manner overriding the security concerns of the displaced themselves.[157]

In northern Iraq, there seems to be little question that many displaced Kurds wish to return to their original homes. In addition to those who were only briefly displaced during the war, thousands of those who had been displaced for longer periods already began to return to areas within the "safe haven" zone even before the fall of the Saddam Hussein regime. It is thought that more will come this fall with the harvests and with the gradual reconstruction of destroyed villages. Moreover, unlike in Georgia, the local Kurdish authorities are ready to welcome dis-

---

[153] *Ibid.,* ¶111.

[154] *Ibid.,* ¶76.

[155] *Ibid*

[156] *Global IDP Database*, entry for the Former Republic of Yugoslavia.

[157] United Nations Office for the Coordination of Humanitarian Affairs—IDP Unit, "The Internally Displaced in Afghanistan: Towards Durable Solutions, Report of the Inter-Agency Mission," May 2003, p. 5, on file with author.

placed Kurds back, seeing their return as a symbol of their success as well as a reversal of ethnic cleansing and genocidal acts.

However, even before the 2003 war, Kurdish authorities are reported to have openly applied "political criteria" to assistance levels for IDPs so as not to encourage them to resettle on a permanent basis. Moreover, the authorities are said to have "adamantly insisted" that displaced Kurds must return to their homes, with the goal of ensuring that a sufficient number of Kurds return to the Kirkuk area to outweigh the Turkman, Arab and Assyrian populations and consolidate Kurdish control of an area and its resources considered historically Kurdish.[158] Such an approach risks subordinating the interests and rights of the displaced themselves, should there be some among them who do not wish to return to these areas. Moreover, as in Afghanistan and Russia, there are lingering security concerns in some of the return areas, as discussed below.

On the other end of the spectrum, both the CPA and UNHCR have been extremely cautious about encouraging returns.[159] In the case of UNHCR, this is borne in part out of its fear that large returns will spark new conflict, in particular due to property disputes (also discussed in greater detail below).[160] While such caution is understandable, it is crucial, as a matter of simple justice, that Kurds' ability to exercise their right to return not be long delayed.

Ensuring Safety and Dignity.
The remaining requirements for return and resettlement programs emphasized by Guiding Principle 28 are those of safety and dignity. There are many factors that go into achieving both of these aims, of which a few are addressed here.

---

[158] Fawcett & Tanner, *The Internally Displaced People of Iraq*, p. 23.
[159] This issue was discussed by High Commissioner Ruud Lubbers and his Special Envoy Dennis McNamara at a meeting on Iraq attended by the author and held in Geneva in July 2003.
[160] *Ibid.*

1. Maintaining Law and Order.

In the center and south of Iraq, the absence of law and order are clear dangers to displaced persons and an important barrier to their successful return or resettlement. This appears to be less the case in the north of Iraq, where the KRG has maintained its armed forces intact throughout the war. However, as noted above, some violence has already been reported in connection with returning IDPs. Moreover, it has been reported that Islamic fundamentalist groups are again becoming active in Sulaymaniya and the PKK has become more active along the border with Turkey, raising the specter of renewed conflict in the area.[161]

As noted above, the Authority has direct responsibility for ensuring law and order pursuant to its duties under humanitarian law. More directly implicated, however, are the forces of KRG, given their strong presence on the ground. Pursuant to the Guiding Principles, Kurdish authorities will need to ensure that law and order prevails not only for Kurds but also for Arabs, Turkmans and other ethnic groups in the territories they control.

2. Addressing the Dangers of Landmines, Unexploded Ordinance, and Biological Chemical Weapons.

The north—and particularly areas of likely return such as Kirkuk—have not escaped from contamination by landmines, unexploded ordinance, and the fallout from the use of chemical and biological weapons. An UNOPS survey in 2001 found that 339 square kilometres in the northern governorates contained landmines as well as other unexploded ordinance.[162] The Mines Advisory Group identified 2,241 separate minefields in the north, affecting 760 villages.[163] With movements incident to the war, casualties in May 2003 alone numbered in the hundreds.[164] Iraqi forces reportedly made extensive use of mines around

---

[161] UN Office of the Humanitarian Coordainator for Iraq, "Weekly Update: 4 Jul – 10 Aug 2003," available at www.reliefweb.int.

[162] Office of the Iraq Program, "Oil-for-Food, Landmine Mapping and Clearance," www.un.org/depts/oip/sectorland mines.

[163] Landmine Monitor Report 2002, "Northern Iraq (Iraqi Kurdistan)," available at www.icbl.org/lm/kurdistan.html.

[164] UNOPS, "UNOPS-MAP Situation Report 8," May 2003, available at www.reliefweb.int.

Kirkuk and Mosul and on roads between Arbil and Kirkuk, Guwer, Mosul and Makhmur in the months leading to the 2003 war.[165] The Coalition forces made extensive use of cluster munitions throughout the country, including around Kirkuk and Mosul and some use of landmines.[166] Moreover, there are well-recorded instances of use by Iraqi forces of nerve gas and other agents along the border with Iran,[167] as well as against Kurdish civilians within Iraq itself.[168]

Returning IDPs are at high risk from these kinds of environmental hazards, particularly in situations of spontaneous return to villages. UN agencies, in particular UNOPS and UNMAS, along with their NGO partner organizations, have been active in mapping, clearance, and education in these areas in the "safe haven" areas for some time. However, the potential pullback of international UN and NGO staff due to the UN headquarters bombing in August 2003 may slow these efforts. Moreover, areas outside the "safe haven" zones are strongly affected.

The Authority is under a particular moral responsibility to address the dangers of the munitions it itself has left behind in areas of return, but in light of its general duty as occupying power under humanitarian law to protect the civilian population, its responsibility in this area should be seen to encompass the full range of such environmental threats. Moreover, Kurdish authorities must take additional responsibility for coordinating activities to address mine and other hazards in areas under their control, particularly when and if they encourage Kurds to return.

3. Promoting Orderly Restitution of Property and Minimizing the Effects of Secondary Displacement.
An issue that touches both on security and dignity of IDPs is property restitution. Dennis McNamara, the High Commissioner for Refugee's Special Envoy to Iraq, has identified this as one of the most explosive and complex challenges presented by the re-

---

[165] Landmine Monitor Report 2003, "Iraq," www.icbl.org.
[166] *Ibid.*
[167] United Nations Environment Program, "Desk Study on the Environment in Iraq (2003)," p. 54.
[168] *HRW Anfal Report*, see note 3.

turn process throughout the country, but particularly so in the north.[169] Authorities must take control of this question quickly for a number of reasons.

First among these is to avoid further violence, whose potential has already been demonstrated on the ground. In addition, the uncertainty of the current situation about who owns and may use such lands might have dangerous economic consequences. According to Refugees International, Kurds returning to reclaim farmlands have been told by local authorities to refrain from planting in the fields of their newly regained homes this autumn because of the unresolved property issues.[170] Given the importance of the region for producing food for the whole country, and the precariousness of the current rationing system, this could be a significant problem.

Less calamitous, but also important, is the potential for protracted uncertainty to impede the economic development required to support those moving back to the lands. An example of this occurred in another part of the world, East Timor (now Timor Leste), where protracted uncertainty about land title in the aftermath of the creation of the UN administration in that territory long deterred legitimate investors crucial to the recovery of the ravaged country and encouraged less scrupulous speculators offering ridiculously low prices for properties, damaging the interests of the local sellers.[171]

Finally, authorities must replace ad hoc actions on the ground with a neutral process to ensure that the rights of those involved are upheld. In this respect, the starting point under the Guiding Principles is that the original owners of land wrongly driven away are entitled to restitution. This precept does not appear to be under question in Iraq today, as it has been in other countries facing similar situations, such as Georgia and Croatia, where

---

[169] See note 159 above.

[170] Brenda Oppermann, "The Many Causes of Internal Displacement in Central and Northern Iraq: Consequences and Recommendations," available at http://www.refugeesinternational.org.

[171] Daniel Fitzpatrick, "Land Policy in Post-Conflict Circumstances: Some Lessons from East Timor," UNHCR Working Paper No. 58, February 2002.

hostile local authorities and discriminatory laws have complicated the return of property.[172]

At the same time, the needs and rights of the secondary occupiers must also be taken into account. The Guiding Principles
require that authorities ensure that any displacement—even to
restore property wrongly taken—takes place to the extent possible through a predictable and fair process. Procedures should be
provided to guard against fraud, to account for investments made
in the land by the secondary occupiers (such as houses built on
previously open land, or the harvest of crops they have planted
and tended)—in particular where there is evidence that occupiers
were themselves coerced by the Iraqi regime to take over Kurdish properties, and that adequate provision is made to attend to
the needs of dispossessed Arabs so that they do not end up
"squatting" in public buildings or suffering other privations of
basic needs. Also, the procedure must fairly address claims by
those from all ethnic groups, whether Kurdish, Assyrian or
Turkman. This should be done in an expeditious manner so that
the exclusion of rightful property owners is not unreasonably
prolonged.

As can be discerned from the preceding section on roles and
responsibilities, the various authorities are not yet coordinated on
this issue. Whereas the UN has assigned UNHCR, in collaboration with other agencies, to play the lead role in working with
authorities to address questions of property restitution, the CPA
has contracted with IOM to collect property claims. It is unclear
whether the CPA has a particular mechanism in mind for dealing
with these claims.

One possibility is for the CPA to impose an international dispute mechanism, through IOM or by other means. This was the
model used in Bosnia with the Commission on Real Property
Claims and in Kosovo with the Housing and Property Directorate and Claims Commission. Both bodies were authorized to
make binding decisions on property disputes and their interna-

---

[172] Scott Leckie, "Housing and Property Issues for Refugees and Internally Displaced Persons in the Context of Return: Key Considerations
for UNHCR Policy and Practice," *Refugee Survey Quarterly* 19:3
(2000), pp. 5-63.

tional nature was perceived as the only way to counter the potential for local biases. However, these bodies have experienced serious problems.

Both began very slowly causing frustration and confusion.[173] Even after their procedures were accelerated, both have had difficulty, despite de jure legal authority, achieving actual enforcement of their decrees because of local hostility.[174] Thus, although the CPRC has decided thousands of claims, the actual number of properties returned has been small.[175] Likewise, in Kosovo, a lack of cooperation from local courts and municipal officials led to a lack of enforcement despite the solid legal framework.[176] Given the generally more favourable relationship between Kurdish authorities and the Americans, a different dynamic would likely prevail in northern Iraq. However, the lack of a legal framework agreed to by the relevant parties, like the Dayton Agreement that led to the Bosnia Commission, could prove an impediment to perceptions of legitimacy.

In a statement issued in May 2003, the Representative suggested that an Iraqi, i.e. domestic, commission be created with representative ethnic and religious makeup to deal with property disputes.[177] He emphasized that the rights and needs of the Arabs should be taken into account, and that the UN should be called in to advise and assist the commission.[178] Such a commission might be an opportunity for building reconciliation between the communities. Moreover, it would have the immense advantage of empowering Iraqis to address their own problems

---

[173] *Ibid.*, p. 24; Organization for Security and Cooperation in Europe Mission in Kosovo, Department of Human Rights and Rule of Law, "Property Rights in Kosovo, 2002-2003." pp. 12-37.
[174] *Ibid.*
[175] Leckie, "Housing and Property Issues for Refugees and Internally Displaced Persons in the Context of Return: Key Considerations for UNHCR Policy and Practice," p. 24.
[176] Organization for Security and Cooperation in Europe Mission in Kosovo, Department of Human Right and Rule of Law, "Property Rights in Kosovo 2002-2003," p. 22.
[177] UN Information Service, "UN Representative Calls for Action on Displaced Persons in Iraq," May 16, 2003, on file with author.
[178] *Ibid.*

through local legal means. However, who would make up and control such a commission, in particular as between national and Kurdish authorities, would be a thorny question in light of the need for a perception of fairness by the various ethnic groups involved. Coordination with UN and other humanitarian agencies to ensure that the effects of secondary displacement are minimized would be essential.

Most importantly, however, in this uneasy stage, it is important that the various authorities make it known that they are planning together to find a solution. Deliberating about and setting forth serious plans will instill confidence among displaced populations that land and property matters will be settled in a fair and expedient manner, and that their plight will not be forgotten.

4. Finding Justice for the Victims of Internal Displacement.
A final issue that touches on both the safety and dignity of return and resettlement is that of justice for displaced Kurds. As mentioned above, the Baathists' concerted efforts to drive the Kurds and other disfavored minorities from their lands were violations not only of their human rights but, arguably, war crimes (when committed within the context of armed conflict) and/or crimes against humanity as well.[179] Plainly the murders that accompanied the intensification of this drive in the Anfal campaign in the 1980s could also be punished as international crimes, including, as many commentators have argued, the crime of genocide.[180] Prosecuting those deemed responsible for these crimes in a fair and impartial system of justice should be seen as an integral part of any plan of reconstruction and of healing the wounds of displacement and sending a message to would-be abusers in the future.

---

[179] For an analysis under the relevant international instruments, see "HRW, Forcible Expulsion Report," pp. 25-28.

[180] E.g., Catherine Knowles, "Life and Human Dignity, the Birthright of All Human Beings: An Analysis of the Iraqi Genocide of the Kurds and Effective Enforcement of Human Rights," *Naval Law Review* 45 (1998), pp. 152-215.

It is debatable whether such prosecutions should occur in an international setting or a rejuvenated local judicial system, but it is plain that the various authorities, including the Authority, co-operate in preserving and recording evidence of these crimes and in seeking out and arresting those responsible for them. Authorities should also consider the issue of compensation for forced displacement—as well as for other grievous human rights violations—as they make plans to punish the perpetrators.

Conclusion

An historic window of opportunity is opening in Iraq, not only for the Kurds as a people to find some measure of self-determination and protection, but also for the rights of the hundreds of thousands of persons forced from their homes over the past decades finally to be vindicated. However, even at such a time individuals can easily find themselves again trampled by the progress of history. It is the underlying premise of the Guiding Principles that internally displaced persons should be perceived by the relevant authorities first and foremost as human beings with individual rights and needs, and not as an undifferentiated mass of people, a security problem to be controlled, a tool for gaining control of land, or a living symbol of past wrongs. IDPs of every ethnicity deserve better than this and the willingness of the various authorities to give them what they deserve will be an important measure of how serious each of them is about building a fair and just state out of the ruins of the old.

CHAPTER 12

The Kurdish Community in Lebanon and Their Future Prospects

Lokman I. Meho and Farah W. Kawtharani

General Background

The Kurdish presence in Lebanon goes as far back as World War I ; however, their major influx took place in the two decades between Sheikh Said's revolt in 1925 and World War II.[1] This was followed by another major wave in the period between the mid-1940s and early 1960s. While a significant number of the second wave moved to Lebanon from Syria escaping the poor economic conditions and the cultural and political repression that began there in 1958, virtually all Lebanese Kurds originated from the villages of Mardin and its surrounding

---

[1] Earlier presence of the Kurds in Lebanon dates back to the arrival of the Ayyubids in the 12th century, as well as to those families that were sent to Lebanon by the Ottomans to maintain order in various parts of the empire. These Kurdish families settled in and ruled many areas of Lebanon for long periods of time. Examples of these families include: the Ayyubis, the Sayfa *emirs* (princes) in Tripoli, the Mirbi family in Akkar, the Jumblats and the Imads in Mount Lebanon, and the Hamiyeh family in Baalbeck. Detached from their homeland for many generations, these Kurdish families became fully integrated into Lebanon's social and political structure and have centuries ago been completely assimilated.

areas. Oral accounts of the success of Kurds who had already moved to Lebanon, as well as the country's proximity to Kurdistan, were important incentives that encouraged the second group to move.[2]

Although Kurds in Lebanon are designated as one coherent group in the perception of the mainstream Lebanese population, a closer look at the community uncovers a great deal of internal ethno-linguistic divisions. In contrast to its religious homogeneity (all being Sunni Muslims), the Kurdish community in Lebanon is divided into two main groups: those who speak the Kurmanji (or Bahdinani) dialect and those who speak an Arabic dialect imbued with Kurdish, Syriac, and Turkish influences. Kurmanji speakers understand this Arabic dialect (which many members of the community call "Mhallami" or "Mardalli" more easily than vice versa.

The Kurmanji speakers, often referred to as "Kurmanj," account for approximately one-third of the community. Most of them originated from the villages of Fafeh, Jibl-Graw, Kinderib, Marjeh, Marska, and Matina and speak Kurdish as their first language and Arabic as their second. Some of them, however, have forgotten Kurdish, primarily because there is no school in Lebanon that teaches it, which makes it very difficult for the community to preserve the language after generations of residence in the country.

The Arabic-dialect-speaking Kurds are referred to in a variety of different ways. For these Kurds, the process of defining oneself is often a laborious and vague process that entails a lot of confusion and shifting from one label to another. When they are invited to talk about their ethnicity, members of this group refer to themselves as "Arab Kurds" or "Mardallis" and, in some cases, as "Arabs" or as "Kurds." The context and identity of people they interact with determines how they identify themselves. The majority, however, refer to themselves after the clusters of villages from where they came, such as "al-Rashdiye"

---

[2] Ahmad Muhammad Ahmad, *Akrad Lubnan wa-Tanzimuhum al-Ijtima'I wa-al-Siyasi* (Beirut: Maktabat al-Fakih, 1995), p. 83.

and "Mhallamiye."[3] For the purposes of this paper, we will label the Kurmanji-speaking Kurds as Kurmanj and the non-Kurmanji-speaking group as Mardallis.[4] Among the largest families of the Mardalli group in Lebanon are: Atriss, Fakhro, Fattah, Harb, Miri, Omari, Omayrat, Ramadan, Rammu, Shabu, Sharif, Shaykhmusa, Siyala, and al-Zein.

Today, Kurds represent the second largest ethnic minority group in Lebanon, outnumbered only by Armenians. An accurate number, however, is not available because there has been no census conducted in Lebanon since 1932 and because the identity cards that Kurds hold do not specify their ethnic background. Most sources though have estimated their number prior to 1985 to be between 60,000 and 90,000, with more than two-thirds of them living in the capital Beirut.[5] Given that thousands of Kurdish families fled the country during the second half of the 1975-1990 Lebanese civil war, it is believed that their number is below that range today. Most of the Kurds who fled the country in the 1980s currently live in Western Europe but continue to visit Lebanon on a regular basis, while investing in the real estate and sending remittances to family members who remained in Lebanon.

Kurds who moved to Lebanon between the 1920s and 1960s arrived with very little education and very few skills other than in agriculture. Most of them settled in low-income areas in Beirut, including: Ayn al-Mreisseh, al-Basta, Bourj al-Barajneh, the downtown sector, Furn al-Shubbak, Raml al-Zarif, and Zukak al-Bilat, as well as the al-Karantina/al-Maslakh area. Their agricultural skills served them very little in their new urban setting. As unskilled laborers, they first entered the labor market as por-

---

[3]The Mhallamis are originally a group of Arab families, most of whom centuries ago moved from northern Iraq to the Kurdish area located between Mardin, Midyat, and Diyarbekir. Over the years, they adopted a considerable number of traits of Kurdish origins. Mhallamis who moved to Lebanon all came from the Mardin region, more specifically from an area called Mhallamiye, a cluster of about 15 villages.

[4]The word "Mardalli" is used after the region of Mardin. It is used by many non-Kurmanji speakers to refer to their language and ethnic identity.

[5] Ahmad, *Akrad*, pp. 84-86.

ters and box manufacturers in the vegetable market of downtown Beirut. A few decades later, some developed new occupational skills in such areas as house painting, construction, auto mechanics, tailoring, and carpeting; others became merchants of vegetables; and still others were able to establish gradually-expanding business enterprises. The majority, however, were stuck in a self-reproducing cycle of poverty and illiteracy. Due to financial difficulties, many of their women needed to work as janitors and housekeepers in order to survive. After more than five decades of residence in Lebanon, most Kurds in Lebanon still have meager socioeconomic means and are considered among the least literate communities in the country.

The Citizenship Dilemma

The adverse socioeconomic and political conditions of the Kurds in Lebanon are not exclusively a result of the poor economic and educational background of the members of the community, but also a result of the lack of the majority of them having obtained Lebanese citizenship—at least until the mid-1990s. Their poverty, lack of property and occupational skills, high illiteracy rate, feelings of insecurity and alienation, and ill-treatment by various Lebanese groups were found to be significantly related to the Kurds' status as noncitizens.

The naturalization process of the Kurds (and that of several other communities who resided in Lebanon for decades) was not an easy one. Since the establishment of Greater Lebanon by France in 1920, the numerical balance of the different confessional and ethnic communities in the country has been a critical matter. At that time, Christians were slightly outnumbering Muslims. However, that predominance increased with the influx of thousands of Armenian refugees who escaped the Turkish genocide during World War I. Most of these refugees were allowed to acquire Lebanese citizenship. Following the naturalization of Armenians, Christian hegemony in the country was formalized in the 1932 census, which showed that Christians outnumbered Muslims by a ratio of 6:5. Since then, no census has been taken and citizenship for new immigrants, such as the Kurds, became very restricted until the mid-1990s.

Most Kurds failed to recognize the value of citizenship until it was nearly impossible for them to acquire it. They failed to apply for citizenship for several reasons. First, many thought of Lebanon as a temporary place of living and believed that sooner or later they would go back to an independent Kurdistan after raising enough money. Second, many Kurds were afraid of military conscription, a fear they carried from Turkey where the terms of the compulsory military service were very harsh and long. Third, before World War II, travel across borders to neighboring countries did not require the carrying of a Lebanese citizenship; noncitizens were able to travel from and back to Lebanon by means of certificates issued by the French authorities. More Kurds would have applied for citizenship had it been a requirement for travel, especially since many Kurds regularly traveled to Syria and Turkey. Perhaps the most important reason why Kurds did not apply for Lebanese citizenship was because of their unfamiliarity with civil rights and the legal significance of citizenship. In the peripheral regions of Turkey from where they came, state institutions, apart from the military, were practically nonexistent.

The Kurds realized the value of citizenship upon the introduction of war-time rationing in 1941. During World War II, the majority of Kurds were denied food ration cards because they did not have Lebanese citizenship. In response, many Kurds rushed to apply for citizenship, but found it was too late to do so. Prior to 1940, citizenship was granted to all applicants who had lived continuously in Lebanon for at least five years, or who had married a Lebanese citizen and lived in the country for at least one year after marriage. Legislation passed in 1940, however, made Lebanese naturalization theoretically impossible.

In the early 1960s, Kurds who did not have citizenship sought the help of Kemal Jumblat, a prominent socialist leader who was serving as the Minister of Interior.[6] He granted them what was known as "unspecified citizenship" which enabled the children of the holders of this identification card to obtain citizenship,

---

[6]Many Kurds argue that Jumblat helped the community because of his Kurdish roots. Upon an official visit to Iraq in the early 1970s, Jumblat met with Mulla Mustafa Barzani in Salah al-Din in northern Iraq.

provided they were born in Lebanon. Due to Christian opposition, however, the granting of non-specified citizenship was soon abandoned and was replaced in 1962 with "under-study" identification cards (*qaid al-dars*), which were transmitted hereditarily and enabled their holders to leave and reenter Lebanese territories and gave them the right to enroll in public schools, but denied them citizenship rights. Thus, the holder of the "under-study" IDs could neither vote nor seek public employment.[7] Despite the fact that the issue of the naturalization of noncitizens was raised in the Lebanese Parliament by more than a dozen cabinets between the 1970s and early 1990s, all efforts to resolve the problem failed because of objections from Maronite representatives.[8]

It was not until the rise of the government of Rafik al-Hariri to power that the citizenship problem was resolved. His government issued a naturalization decree on June 21, 1994 to settle the legal status of all qualified non-naturalized individuals living on Lebanese territories. The decree allowed the majority of the non-naturalized Kurds to acquire citizenship. To their dismay, some-

---

[7]The "under-study" identification cards were usually granted to applicants for periods of three years, after which they could be regularly renewed. Applications, fingerprints, and application fees were required from each individual to obtain the ID card. Kurds residing outside Lebanon had grave problems when Lebanese embassy officials refused to renew their cards. These Kurds were forced to travel to Beirut with their families, incurring severe financial expenses, in order to complete the transactions.

[8]For instance, in November 1974, Prime Minister Rashid al-Sulh insisted that the inaugural government statement include an article committed to resolving the issue of naturalizing Lebanese noncitizens. Following an intense debate with the Christian Phalangist Party (*al-Kata'ib*) and the National Liberals' Party (*Hizb al-Wataniyyin al-Ahrar*), George Saadeh, the Phalange representative in the government, drew attention to the political ramifications of naturalizing the Kurds by stating: "We, the Phalangists, have worked hard in the past to give the Armenians Lebanese nationality and this was accomplished. But what was the result? They have become the electoral balance in the districts they live in. So if the Prime Minister wants his electoral fate to be determined by the Kurds, we are with him." Cited in *Rohilat*, no. 9 (November 1974), p. 2.

where between 3,000 and 5,000 Kurds missed out because they were unable to afford the cost of the application, were abroad and could not travel to Lebanon to file, or simply because they did not believe that the granting of citizenship would materialize. The decree raised a storm of political opposition from Maronite officials who argued that many of the citizenship recipients did not meet the minimum qualifications required for naturalization. The main argument of the opposition was that the naturalization has disrupted the confessional balance of the country. For Kurds, however, the decree represented the salvation that they had long been awaiting. Estimates of the number of naturalized Kurds ranged between 10,000 and 18,000.[9]

Socioeconomic Conditins

Just as it could on the eve of the civil war in 1975, Lebanese society today can be easily divided into five broad definable social classes: the national elite, the upper class, the middle class, the upper lower class, and the lower class. In general, the Kurds belong to the lower class, which for the most part includes working people who possess neither office nor wealth, and little or no education. They include taxi drivers, vegetable peddlers, barbers, sharecroppers, unskilled day laborers, servants, office boys, and craftsmen or tradesmen who work as employees or apprentices. Many are employed in other menial jobs in construction, road building, and small industry, most often with no social or medical insurance or trade-union rights. Low-paid lower class people often work on a temporary basis and are easily dismissed from their jobs. They also do not have adequate property or savings to use as insurance when work becomes slack. Additionally, many members of the lower class—especially those who were denied citizenship—are perceived as aliens and are severely vulnerable to discriminatory and unjust treatment. Kurds, in particular, still face greater adversity than most other members of the lower class, largely because they are not Arabs. This ethnic differentiation denies many of them employment, humanitarian support,

---

[9] Salah Abu Chakra, *Al-Akrad: Sha'b al-Mu'anat* (Beirut: Dar al-Hadi, 1999), p. 150.

and equal treatment in government offices, even after they became citizens.

As in most other developing countries, education in Lebanon both reinforces the position of many traditionally high status groups and provides other groups with an important channel for upward mobility. However, the fact that lower class people are relatively overwhelmed by the pressure to provide their families with basic resources for survival means that they have neither the money nor the time to send their working-age children to schools. As a result, the lower class becomes the least literate class in Lebanon and the easiest for others to exploit and manipulate. In 1995, Meho[10] found that 85 percent of the Kurds live at or below the poverty line. He also found that the Kurds' educational attainment is extremely deficient; almost 60 percent of them are virtually illiterate, and the figure goes up to over 95 percent among the elderly. Kurds also overwhelmingly lack property; most of them rent their places of living.

Mobility from the lower to higher class requires not only education and wealth, but also social and psychological mobility; that is, the family must transform itself from an extended family sub-culture—a characteristic of lower class communities—to a new model of family ties and duties often represented in the nuclear family. The family must also transform itself from social and economic dependence to social and economic independence. Such a transformation process is still in its infancy among the Kurds, let alone the fact that most of them have large families, exceeding six children in about 44 percent of the cases.[11]

This bleak picture of the socioeconomic conditions of the Kurds started to change following the end of the civil war in 1990 and the attainment of citizenship in 1996. However, the extent and speed of this change remains to be seen. One noticeable change that took place in the last decade has been the rise of Kurds' participation in local politics and associational organiza-

---

[10] Lokman I. Meho, *The Dilemma of Social and Political Integration of Ethnoclass Groups within Pluralistic Societies: The Case of the Kurds in Lebanon*. Master's thesis. (Beirut: The American University of Beirut, 1995).

[11] *Ibid.*

tions. As a result, they started to attract considerable interest and care from various Lebanese politicians, particularly from Prime Minister Hariri and the two influential Sunni Islamist groups: The Association for Charity Projects (*Jam'iyat al Mashari' al-Khayriyya*), better known as *al-Ahbash*, and the Islamic Group (*al-Jama'a al-Islamiyya*). The following section provides a brief account of the most important Lebanese Kurdish organizations.

Associational Organizations

Despite the frequent attempts of, and encouragement by, Prince Kamuran Bedirkhan, Kurds in Lebanon were virtually uninvolved in any major social or political activity before the 1950s. This changed dramatically after the events that took place in the region in the late 1950s and early 1960s. The union between Syria and Egypt in 1958-1961 had significant repercussions on the social, economic, and political conditions of the Kurds in Syria, and the end result was ultimately felt in Lebanon. The union, which ushered in a period of intense Arab nationalism, initiated the first oppressive measures against the Kurds in Syria.[12] In due course, several thousands of Syrian Kurds— mostly politicized students, workers, refugees, and asylum seekers—moved to Lebanon. Despite the temporary presence of most of these Kurds, they were instrumental in raising awareness among Lebanese Kurds regarding the significance of social and political activism.

Another, and perhaps a more important, factor leading to social and political awareness among the Lebanese Kurds was the 1958 fall of the Iraqi monarchy, which ultimately led to the outbreak of the 1961-1975 Kurdish war. Mulla Mustafa Barzani found a needed publicity platform for the war in the liberal city of Beirut, where thousands of Kurds lived. As the Kurdish war boosted the national self-awareness of Lebanese Kurds, many of them began to sense their impoverished status and to think about methods of enhancing their living conditions. One such method was the establishment of socio-political organizations.

---

[12] David McDowall, *The Kurds of Syria* (London: Human Rights Project, 1998), pp. 15-19.

Among the first attempts was the establishing of The Kurdish Democratic Party in Lebanon (*Al-Hizb al-Dimuqrati al-Kurdi fi Lubnan – al-Parti*), better known as The Parti. Founded in 1970 by Jamil Mihhu, a house painter, The Parti started to operate clandestinely in July 1960 under the name of the Organization of Kurdish Democratic Youth in Lebanon (*Munazzamat al-Shabiba al-Dimuqratiyya al-Kurdiyya*). It was formed by a cluster of young Lebanese Kurds with the assistance and encouragement of the Kurdish Democratic Party in Syria (KDPS), and was considered the Lebanese affiliate branch of the Kurdistan Democratic Party in Iraq (KDP). Initially, the activities of the Organization were limited to communication with local Kurds and dissemination of statements explaining methods of improving the social, cultural, and political conditions of the Kurdish community, with particular emphasis on education and naturalization. As of 1961, and upon the recommendation of the KDPS, activities developed to include assisting Kurdish representatives sent by Mulla Mustafa Barzani to publicize the Kurdish national movement in Iraq.

The group's political activities remained underground until Barzani informed Mihhu of the significance of organizing Kurdish political activities into a legal body, which would serve both the Lebanese Kurds and the Kurdish national movement. Given the popularity of Barzani among Lebanese Kurds and his support of Mihhu, the latter succeeded in mobilizing many Kurds to rally behind him. He asked the Lebanese government to legalize the party's status and was given the license on September 24, 1970. Soon after its founding, Mihhu was lured by the Iraqi government for financial gains and his popularity among Lebanese Kurds eventually deteriorated. Consequently, The Parti was dismantled into several factions and subdivisions that recreated in Lebanon the inner divisions of the Kurdish leadership in Iraq and Syria, until almost all of them were disbanded during the 1980s and early 1990s.

Currently, the most active and influential Lebanese Kurdish associations are: The *Rawdah* Delegation, The Lebanese Kurdish Philanthropist Association (*Al-Jam'iyya al-Khairiyya al-Kurdiyya al-Lubnaniyya*), The Cedars Sports and Cultural Club (*Jam'iyat al-Arz al-Riyadiyya al-Thaqafiyya*), The *Rezgari*

(Freedom) Party, The Omayrat Family League, The Lebanese Social Association (*al-Jam'iyya al-Lubnaniyya al-Ijtima'iyya*), The Kurdish Cultural and Humanitarian League in Lebanon (*al-Rabita al-Thaqafiyya al-Insaniyya al-Kurdiyya al-Lubnaniyya*), and The Future Generation (*Jil al-Mustaqbal*), all officially recognized by the Lebanese government. The following is a brief account on each.[13]

The Rawdah Delegation.
This Mhallami-based association was established in 1960 by members of the Omari family, who migrated to Lebanon in the 1940s. Starting in the 1950s, they gradually moved from the traditionally Kurdish-populated areas of Beirut, such as Zukak al-Bilat and Ayn al-Mreisseh, to the poorer slum areas around the Palestinian refugee camp of Bourj al-Barajneh in the southern suburbs of Beirut. The Omaris are the only Kurds who live in the suburbs of Beirut surrounded by non-Sunni non-Beiruti neighbors.

This association sponsors several institutions that are vital for the basic needs of the community for which it caters. It has a mosque and an infirmary that serves the needs of approximately 300 patients per month, and is run by six medical doctors covering the most basic medical specializations. The association also owns a secondary school, *al-Iman* (Faith), which enrolls over 500 students. According to its president, the association has over 6,000 informal affiliated members, most of them from the Omari family.

Since the early days of its establishment, the *Rawdah* Delegation had very close ties with the Islamic Group, a powerful Islamic group that has strong relations with the country's Islamic Sunni Council (*Dar al-Fatwa*), the highest Sunni religious

---

[13]This section is largely adopted from Farah W. Kawtharani, *The Interplay of Clientelism and Ethnic Identity in Pluralist States: The Case of the Kurdish Community in Lebanon.* Master's thesis. (Beirut: The American University of Beirut, 2003), pp. 69-96, who conducted face-to-face interviews with presidents, board members, and regular members of the associations.

authority in Lebanon. Through their favorable connections with the Council, the Islamic Group and the *Rawdah* Delegation have been able to raise significant amounts of money to fund their medical and educational institutions.

The members of the Delegation, like many other non-Kurmanji speakers, exhibit ambiguity in relation to the definition of their ethnic identity. They maintain the general myth that they are descendants of the Arab tribe of Banu Hilal that centuries ago settled in Eastern Turkey. Although they preserved their Arabic language, they admit that they had gained considerable Kurdish traits from their surroundings. When they arrived in Lebanon, they were labeled as "Kurds" and the label remained part of their identity. Like most other non-Kurmanji groups, the Omari clan does not want to dissociate itself from the rest of the Kurdish community. If they refute Kurdish ethnicity, they will run the risk of being excluded from the Kurdish community, yet without guarantees of being fully accepted by the mainstream Sunni community. The fact that the *Rawdah* Delegation constantly participates in the Lebanese parliamentary elections compels them to preserve its solidarity with other Kurdish associations and clans in order to acquire their support during election times, however challenging this proves to be.

The Lebanese Kurdish Philanthropist Association (LKPA).
The LKPA was the first legal Kurmanji association to be established in Lebanon. It was founded on September 19, 1963, when Kemal Jumblat was the minister of interior. Today, its main goals are to distribute material aids whenever they are available and to follow up on individual legal cases pertaining to the citizenship status of Kurds.[14] Occasionally, it offers to members of the community night and weekend Kurdish language courses. The LKPA is currently considered one of the largest and most active Lebanese Kurdish associations. According to its president, the association has over 200 families officially registered which make the number of affiliated adult family members approxi-

---

[14]There are a number of Kurds who were entitled to and applied for citizenship but were not naturalized because of bureaucratic mistakes. The association negotiates with the government to resolve these issues.

mately 1,000. Almost every year since the mid-1990s, the LKPA has organized *Newroz* concerts, each attended by over 1,000 people.

The majority of the LKPA members are Kurmanji speakers. Over the past few years, however, there has been a lot of effort to attract and recruit non-Kurmanji speakers to foster the relationship between the two groups. In the most recent board elections, two out of the five elected candidates were from the non-Kurmanji group. Today, most members of LKPA hold Lebanese citizenship. Despite having lived in Lebanon since the 1940s, they continue to view both Lebanon and Kurdistan as "home" and many of them regularly visit the latter on short trips. As most other Kurdish associations, the LKPA survives on membership fees and meager donations and external funds.

The Cedars Sports and Cultural Club (CSCC) and the Rezgari Party.
The CSCC and the *Rezgari* are treated in the same section because of their common origins. The Club was founded on March 18, 1969 to enhance Kurdish athletic and cultural activities. It was essentially instituted as the platform of the Rashdiye group of Kurds. The headquarters of the Club, an apartment in a lower middle-class building in Beirut, is fully decorated with portraits of the founding members who are all from the Fakhro clan and their kin families, including: Ali, Atriss, Hasan, al-Kurdi, and Rammu, among others. One of the distinguishing activities of the Club was the establishment of a soccer team that won several nationwide championships in the early 1970s. Another distinguishing activity was the publication of a bulletin named *Rasti* (The Straight Path) that dealt with the general conditions of the Kurds in Lebanon and the affairs of Kurdistan. The bulletin is still being published but irregularly and now focuses primarily on the general news of Lebanese Kurds and particularly those of the Club's closely associated families. Currently, most of the athletic and cultural activities of the club have either been relinquished as a result of lack of resources or have been significantly reduced in scope. According to its president, the number of members in the club has fluctuated over the years between 200-300.

The *Rezgari* Party was founded on April 3, 1975 by Faysal Fakhro as a political wing of the Cedars Club. Fakhro claimed that the *Rezgari* is needed because of the failure of The Parti to appeal to non-Kurmanji speakers and because of Mihhu's support for the Iraqi regime's one-sided plan for Kurdish autonomy. Fakhro also claimed that The Parti was transformed into a Mihhu family organization rather than one that represents the interests of the whole Kurdish community. Once a very popular party, membership in the *Rezgari* has dropped significantly over the years due to internal divisions, lack of financial resources, and the emigration of most of its members to Europe. It halted the publication of its popular monthly magazine, *Xebat* (The Struggle), in 1995 as a result of financial difficulties.

Despite the fact that the presidents and all members of both the *Rezgari* party and Cedars Club descend from the non-Kurmanji-speaking Mardalli group, a thorough embrace of Kurdish identity is spelled out in their bulletins and publications. The constant reference to Kurdish history, language, and literature in *Rasti* and *Xebat* attest to their interest in preserving their Kurdishness and in representing all Lebanese Kurds. Although some, especially members of CSCC, acknowledge the linguistic differences between them (i.e., the Mardalli) and the Kurmanji group, they stress the unity of the larger community. Their argument is that despite the existence of linguistic differences, they are unified by their Kurdishness. Such an embrace of Kurdishness carries with it many benefits for both the Club and the *Rezgari* party. It enables the president of the Club to establish himself as a leader and a spokesman of the Kurds vis-à-vis the community and the state. It also helps the Club establish better relations with the Barzani leadership, which could lead to material support in the future.

The Omayrat Family League and the Lebanese Social Association.
The dominance of the Fakhro lineage and their kin families in the Cedars Club and the *Rezgari* party alienated several other large Mardalli clans, particularly the Omayrat, whose members decided to establish their own association or join others. They founded the Omayrat Family League in 1979 to serve the inter-

ests of the members of the clan and their kin families. Many
other members of the clan joined the Islamist group, the Lebanese Social Association (LSA). Nothing in the name of the LSA
denotes its Kurdishness or its Islamist vocation. Yet, it is well
known as the official platform of the Islamist Kurds affiliated
with *al-Ahbash*. While the majority of LSA's members are from
the Omayrat family, other smaller Mardalli families are well represented, such as the Madani, Simmo, Sado, and others. LSA has
300 official members, but claims the support of many more individuals and families. It was founded in the 1980s by a group of
Beiruti Arab families. Its original founders, however, gradually
abandoned it, leaving it entirely in the hands of the Kurds in
1998. LSA receives considerable legal and material support from
al-Ahbash.

The *Al-Ahbash* group are well known to have always enjoyed
good relations with the officials in power, which allows them to
act as an intermediary between the Lebanese state and the various social groups. By virtue of their privileged contacts, the *al-
Ahbash* group were able to help their Kurdish affiliates in their
dealings with the government before and after they received
Lebanese citizenship. They protected them from the infringe-
ments of power and arbitrary prosecutions often undergone by
weak minority groups. *Al-Ahbash* also provided their Kurdish
followers with unrestricted access to their educational and medical institutions, services that historically were not easily accessed
by Lebanese Kurds. *Al-Ahbash*, in return, gains new recruits who
in time of elections cast their votes to *al-Ahbash* candidates.

The LSA, despite its open affiliation with *al-Ahbash*, claims
to be open to all Kurdish groups and is at the service of the general community. Their attempts to approach other Kurdish associations, however, have been viewed suspiciously because the
association is not being perceived other than as an affiliate of *al-
Ahbash*. In the discourse of the association, inter-group ethnic
distinction among the various Kurdish groups is clearly stated.
To the larger Lebanese society, members of the LSA identify
themselves as "Kurds." But when compared to Kurmanji Kurds,
they prefer to identify themselves as "Mardallis" or "Mardalli
Kurds." They justify this discrepancy in that they do not desire to

create tension and conflict that will only undermine the general well-being of the community.

As members of the Omayrat clan, the same rationale of LSA is used by members of the Omayrat Family League in the expression of their ethnic identity. However, one important characteristic distinguishes them from each other. The members of the League limit their support of *al-Ahbash* to the religious aspect of the relationship and deny the Islamist group their political allegiance. Instead, the League members stress their loyalty to Prime Minister Rafik al-Hariri. They justify this in that as a group they prefer to have an official *marjaiya* (or someone in power) to speak up for them.[15] An official *marjaiya* can extend legitimacy and protection to Kurds more so than someone who is not in power.

The Kurdish Cultural and Humanitarian League in Lebanon (KCHLL).
Among Lebanese Kurds, KCHLL is considered as the unofficial representative of the Kurdistan Workers Party (PKK) in Lebanon. Apart from members of the administrative board, who all hold Lebanese ID cards, most members of this group are Syrian and Turkish Kurds who reside temporarily in Lebanon or visit the country periodically. The main activities of the League include providing classes in the Kurdish language, organizing exhibitions of Kurdish artifacts that raise revenues, and organizing folkloric events on national occasions, such as *Newroz*. According to Kawtharani,[16] the number of people who attended KCHLL's 2002 *Newroz* party amounted to approximately 5,000 individuals, including celebrants from Syria. The association also issues a magazine in Arabic called *Sorghul* (Red Rose), fo-

---

[15]"The *marjaiya* in Lebanon is a concept that denotes, in addition to an official political framework within which public legality or legitimacy is ensured vis-à-vis the authorities, an access to not-necessarily monetary benefits but protection from the law and the security authorities, as well as access to otherwise inaccessible resources. A *marjaiya* could be a political party, a *zaim*, or any public figure that has solid relations with the political and security forces of the country" Kawtharani, *Clientelism and Ethnic Identity*, pp. 78-79.

[16] *Ibid.*, pp. 72-73.

cusing on the cultural events of Kurds in Lebanon and Syria. In spite of the display of numerous political referents that underly a strong identification with the Kurdish national cause, and a fervent involvement in Kurdish affairs in Turkey with an assertive nationalist spirit, members of the board stress the supremacy of their loyalty to Lebanon.

The Future Generation.
Three important features characterize this association: All members are from the Mardalli group, particularly from the Mhallamiye area, are staunch allies of Prime Minister Hariri, and refuse to be identified as Kurds. Founded in 1997, the goal of the association is to provide aid to its members and followers. The association's loyalty to Hariri is symbolized by the use of the word "Future" that features in its name. The motto has been used in the campaigns of Hariri for several years and has become his trademark. Leaders and members of this association completely dissociate themselves from Kurmanji-speaking and non-Kurmanji-speaking groups and prefer to call themselves Arabs. They insist they have absolutely no involvement or sympathy with the Kurdish cause and that full assimilation in Lebanon is their ultimate goal. This association is discussed here because they are still considered Kurds in the perception of the mainstream Lebanese population.

In summary, it is evident that most of the existing Lebanese Kurdish associations act as extended kinship networks that are based on ethnic and tribal backgrounds which address in particular the well-being of the members of the kinship or village group rather than the community as a whole. This explains why there have been and still are more Kurdish associations and organizations than might be expected, considering the size of the community and its human and financial resources. The common goal that animates all of the associations is, first, to acquire needed resources to help their group members and, second, to perpetuate solidarity among their affiliates and create provision for social and cultural activities.

As for the political parties, in particular, Kurds took little part in their activities. For the majority of Kurdish men, participation seemed irrelevant to their primary concerns, which centered on finding jobs and securing food and medical aid for their families. Their lack of interest was also related to the fact that most of the political parties did not emerge out of Lebanese Kurdish political consciousness; instead, they were instigated by outside actors or were haphazardly established as a reaction to dissatisfaction with existing parties. Moreover, the predominantly "self-appointed" leaders not only dominated the power apparatuses of the parties, but also exploited its resources for personal goals. These leaders lacked both the education and skills necessary to run organizations effectively and efficiently and, at a time when most of them were incapable of supporting their parties financially, they still promised to build schools and health care centers—plans that were completely beyond their means. At various times, national issues (i.e., events in Kurdistan) prevailed over local ones and interfered with the primary activities of the parties, often leading to the neglect of efforts to improve the general status of the community in Lebanon. Perhaps most importantly, the various Kurdish groups rarely coordinated their efforts or cooperated with each other. The impact of this on the political status of the Kurds in Lebanon is discussed below. Not unreasonably, many Kurds also feared that if they are very active in politics, they will be threatened or detained by Syrian intelligence that has had a strong presence in Lebanon since the outbreak of the civil war in 1975.

Kurds in the Lebanese Political System

Throughout its modern history, Lebanon has been characterized by the division of its population into competing families and religious groups politically organized in what is known as patron-client relationship.[17] Such a relationship, involving an interchange of unequal goods and services between patrons (*zaims* or leaders) and clients (followers), has profound effects on the so-

---

[17]Lebanon is a country of minorities. It is a mosaic of many ethnic and religious groups, the most prominent being the Shiite and Sunni Muslims, Druzes, Christian Maronites, Greek Orthodox, Greek Catholics, and Armenians. Other smaller groups include Kurds, Alawites, Syriacs, Assyrians, Protestants, and Chaldeans.

cial and political culture of the Lebanese. In exchange for their support of a *zaim*, usually in the form of votes or more active forms of political participation, the followers expect to receive assistance or favors in securing employment, government benefits, and mediation with government officials or other prominent persons.

Lebanon's population of clients can be divided into three main categories that comprise the *zaims'* resources of patronage:[18] First, and most important, are the rich clients who usually belong to large families and have adequate financial resources to support the *zaim*. Second, are the financially and politically less important voters, who make up the majority of the *zaim* support base. Such people generally have simple requests, which can be dealt with by the assistants of the *zaim*. The third category of clients is comprised of two groups of people: those who vote in another constituency and the disenfranchised Kurds and Palestinian refugees who are largely noncitizens. Members of this third category have little to offer the *zaim* and, as a result, are largely excluded from cliental networks. As more Kurds became citizens as of the mid-1990s, more attention was given to them by local *zaims*, even though they are not promoted yet from the third to the second category of clients.

By virtue of their residence in Beirut, Kurds came to identify themselves with the politics of the city. As an ethnic immigrant group that did not have adequate educational and economic resources to participate fully in social and political activities, and with the lack of outside support from fellow Kurds, the Kurds of Lebanon looked to Sunni *zaims* in Beirut to provide them with the missing leadership and protection. Kurds have always been keen to be enlisted by whatever Sunni leader was in power. In the 1940s and 1950s, they were strong supporters of members of the al-Sulh family, more specifically Prime Ministers Riad and Sami, who were responsible for naturalizing hundreds of Kurdish families. In the 1960s and early 1970s, many Kurds shifted their loyalty to Saeb Salam, another Sunni leader belonging to a

---

[18] Michael Johnson, *Class and Client in Beirut: The Sunni Muslim Community and the Lebanese State, 1840-1985* (London: Ithaca Press, 1986), p. 94.

wealthy notable family. Unlike Riad and Sami al-Sulh, however, Salam was not as popular among Kurds because his favors for them (e.g., schooling and access to health care) were not provided on a collective basis. Rather, they were specifically channeled to those Kurds who held Lebanese citizenship, that is, to those who could return the favors with electoral votes. In the 1960s and 1970s, Kurds also became supporters of Rashid al-Sulh and the Druze leader, Kemal Jumblat, who provided the noncitizens with the under-study identification cards.

During the 1975-1990 civil war, Kurdish allegiance spread out among different factions. Although Kurds had little reason to take sides in the war, the situation changed when the Christian Maronite Phalange forces purged them and the Palestinians from East Beirut. Consequently, many Kurds decided to take up arms against the Christian-dominated Lebanese Front (*al-Jabha al-Lubnaniyya*). They did so by joining the Lebanese Communist Party, the Movement of Independent Nasserites (*Harakat al-Nasiriyyin al-Mustaqllin* better known as *al-Murabitun*), and other Sunni militia groups. Several joined Palestinian organizations, especially the Popular Front for the Liberation of Palestine (PFLP) and the Democratic Front for the Liberation of Palestine (DFLP). The Kurds sought common cause with these parties not only because they were assaulted by Christian militias, but also because they thought that, upon victory, the parties they joined would deliver them from permanent political, economic, and social misfortunes imposed by the existing political system.

In the early years of the war, Kurdish participation focused primarily on fighting Christian militias in East Beirut. Then in 1984, they started to fight Amal, the main Shiite militia group. At the time, Amal was trying to control south and west Beirut on behalf of Syria. Although its main focus was the suppression of Palestinian guerrilla factions, Amal also fought *al-Murabitun* and other Sunni militias and rapidly eliminated them to gain full control of the city. Unhappy about Shiite encroachments into vital areas of the Sunni-dominant west Beirut, the Kurds joined forces with the Druze Progressive Socialist Party (*al-Hizb al-Taqaddumi al-Ishtiraki*) to resist Amal's supremacy. Fighting lasted until 1987 when Syria and the warring factions reached an agreement to withdraw all militias from Beirut and hand over public order and security to Syrian forces. As part of the agreement, the Druze Progressive Socialist Party (PSP) retreated to its heartland in the Shouf mountains; however, the Shiite forces remained in Beirut because they were still needed to maintain control over the areas surrounding Palestinian camps. This left the Kurds vulnerable to Shiite dominance and to Syrian surveillance and harassment. Many Kurds—primarily those who were members of PSP and other anti-Syrian Palestinian organizations—were jailed and thousands others either fled to Europe or moved to the Biqa' region and the Druze mountains. The exodus of these Kurds had also to do with the deteriorating economic conditions in Lebanon as well as the feeling of the need to find a more secure place of living (as opposed to continue living in Lebanon as noncitizens).

Kurdish involvement in the war not only cost them lives and resulted in their displacement, it also exposed the extent of the prejudice they faced in Lebanon. For instance, during the civil war, the Kurds were asked to volunteer their services as auxiliaries to the Sunni *al-Murabitun* militia. The Kurds willingly gave these services, yet lost out when it came to sharing relief supplies from Europe: "Supplies were usually divided into four parts and handed over to the Maronites, the Druze, the Shiites, and the Sunnis."[19] As Christians, Armenians received a share from Maronites. Although Kurds should have received a share from their fellow Sunnis, they did not because they were not viewed as insiders or as members of the Sunni community.

The end of the civil war in 1990 and the naturalization of Kurds a few years later presented the Kurds with new opportunities to establish, and benefit from, fresh patron-client relations. Being the most powerful Sunni leader in the country, Prime Minister Hariri was their main target as a patron. Kurds sought Hariri not only because of his power and wealth, but also because of his role in the promulgation of the naturalization decree

---

[19]Interview with a Lebanese Kurdish refugee in Sweden, cited in Ismet Cheriff Vanly, "The Kurds in Syria and Lebanon," in *The Kurds: A Contemporary Overview*, ed. by Philip G. Kreyenbroek and Stefan Sperl (London: Routledge, 1992), p. 167.

in 1994. He was considered by the majority of Kurds as their new champion. Naturally, in the aftermath of their naturalization, Kurds started to express a set of demands to Hariri, including: representation in the parliament and the municipality of Beirut, recruitment in the civil service administration and military bureaucracy, and financial support to establish health, cultural, and educational centers.

Although more than half of the 15,000 Kurdish voters have willingly voted for the Prime Minister and his associates in the 1996 and 2000 parliamentary elections, Kurds gained very little in return. Even members of the *Jil al-Mustaqbal* association, who claim total allegiance to Hariri, expressed their dissatisfaction at the level of benefits received from him and his institutions. Overall, even after most Kurds became citizens, they are still excluded from virtually all the spoils that other religious and ethnic groups and family and communal associations receive (e.g., employment in the public sector, official representation, and government subsidies and aids). In describing the relationship between the Kurds and the office of the Prime Minister, most Kurds claim that it is a policy of exploitation and manipulation.

Despite the disproportionate support of and from Hariri in comparison to the electoral votes he gets from Kurds, the latter rarely criticize him for that and remain loyal to his leadership. This policy is evidenced by the Kurds' constant casting of their votes in the parliamentary elections of 1992, 1996, 2000 and municipal elections of 1998, the frequent visits they pay to his assistants and political aides, and the continued requests they make. This continuous Kurdish loyalty to a patronage that does not provide concrete and fair benefits is justified by: (1) the hope that the benefits may be gained in the future and (2) the fact that there is presently no other alternative source of patronage than Hariri's.

The aides of Hariri justify their minimal support by arguing that the Kurds are subdivided into several antagonistic groups that hamper the crystallization of a coherent and representative leadership that can speak in the name of all Kurds. For example, before the 1996 elections, Hariri asked all seven Kurdish associations to convene with him to discuss issues of interests. In return for their votes, Hariri promised to assign a Kurd the position of "councilor in charge of Kurdish affairs" within his institutions whose task would be to look after the interests and needs of the community. He asked the associations to select one representative for all of them. Unable to agree over the selection of a representative, the whole idea was dropped. In conclusion, only when the Kurds are united, will officials give them greater attention. Hariri's aides realize that Kurds have very few other options, and the meager benefits they provide are enough to maintain the support of the Kurds.

In summary, the allegiances of the Kurds have almost always been driven by their need to secure patronage. Despite some individual small-scaled and basic gains that Kurds have been able to extract from some *zaims*, they have in general been excluded from the main flow of resources. The problem is that Kurds are very much divided and, therefore, do not exert any real threat to traditional Sunni patronage, which is aimed at serving the "local" (i.e., Arab) Sunni population. Because of this, no real, efficient cliental networks are available for Kurds.

The nature of the patronage that Hariri offered the Kurds is considerably below the expectations of the community. Few medical and financial benefits were granted to members of the community, and these are considered very meager in comparison to what fellow Sunnis and Armenians receive. In the future, Kurdish success and integration will be contingent on the internal cohesion and accord among the members of the community and their socioeconomic development. It will also be contingent on their ability to become a more powerful pressure group that politicians cannot but account for.

Lebanese Kurds and Kurdish National Politics

Although Lebanon has been a center of Kurdish politics and politicians since the 1920s, the Kurds of Lebanon became involved in Kurdish national politics only with the outbreak of the Kurdish war in Iraq in 1961.[20] Since then, Kurds, especially

---

[20]To illustrate, the Kurdish National League, *Khoybun*, was formed in Bhamdoun, Lebanon in October 1927. Among several other figures,

Kurmanjis, have proclaimed their support of Mulla Mustafa Barzani and his successor, Massoud.[21] Their involvement included disseminating news (through bulletins, reports, and so on) about the war to members of the community, accommodating and assisting Kurdish delegates sent by Barzani, helping out Kurdish political refugees from Syria, and sending material aid to refugees in Iraqi Kurdistan. Following the collapse of the Kurdish revolt in 1975, there were even calls in Lebanon to recruit fighters and send them to Iraqi Kurdistan to continue the war.

Lebanese Kurds' involvement in Kurdish national politics also included forming their own political parties, some of which were extensions of Barzani's Kurdistan Democratic Party of Iraq (KDP), such as The Parti and The Parti/Central Leadership (*Al-Parti/al-Qiyada al-Markaziya*). Others participated in political parties that were formed by Syrian Kurds living in Lebanon, such as *Rezgari* II and The Leftist Kurdish Democratic Parti Organization in Lebanon (*Munazzamat al-Parti al-Kurdi al-Yasari fi Lubnan*). Following the Israeli invasion of Lebanon in 1982, Kurdish contacts with representatives of Barzani's KDP virtually ceased, and all Kurdish political parties, with the exception of *Rezgari*, were dismantled.

As of the mid-1980s, many Kurds started to sympathize with, and even join, the Kurdistan Workers Party (PKK), which seemed to respond to ambitions and concerns of the Kurdish people, particularly in overcoming the tribal divisions and factionalism that characterized the other Kurdish political movements. The PKK promoted a vision of a united Kurdish nation fighting for independence. Kurds who supported the PKK found in it and its leader, Abdullah (Apo) Ocalan, the

---

Bhamdoun, Lebanon in October 1927. Among several other figures, Kamuran Ali Bedirkhan stayed in Lebanon for several years and from 1943 to 1946 he published in Beirut the weekly *Roja Nu* in Kurdish and French. He moved to Paris in 1948 where he taught Kurdish at the National Institute of Oriental Languages and Civilizations and published a bulletin on Kurdish studies. He died in Paris in 1978.

[21]Despite their participation in and celebration of Kurdish national festivals, such as *Newroz*, non-Kurmanji Kurds rarely speak of, or relate to, Kurdish national politics.

embodiment of a national dream and a renewed claim of an identity forged out of national dignity and pride. The popularity of the PKK, however, diminished rapidly with the capture of Ocalan in 1999 and his subsequent apology to the Turkish government for his war. The popularity of the PKK was receding even before 1999 though. Very few Lebanese Kurds took pleasure in the violent means (sometimes against Kurds themselves) used by Ocalan to achieve autonomy in comparison to the more successful Massoud Barzani, who was able to reconstruct Iraqi Kurdistan by relatively more peaceful means and establish himself as the most prominent representative of the Kurds in Iraq.

Symbolic loyalty for Barzani remained throughout the 1980s and 1990s and ultimately led to the renewal of direct interaction between Lebanese Kurdish associations and the KDP. Several meetings took place between the two in the past five years or so, most of which focused on Lebanese Kurds voicing their urgent needs for services, such as a community school, a cemetery, and health center. When Lebanese Kurds speak about Barzani, the general discourse is that Barzani has responsibilities to help them improve socially, economically, and politically. Despite their continuous efforts to secure benefits from the Barzani administration, the latter has not committed itself yet to the provision of any material help to the community in the post-civil war era. Promises have been made to assist, but it remains for the future to verify the credibility of these promises. This situation can be expected to continue in the post-Saddam era.

Summary and Recommendations

Since their arrival in Lebanon in the early 1920s, Kurds have been held in low esteem by most Lebanese communities and have often been objects of contempt, ridicule, and mistreatment. This situation forced most Kurds to maintain their ethnic boundaries and to fall short of integration into the Lebanese political system, the effect of which is acutely exemplified in barring them access to a share in the Lebanese quota system and denying them representation in parliament and state institutions. In addition to waiting for over 70 years before the majority of them became naturalized citizens, Kurds suffered at the hand of almost every major sectarian group in the country. The Christian Maronites denied them citizenship to avoid tilting the sectarian balance of the country towards Muslims. The Sunnis did not fully embrace their coreligionist Kurds and continue until today to reject them as equal. Both the Druzes and the Sunnis used the Kurds to fight their wars, ignoring and disregarding them when no longer needed. Despite all this, after living for several decades in Lebanon, the majority of Kurds seem to have acquired a dual life style and have not given up their efforts to identify themselves as Kurds as well as Lebanese.

Kurdish misfortunes have also been a result of their own lack of effort and vision. In comparison to other countries where Kurds live, Lebanon has been more than a safe haven for them. Kurds were allowed to create their own political parties and social organizations, establish their own schools and health care centers, use their own language, openly celebrate their cultural events, and participate in the political process of the country. In general, Kurds missed a lot of opportunities that were presented to them in Lebanon. It took many of them two decades before they realized the significance of applying for Lebanese citizenship. That was at a time when acquiring it became theoretically impossible. Originating from extremely poor and isolated villages of Mardin, it was not until the mid-1960s that Kurds started to appreciate the value of education. Even then, many parents did not send their children to school, and very few allowed their daughters to attend school beyond the early teenage years.

Today, there are more Kurds who hold degrees higher than a bachelor, but the majority of Kurdish youths still do not study beyond high school. In addition, while the number of Kurds acquiring and learning new, more respected professional skills is rising, there are still many Kurdish men who inherit their fathers' menial, low-income occupations. As a result, Kurds still need to fully embrace the two important channels for upward mobility (i.e., higher education and better occupations) that could help reinforce their position in the Lebanese society and would allow them to produce leaders or cadres who would more influentially appeal to the majority of Kurds and Lebanese politicians.

While the goal of all Kurdish associations was and still is to improve the general conditions of members of the community, virtually none of the associations function with any form of an agenda or plan. They all conduct their activities haphazardly and with minimal or no cooperation from each other. Their lack of resources and unity has allowed, and continues to allow, others to manipulate them and deny them the bargaining power they need to get their fair share of state resources. The lack of vision and poor leadership skills among the heads of these associations have rendered the latter ineffective in changing Lebanese politicians' view of the Kurds.

The future of the Kurds in Lebanon is not as bleak today as it was before the naturalization of the majority of them in the mid-1990s. However, the improvement in the general conditions of the Kurds and their integration into the Lebanese society will be contingent on the internal cohesion and harmony among the members of the community, their attainment of and focus on education, as well as on the ability of the associations to attract the young and educated generations of Kurds who will eventually lead these associations. All these are prerequisites for creating a stronger community that would be able to exert enough pressure to attract better services and more recognition from Lebanese politicians, particularly the Sunnis.

Given the current lack of resources necessary to do the aforementioned, Kurds will need help from Lebanese leaders such as Prime Minister Hariri, as well as from leaders in Kurdistan, particularly from Barzani's administration because of its historical relationship with Lebanese Kurds and because of its national, regional, and international status. With growing opposition and competition to Hariri's leadership in Beirut and the increasing number and concentration of Kurdish population in Sunni Beirut, Hariri (perhaps more so his associates) will need to maintain and depend on the Kurds' allegiance and even strengthen it. The Kurds can earn, and Hariri will most likely have to provide, more benefits from their mutual alliance. What Kurds need to do is to know how to exploit this dependence and alliance and use them towards improving their social, economic, and political conditions. Help from leaders in Kurdistan will not only contribute to improving the general conditions of the

Lebanese Kurds, but also help them preserve their ethnic identity while integrating into the Lebanese society. Kurds will need help especially in bolstering the activities and image of their associations among the masses. This can be done by providing these associations with material and logistical support that would enable them to develop projects that would make people highly dependent on them (e.g., by founding basic medical centers, owning a cemetery, and providing academic scholarships).

Today, many Kurds, especially the younger generations, have forgotten their language and know little about their culture, civilization, and history. Therefore, projects in the areas of teaching the Kurdish language and history and in the areas of celebrating cultural events are also highly recommended. Leaders from Kurdistan should encourage Lebanese Kurdish associations to collaborate. The unity of the Kurds in Lebanon is a key factor for them to become a more influential community. A more vigorous and united Kurdish community in Lebanon could uplift its own social, economic, and political status, as well as play a catalytic role in promoting the Kurdish cause in the Middle East.

Index

CONTRIBUTORS

Mohammed M. A. Ahmed

Dr. Ahmed was Assistant Professor of Economics at the University of Baghdad in the 1960s and joined the United Nations as an Economic and Social Affairs Officer in 1969. He spent 24 years working for the UN in different capacities, first in the field and then at the UN headquarters in New York. The last post he held at the UN was Chief of the Policy and Development Planning Branch of the Department of Development Support Services. After retiring from the UN, he founded the Ahmed Foundation for Kurdish Studies, which is a non-profit and non-partisan organization. Dr. Ahmed has so far organized three conferences on Kurdish topics and published, in cooperation with Professor Michael Gunter, their outcomes in the following book forms: *The Kurdish Question and International Law*; *Kurdish Exodus: From Internal Displacement to Diaspora*; and the present volume.

Hamit Bozarslan

Dr. Bozarslan is Assistant Professor of History and Political Science at the Ecole des Hautes Etudes en Science Sociales. Bozarslan is also Co-Director of the Institut d'Etudes de l' Islam et des Societes du Monde Musulman. He has published: *From Political Contest to Self-Sacrifice: Violence in the Middle East; Network-Building, Ethnicity and Violence in Turkey* (Abu Dhabi, ECSSR, 1999); *La Question Kurde: Etats et Minorites au Moyen-Orient* (Paris Presses de Sciences-Po, 1997); *Some Remarks on Kurdish Historiographical Discourse in Turkey* (1919-1980); and *Essays on the Origins of Kurdish Nationalism* (California: Mazda Publishers, Inc., 2003).

Nader Entessar

Dr. Entessar is Professor of Political Science and Chair of International Studies at Spring Hill College in Mobile, Alabama. He was previously a senior research fellow at the Institute for

International Political and Economic Studies in Tehran, Iran. Entessar is the author or editor of several books, including *Kurdish Ethnonationalism* (Lynne Rienner Publishers); *Reconstruction and Regional Diplomacy in the Persian Gulf* (Routledge); and *Iran and the Arab World* (St. Martin's Press). He has also authored more than sixty book chapters and articles in scholarly publications in the United States, Europe, and the Middle East.

David Fisher

David Fisher is the Senior Legal and Research Officer at the Brookings Institution-SAIS Project on Internal Displacement. He is based in Geneva, where he also serves as a consultant and researcher in support of the mandate of the Representative of the United Nations Secretary-General on Internally Displaced Persons in the Office of the High Commissioner for Human Rights. Prior to his current post, Fisher served as a legal researcher at the Institute for the Study of International Migration and practiced law as a commercial, criminal and public interest lawyer.

Michael M. Gunter

Dr. Gunter is a professor of political science at Tennessee Technological University in Cookeville, Tennessee. He is the author of five critically praised scholarly books on the Kurdish question, the most recent being *Kurdish Historical Dictionary*, 2004; *The Kurdish Predicament in Iraq: A Political Analysis*, 1999; and The *Kurds and the Future of Turkey*, 1997. He has also published numerous scholarly articles on the Kurds in such leading periodicals as the *Middle East Journal, Middle East Quarterly,* and *Orient,* among others, and is a former Senior Fulbright Lecturer in International Relations in Turkey.

Gulistan Gurbey

Dr. Gurbey is a professor of Political Science and International Relations and currently teaches at the Free University of Berlin. Her research focuses on conflict resolution, peaceful approaches to settling ethno-nationalist conflicts, protection of minority and human rights, and international migration and foreign policy.

Her publications include articles on the Kurdish conflict, Turkish democracy, and Turkey's foreign policy and decision making process.

Farideh Koohi-Kamali

Dr. Koohi-Kamali is an adjunct Professor at the New School University in New York with focus on the politics and history of the Modern Middle East and Women and Islam. Her publications include *The Political Development of the Kurds in Iran: Pastoral Nationalism* (Palgrave Macmillan); *Economic Transition of Kurdish Nationalism in Kurdish Identity: Past and Future*; and *Aging Baby-Boomers and Their Impact on the Financial Market*. She has produced a number of other significant articles on the Kurds and Iranian women. She is also "Acquisition Editor" at Routledge and Research Consultant/Analyst.

Farah Kawtharani

Farah Kawtharani is a recent graduate of the American University of Beirut. Her Master's thesis was entitled *The Interplay of Clientelism and Ethnic Identity in Pluralistic States: The Case of the Kurdish Community in Lebanon*.

David McDowall

David McDowall has worked with the British Council and the United Nations Relief and Works Agency for Palestine Refugees. He became a fulltime writer on Middle East Affairs in the mid-1980s. Among his published works are: *Lebanon: A Conflict of Minorities* (Minority Rights Group, 1983); *The Palestinians: The Road to Nationhood* (Minority Rights Publications, 1994, paperback 1995); *Palestine and Israel: The Uprising and Beyond* (I.B., Tauris, 1989; paperback 1995); *A Modern History of the Kurds* (I.B., Tauris, London, 1996, new edition 2000); and *The Kurds of Syria* (Kurdish Human Rights Project, December 1998). McDowall has authored numerous other significant articles and supported Kurdish asylum seekers from Turkey in UK courts.

Lokman I. Meho

Dr. Meho is an Assistant Professor at the School of Information Science and Policy, University of Albany, State University of New York. He has published *The Kurdish Question in U.S. Foreign Policy: Documentary Sourcebook* (Praeger, 2003). His first bibliographic guide, *The Kurds and Kurdistan: A Selective and Annotated Bibliography* (Greenwood Press, 1997) was selected as one of the best bibliographies in the field of history in 1996-1997 by the Reference and User Services Association of the American Library Association. Aside from articles and book chapters on the Kurds, his Library and Information Science papers have been published in leading journals of the field.

Carole O'Leary

Professor O'Leary is the Scholar-in-Residence for the Middle East Initiative at the American University Center for Global Peace in Washington, D.C. A key area of her research is the politics of identity in the Middle East, specifically in Iraq and Iran. She established the "Iraq Working Group" at the Center in 2001 to examine the feasibility of federalism as a framework for governance in a future Iraq. She is closely associated with the Mustafa Barzani Scholar of Global Kurdish Studies at the American University. Her most recent article on "The Kurds of Iraq: Recent History, Future Prospects," was published in the Middle East Review of International Affairs (MERIA) Journal in December 2002.

Robert Olson

Dr. Olson is Professor of Middle East History and Politics at the University of Kentucky. He is the author of *The Siege of Mosul and Ottoman-Persian Relations, 1718-1743: A Study of Rebellion in the Capital and War in the Provinces of the Ottoman Empire* (1975); *The Emergence of Kurdish Nationalism and the Sheikh Said Rebellion: 1880-1925* (1989); *The Kurdish Question and Turkish-Iranian Relations: From World War I to 1998* (1998); *Turkey's Relations with Iran, Syria, Israel, and Russia, 1991-2000: The Kurdish and Islamist Questions* (2001); *Turkey's Relations with Iran, 1979-2004: War, Revolution, Ideology, Coups and Geopolitics* (2004). He also has published many scholarly articles on the Kurds in leading academic journals.

Hakan Yavuz

Dr. Yavuz is an Associate Professor of Political Science at the University of Utah. His current projects focus on transnational Kurdish networks in Europe and Turkey; Turkish and Kurdish nationalism; and ethno-religious conflict management. Professor Yavuz recently published *Islamic Political Identity in Turkey* (Oxford University Press, 2003). He also has published more than 20 scholarly articles in internationally renowned journals, is a regular contributor to several Turkish newspapers and magazines, and an editorial member of *Critique* and *Journal of Muslim Minority Affairs.*